Working Through Setbacks
in Psychotherapy

D0269003

This book to be returned on or before the last date below.

6 . 12 . 0 L

" 16/04

WITHDRAWN

616.8914

Leiper, Rob

Working through setbacks in
psychotherapy: crisis, impasse and
relapse

COLEG SIR GÂR

Working Through Setbacks in Psychotherapy

Crisis, Impasse and Relapse

Rob Leiper with Rosemary Kent

SAGE Publications
London • Thousand Oaks • New Delhi

COLEG SIR GAR	
Cypher	04.07.02
616.8914	£17.99
Am Co45771	

© Rob Leiper with Rosemary Kent 2001

First published 2001

Apart from any fair dealing for the purposes of research or
private study, or criticism or review, as permitted under the
Copyright, Designs and Patents Act, 1988, this publication may
be reproduced, stored or transmitted in any form, or by any
means, only with the prior permission in writing of the
publishers, or in the case of reprographic reproduction, in
accordance with the terms of licences issued by the Copyright
Licensing Agency. Inquiries concerning reproduction outside
those terms should be sent to the publishers.

SAGE Publications Ltd
6 Bonhill Street
London EC2A 4PU

SAGE Publications Inc
2455 Teller Road
Thousand Oaks, California 91320

SAGE Publications India Pvt Ltd
32, M-Block Market
Greater Kailash – I
New Delhi 110 048

British Library Cataloguing in Publication data

A catalogue record for this book is available
from the British Library

ISBN 0 7619 5314 0
ISBN 0 7619 5315 9 (pbk)

Library of Congress Control Number: 2001132925

Typeset by Mayhew Typesetting, Rhayader, Powys
Printed and bound in Great Britain by Biddles Ltd, Guildford, Surrey

To Our Parents

Neil and Mamie Leiper
Jack and Eileen Kent

Contents

Preface and Acknowledgements

As approaches in psychotherapy and counselling proliferate, we might be seduced by the idea that eventually the right technique will be found which can solve every problem. Each theory implies that it has *the answer* – correctly implemented it would prevent difficulties arising or provide ready solutions for overcoming them. Experience suggests otherwise. We have written this book in the hope of helping readers cope with some of the realities of the practice of therapy: the way things often don't seem to work out how we, or our clients, had hoped.

In addressing such difficulties, we have to avoid sinking into cynicism or despondency and encourage movement towards thoughtful experimentation and a creative freedom from ready-made answers. Experiencing a sense of failure, finding oneself blown off course, having to face disappointment – these challenge therapeutic self-importance and omnipotence and can act as a productive stimulus to our own growth as therapists. With the trend towards a more integrative view of psychological therapies, these challenges can also provide opportunities to extend and remodel the therapeutic frameworks which guide our practice. An excess of loyalty to our particular approach blinkers us to new perspectives, causing us to do more of the same and leading us further into the mire.

The topics of crisis, impasse and relapse encompass an enormous range of the types of setback encountered in daily practice with a wide variety of client groups. We frame our ideas in terms of a developmental approach – seeing difficulties in the therapeutic process as being intimately linked to blockages in the process of growth and part of the complex, fluctuating course of personal evolution across the lifespan. As such, these challenges may also be opportunities – points at which things can take a new turn. The book is structured so as to deal with each of the topics sequentially, but the issues overlap so that some repetition becomes inevitable. Certain themes recur in relation to each topic: the centrality of the therapist's personal response and its contribution to the therapeutic relationship; the dilemma of whether to 'hold the line' in terms of technique and framework or to respond flexibly and inventively; the need to accept difficulty without becoming either passive or impulsive. We hope that our thoughts on these issues will enable therapists of all orientations to think about and respond to developmental setbacks more resourcefully.

It would have been much more difficult to undertake such a wide-ranging project without the help of many friends and colleagues. We owe a debt to Colin Feltham for the original inspiration of collecting these three topics together and for his encouragement during the writing of the book. We would particularly like to thank Rudi Dallos, Robin Davidson, Tony Lavender, Tony Roth and Jeremy Safran who generously suggested sources, provided access to unpublished manuscripts or commented on sections of the text. Finally, we are enormously grateful to Karen Hinchliffe whose patience and hard work in providing secretarial support saw the project through its many revisions.

For reasons of confidentiality none of the case material cited in the text is directly from our own therapeutic work. Case examples are often composites of people with whom we have worked, or are disguised clients whom we have encountered through supervision, or are derived from the therapeutic literature of other people's work. Throughout the text, we have used the female gender in referring to both therapists and clients, in order to preserve stylistic simplicity. In general, we have used the term 'therapist' to apply to practitioners of all forms of psychotherapy and counselling, since the practice of the psychological therapies – although containing important stylistic and technical distinctions – has no clear demarcation lines.

1 Setbacks in the Developmental Process

A sense that things are falling apart; the apprehension that we are completely stuck in our lives; the feeling that, in spite of our best efforts, we are back to square one: these are the experiences that bring people in search of psychotherapy or counselling. We hope for growth and change – but these very obstacles often recur in the therapeutic relationship which was supposed to transform them. Therapy is difficult. For the therapist – as for the client – the process is often painful: alarming, overwhelming, disorienting, confusing, boring or disappointing. Too much writing on psychotherapy glosses over this, ignoring such experiences or placing a positive 'spin' on them. Of course, therapy is often rewarding, enlivening, even inspiring – but encountering setbacks and struggling to respond to them is often at the very heart of the process. Crises, impasses and relapses in therapy – and in life generally – seem to play a central part in the drama of change and development.

Frequently, psychotherapy and counselling do not go smoothly. Real therapy often does not seem to work out in the ways projected in the advertisements which are our therapeutic theories, even those of our favourite brand. Instead, we find ourselves bogged down and immobilized – fearful that our client or the therapy itself might fall apart, or demoralized by a lack of progress or the reversal of hard-won gains. At moments like these, we need to be able to sustain our commitment to the work and a sense of efficacy in our therapeutic role in order to be able to respond in a skilful way. To do this, it is helpful to view crises, impasses and relapses in the light of an overall framework of growth and to reframe these setbacks as challenges which may carry within them the potential for a more fundamental transformation: we need psychological theories which promote images of human development which encompass and validate the complexity of change.

Joanne was 32 when she first saw a counsellor at the surgery of her GP. She had been separated for three years from the husband she had married when she left college and the divorce was just coming through. He was an older man whom she was aware she had hoped would provide the security lacking in a childhood marred by the drinking and arguments of her parents. However, she had never been able to feel close to her husband and throughout her 20s had felt flat, directionless and rather stuck. An affair with someone at work created the crisis which ended the marriage. She felt anxious but more alive, threw herself into her career as a journalist and experimented with a series of brief relationships. Her sense of anxiety grew and she started to withdraw socially once more. Her GP prescribed anti-depressants but she didn't take them consistently. When she lost her job due to restructuring, it felt as though her world had collapsed. The counsellor was able to see her quickly, assessed the risk of her making the suicide attempt which she had contemplated and worked with her to ensure her safety. They worked intensively for eight sessions in a six-week period in a way that enabled Joanne to marshal her resources, find a new job and make some sense of why the loss of employment had hit her so hard. At a follow-up session, she agreed to accept a referral to a private psychotherapist.

The male therapist saw her weekly and the rapid improvement in her mood and energy level continued. After five months however, a growing feeling of stuckness and emotional distance crept into the therapy and persisted in spite of efforts to make sense of it. The therapist's frustration increased but in supervision he became better able to see the feelings of dependency and anger which Joanne was frightened of and his own anxious efforts to be calm and dependable. He stopped trying so hard to be 'empathic' and this initiated a much more stormy period in the therapy, with Joanne feeling much angrier and even making one suicidal gesture. However, with persistence, this period proved productive and over the next year she worked through and understood many painful feelings, achieving a new level of awareness and independence. She started a new relationship and ended the therapy in a planned way, in spite of withdrawing emotionally somewhat towards the end.

When some nine months later the relationship broke up, Joanne felt quite suicidal again. She contacted her former therapist, who was able to see her for an emergency consultation. This rapidly stabilized the situation and he found space for a further 12 sessions of deliberately short-term work in which many of the patterns and issues of the previous therapy were reviewed in a compressed way. The ending was positive. When, a few years later, Joanne looked back on this whole period of her life, she felt it was the time when she had made a new beginning.

This is an example of a 'success story' – not all are. Nonetheless, setbacks in development are not 'pathological' but a feature of our struggles to adapt and grow. Understanding normal developmental change provides a context from which to approach crises, impasses and relapses in a balanced way, seeing them as normal fluctuations in the experience of an evolving person. In attempting both to tolerate and respond to these challenges, the therapist needs a degree of faith in the capacity of human beings to grow and an acceptance of their difficulties in doing so. Developmental theory is a support in sustaining hope and making sense of the often confusing alterations and reversals which clients go through as they change. Some central theoretical principles can provide a framework for thinking about developmental and therapeutic challenges.

The dialectic of change

Change and continuity define each other: we cannot recognize or understand one without the other. They are co-dependent concepts. The spiritual traditions of both East and West have long sought to elucidate the nature of reality as the dynamic interplay of order and disorder, constituting a unity of opposites (Fingarette, 1963). Psychologically this can be understood in terms of self-organizing processes operating at the core of a person's functioning in which there is a dynamic interplay between the maintenance of existing psychological structures and their transformation, and between the elaboration of existing structures and their replacement with new forms of organization. Piaget (Piaget and Inhelder, 1969) identifies these two contrasting processes in cognitive terms as:

- *assimilation* – understanding new information in terms of established ways of knowing (or 'schemas'); and
- *accommodation* – transforming existing schemas in response to novel experience.

These processes of integration and differentiation are experienced at the level of our sense of self in terms of self-protection or self-elaboration. Psychological growth means movement towards greater complexity of the person's inner world: a wider range of awareness and clearer differentiation of emotional experience, together with a greater capacity for integration and containment of that emotional range which affects the quality of the openness and liveliness of a person's response to life. All the time and at different levels within the self, a struggle takes place between stasis and change, between building and destroying psychological structures. The tension between these creates a situation of constant dynamic conflict that lies at the heart of our human experience.

There is thus a dynamic balance between states of stability and transformation: psychological change is a solution to disequilibrium, to feeling off-balance. The extensiveness of the change required depends on the extent of the conflict that needs to be resolved within the person's experiential world. There is always a choice about whether an assimilating or an accommodating approach is taken: whether a discrepancy between novel experience and existing ways of viewing the world can be 'glossed over', or whether the work of significant internal transformation is undertaken. This is similar to the systems theory distinction between first and second order change: altering tactics within the rules of the present 'game' or changing the rules themselves (Fish et al., 1982). Both moments in the dialectic of development have value and require respect – even when they seem 'inconvenient' to us in the role of therapist. Change is more difficult than is sometimes admitted. There are 'limits to how much and how quickly an individual can change without jeopardizing his or her psychological integrity – that is, the sense of self and reality' (Mahoney, 1991: 18).

Resistance to change, including its chronic forms such as a therapeutic impasse, has to be understood in terms of its function in maintaining the integrity and coherence of our psychological structures. Continuity and stability have value, even when they play a role in maintaining painful or self-defeating ways of living. Equally, periods of personal disequilibrium and disorganization, even when they take the form of major crises or episodes of significant disorder, may be valued for their role in the genesis of new developmental achievements. Breakdown in existing structures may be needed for the emergence of creative new solutions to seemingly intractable life problems – achieving a breakthrough.

This continual interplay between change and stability is pervasive and relentless; it is the ever-present undercurrent of our experience of who we are and the world we live in. It exists in continual dialogue with the events and circumstances of our lives as they arise in both predictable and unpredictable ways. These dynamics are complex and non-linear: growth does not take place as a smooth progression; it is not an accumulation of elements. There is little certainty and there are no guarantees. At best, it is possible to distinguish cycles of change and repetition, a spiral pattern of revisiting similar issues again and again from slightly different – perhaps more 'developed' – starting points. Relapses need to be understood in the context of these non-linear and cyclical processes. It may be possible to distinguish alternating phases of change and revision or stability and consolidation in psychological structure during extended episodes in a person's life-cycle (Levinson, 1986). On a smaller time scale, Mahoney (1991) suggests that experience itself has a rhythm of expansion or contraction – of feeling more collected and centred and then of falling apart, being 'untogether' – which parallel these structural phases of integration/assimilation and differentiation/accommodation.

Change is seldom easy and even when it seems to take place quickly, it is likely to continue to unfold over a significant period of time. It is important to respect a person's individuality in the rhythm of this cycle of change: there may be times for challenge and demand which alternate with periods needing patient acceptance and support. Oscillations in the quality of our experience are normal and it should not be the aim of therapy to eliminate them. It may be important to 'normalize' these cycles for a client and to enable her to relate to her own fluctuating experiences more respectfully and compassionately. Our image of what it is to be human must be informed by an understanding that periods of difficulty and despair are part of our common condition and can contain the seeds of creativity and transformation.

The dynamics of transition

The cycles of change may be long or short depending on the scale of the change which has to be accommodated. Where there is significant discontinuity in the person's 'life space' they are likely to enter a 'transition state' (Golan, 1982). This is a period of persisting disruption and fluidity in which the need for a new, stable life organization and identity can be addressed. This may be the result either of internal developmental pressures (such as adolescent or mid-life 'crises') or significant psychosocial role shifts (such as marriage, relocation or retirement). Patterns within such transitional phases have been identified which provide a working model for any significant change process.

Transitional states constitute a period of uncertainty suspended between past and future. They might be considered a boundary zone existing between two states of greater stability. It is as though a 'gulf' has to be crossed: the old and familiar must be let go of in order to reach the new. This might be thought of as a 'death and rebirth' model of change (Gordon, 1978). In his classic anthropological work, Van Gennep (1960) noted the universality of ritual around significant developmental role changes; these 'rites of passage' attend to the person's need for a clear separation from the old role, for holding during a transitional phase and for some social marking of her incorporation of the new status. Thus, even positive changes, those which are desired and willed, require the letting go of the security of the known – they involve a process of loss.

The phases of the transition process have been analysed in detail in relation to many major change events. A simplistic stage model of mourning no longer seems adequate (Littlewood, 1992) but the centrality of the experience of loss in all developmental transitions means that the idea of a series of phases to be gone through and tasks to be undertaken provides a useful guide to therapeutic thinking. This sequence involves the destruction of a previous identity; a period of disintegration which may be more or less severe and more or less well managed; and a phase of reintegration of a new and hopefully more adaptive identity. This sequence is outlined in Figure 1.1. It consists of several experiential phases:

- In severe or unexpected changes, there is a phase of immobilization in which the person feels overwhelmed and responds with shock and numbness. This paralysis in the face of the unfamiliar will be less marked where the change is more under control but there may still be a degree of disorientation, unreality and a sense of detachment.
- There is often an early tendency to minimize the significance of a change. There may be some form of outright denial, a pretence that 'this is not happening to me'; or reactions of protest involving anger and outrage and the attempt to reassert control, a refusal of ownership or an insistence that things should be put back to how they were.
- Minimization is a temporary retreat from the distress of the change and from facing its implications. It is often combined with periods of 'dosing', in which manageable amounts of the disturbing reality are acknowledged and feelings of distress alternate with defensive calm (Horowitz, 1974).
- As loss of the old situation is acknowledged, feelings of depression and misery, combined with anger and frustration predominate. There is a need for a period of mourning. This depressive phase can also become a defensive retreat from accepting the need for change, especially if negativity cannot be expressed.

- This phase of depression may also involve a sense of helplessness, anxiety and imminent panic as the need to adapt to the new situation becomes clearer and a sense of security, familiarity and control has to be finally given up.
- The period of mourning for the past and refusal of the future starts to resolve through an acceptance of the reality of the changed situation and the letting go of what has been lost. Attachments to the past are allowed to loosen.
- A bridge to the future is formed as a period of active exploration enables the person to move forward and test herself out in the new situation. Alongside this energy there may also be an irritability and an insistence that things should be in line with expectations.
- This moves into a concern for understanding more fully the ways that things are now different, a phase marked by lower activity. Within the restructured life situation, there is a need to find a wider meaning for the change that provides a framework for a new view of who you are.
- Finally, over time, the changes in behaviour, role and self-concept are internalized and are incorporated in a new overall identity. This requires that psychological work be done to integrate what is new with who you were before in order to create a sense of continuity and self-coherence.

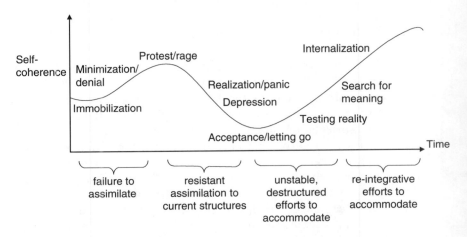

FIGURE 1.1 *The course of transitions (adapted from Adams and Hopson, 1976)*

Viewing these phases as strictly sequential stages is unhelpful and misrepresents many transitions. However, they do point to a series of predictable responses to the tasks of 'working through' a major transition. Such tasks include accepting the reality of the change and of the feelings of loss and separation that it involves; questioning and re-evaluating yourself and your place in the changed world; experimenting, initiating and testing out new ways of being which may include incorporating neglected aspects of the self; choosing and integrating the emergent patterns of living and committing yourself to a new identity. If someone's psychological structures tend to be rigid and absolutist, it will be relatively harder to manage this necessary 'emotional processing' without encountering difficulties.

Setbacks in development – both in life and in therapy – can be understood in relation to these transition dynamics. Crises are not necessarily part of a transitional state, though they may lead into one. However, many life crises bear similarities to the early stages of immobilization, denial, depression and panic; and clients will often need to be helped to move into working through subsequent phases in order to avoid becoming developmentally stuck. Any crisis which might lead into a transition state is an opportunity for growth since people are most open to new learning in a phase when they are exploring what a meaningful new identity might be. Impasses and relapses are understandable as blockages in the transition process which may take place at any of its phases. Both avoidance and certain kinds of depression are alternatives to accepting a changed reality. Equally, some people seem to remain safely in an experimental phase without managing to commit themselves to a new integration – they fail to move on. Regressing to previous phases in the process after apparent progress always seems to be a possibility. It is vital for therapists to accept where people actually are in developmental terms and not try to move them on too soon. To integrate what is new, people need support in their ownership of what is difficult about letting go of past securities.

This focus on separation and loss as central to developmental transition owes a great deal to attachment theory. Bowlby (1988) saw our innate tendency to seek affectional bonds with caretakers as intimately related to our desire for exploration: the safety provided by attachment to a caretaker provides a base for exploring the world. These needs are reciprocals of each other and have to be kept in a stage appropriate balance to ensure healthy development. Experiences of separation are linked to the progressive differentiation of self from others and the gradual elaboration of individual experience. The reliability and responsiveness of our attachment figures provides the sense of security from which we learn and grow. The predictable patterns of distress upon separation is a kind of template for our experience of future losses and those who experienced insecure or unempathic early relationships have this pain revived by subsequent transitional events.

The therapist's role is analogous to that of the caretaker: to provide a secure base to enable the client to manage the novelty of a transition and to help her explore more effectively (Holmes, 1993). The personal relationship is the vital element in helping, since it can create a safe and protected space in which a degree of disintegration can be contained: this security helps people work through the tasks of separation during a transitional state. However, for many therapy clients, early attachment experiences have left them with a very insecure sense of self in relationship to others: they act – either during periods of stress or perhaps much of the time – in ways which match well-established but ineffective means of providing a sense of security – patterns such as clinging desperately to others or avoiding any involvement and denying distress. The therapist has to understand these defensive responses and recognize in them both the current and the historical roots of the client's attempts at self-protection: her sense of self-integrity feels like it is in jeopardy. The therapeutic situation must be made more challenging or more supportive, depending upon the individual's needs and the amount of anxiety or security, separateness or connectedness, which she can tolerate at a given time. Setbacks often arise due to the client's experiencing her therapist's offer of availability and relatedness as insufficiently safe – too close, too unreliable, too demanding, too rejecting and so on. She cannot take the risks needed to experiment with or sustain change. She clings to the relative safety of familiar patterns of relating.

Evolution in the life cycle

In thinking about patterns of change, writers about development in adulthood have sought to identify more extended cycles which might map out an underlying order to the human life course in all its complexity (Sugarman, 1986). It remains contentious to what extent the psychology of adult life is predictably ordered, with some theories emphasizing the open-ended and unpredictable nature of development (Ford and Learner, 1992), while others uphold evolution according to a 'ground plan' (e.g. Erikson, 1963). It seems clear that there are elements of both, with unpredictable, idiosyncratic and chaotic events and changes interacting with patterned influences which can create identifiable life stages. Such influences involve both internal maturation and the normative age-graded expectations and role structure of a particular cultural environment. There is an understandable anxiety about theories of 'adult development' being interpreted rigidly by psychotherapists in oppressive and constraining, rather than liberating, ways. Nonetheless, life events, developmental setbacks and emergent change take on different meanings depending on their place in an individual's evolving life cycle.

Levinson (1986) proposes the idea of a 'life structure', an evolving pattern encompassing the intersection of the person's beliefs, values and sense of self and the investment of those in the roles and activities of the social world. People go through alternating phases of structure building and structure changing. In the former, the major investment is in consolidating a lifestyle and pursuing the goals to which it is devoted. However, any structure in time becomes outmoded: the balance of rewards and sacrifices becomes less satisfying or the viability of the role structure is compromised by external changes. The person will then move into a lengthy transitional phase in which the old structure is dismantled, goals reappraised, other possibilities explored and different commitments made. This is very much like the account of a transition state, but Levinson is describing a cycle which takes place over a longer time scale, with alternating five-year periods of change and consolidation. Gould (1980) chooses the attachment–separation dynamic as an underlying perspective to orient understanding of the course of adult development. Repeatedly, safety has to be given up in order to attain an expanded sense of self, one in which we are more accepting of ourselves and more autonomous and empowered, less governed by a 'childhood consciousness' in which we feel determined but protected by rules and standards set by others. Both authors map out a specific pattern of predictable phases with their own themes and developmental tasks of maturation to be mastered at each point in the life cycle: these issues are likely to be much more culturally dependent and open to historical and individual variation. In general, however, it is the failure to negotiate the demands of such transitional periods which are at the root of any developmental setback.

In a sense, such accounts of the life cycle are themselves narratives through which we as a culture, through our psychological theories, find stories which give coherence and continuity in the face of the many changes and discontinuities, both gradual and dramatic, which people's lives go through. Stories with plots are the crucial form by which we integrate the various accounts which we can construct of a complex experience (McLeod, 1997). Many of the developmental setbacks which we encounter – the crises, impasses and relapses – occur when the plot of our life story is interrupted, diverted or fails to progress in a direction and at a pace which makes sense to us. Our sense of 'identity' is perhaps the central narrative device by which we seek to make ourselves and our progression through life coherent and comprehensible (Erikson, 1968), integrating diverse elements of experience and bringing aspects of ourselves into relation with others – past, present and future. Reconstructed progressively across the life span, identity is the crucial focus of revision during any transitional phase: in such an 'identity crisis', we attempt to create a more inclusive sense of self which, if authentically achieved, is more complex and better integrated, providing a renewed sense of coherence and an increased vitality. However, this revision involves risk-taking. During the transition, coherence is let go of, our grasp of previous certainties is loosened and personal boundaries are more permeable. The sense of self is less clear in its separateness and individuality: the person might feel naked, her sense of integrity breached, with a feeling that she might be 'spilling out': it is a time of vulnerability and loss of control, with a need to be held together. In the absence of enough safety and personal containment, the process can result in compromised forms of resolution (Marcia, 1966). The person might 'foreclose' by adopting some protective identity too early, either by rigidly clinging to old, received identifications or by rushing to assume some new, 'pre-packaged' identity received from outside, without doing the work of integrating this with her wider experience. Equally, she might give up on the work of integration and settle for a diffuse, relatively disintegrated sense of self, lacking in personally meaningful values, ideals and goals. The individual needs to be held in order to take the risks that can lead to the renewal of her identity and avoid a developmental impasse.

Developing therapeutic vision

Some vision of maturity – a desired outcome of development – always guides psychotherapeutic interventions and therapeutic theories offer a way to understand the developmental setbacks which might stand in the way of realizing it. This vision underpins the values on which the therapeutic enterprise is based. In this chapter, we have attempted to identify some ways of thinking about the change process which meaningfully link together the diverse themes of this book – viewing crisis, impasse and relapse as challenges to a process of development which are intrinsic to the way in which growth occurs. We have sketched out elements of a 'meta-narrative' which gives coherence to these themes and guides the wide-ranging story told by the book as a whole. The principles of this are summarized in Table 1.1. It views human development as one of increasing complexity achieved through the dialectical process of differentiation and integration, linked to a narrative of progressive separation and individuation. This might run the danger of over-emphasizing the individual person at the expense of her relationship to others, but this need not be so. There is an intimate interconnection of the personal and the social: self and identity are constructed within and totally dependent upon the matrix of human relationships. Values embodied in this developmental narrative concern the creative elaboration of experience, the toleration of dynamic tension, the promotion of dialogue and the search for

TABLE 1.1   *Some principles of developmental change*

- *Development is dialectical*: psychological structures are built and transformed through the interplay of differentiation and integration.
- *Change is continuous and life-long*: the dialectic of development takes place across all time-frames – immediate, medium and long-term.
- *Progress is complex and non-linear*: regressions, pauses and sudden shifts are normal; issues are revisited in a spiral motion.
- *Change involves loss*: to grow, risks must be taken – separation from old securities, the closing of options.
- *Personal identity creates security*: familiar ways of relating provide a sense of a predictable world and a consistent self which is a context for and counterweight to change.
- *Causation in relationships is circular*: established ways of relating safely create predictable patterns of response which confirm expectations, even if these are negative and self-defeating, and so resist change.
- *New events evoke past experience*: change resonates with prior formative relationships and expectations are revived and reinforced.
- *Balance of security and challenge enables growth*: safety encourages openness, flexibility and risk in response to demands for change.
- *Rigidity, closure and withdrawal impede development*: crises, impasses and relapses become problematic when demands overwhelm existing capacities to provide security.

balance between diversity and freedom on the one hand, and awareness and control on the other.

In developing a guiding theoretical narrative for our therapeutic work, it is important to think about what kind of role we wish it to play. It should not be a way of imposing our values and goals on clients or constraining their life stories to fit our model. However, in facing difficult therapeutic situations where there is a danger of the work being pushed off course, progress halted or deterioration setting in, therapists are vulnerable to twin pressures: either falling into paralysis and despair or rushing to impulsive action. There is a real danger of engaging in a desperate search for some method of regaining control of the situation. We need support in the face of these pressures and the foundations provided by a theoretical base (as well as by our personal and professional context) offer the needed stability and confidence. At the same time, when things are not going well we need to respond flexibly and creatively: it may not be enough to just keep doing the same thing. Theory can facilitate 'reflection in action'. The dialogue with a problematic therapeutic situation can be the spur to elaborating theory. In difficult situations, rigid adherence to your specific 'school' seems particularly unhelpful. Some form of conceptual 'base camp', to use Mahoney's (1991) phrase, provides security and discipline, but should also be a starting point for further exploration. We need secure theoretical attachments as therapists that support a creative and non-exclusive developmental vision.

In therapeutic work as in life, there is a dynamic complementarity between stability and change. Throughout the subsequent chapters, we draw eclectically on a variety of different theoretical and technical approaches. To the extent that there is a place of integration, it is within the broad dynamic theory of development that we have sketched in this chapter. However, it is for each practitioner to select from the ideas presented what can effectively be integrated within her own personal approach to her work. Such theoretical choices are embedded in our cultural and personal history: our development as therapists reflects who we are as people – and what we envision becoming. Being sufficiently free and empowered to respond to therapeutic setbacks requires us to be conscious of the choices we are making about how to work and the ethical and value commitments which these embody. We need to do the developmental work of creating a coherent professional identity which supports our practice. Each therapist has to articulate a personal vision of what it means to 'grow' and how to provide the conditions in which that happens.

Psychotherapy and counselling necessarily have a privileged relationship to change. Our social role is to be sanctioned change agents, on the edge of many cultural commitments and identities. It is part of that role to maintain an optimistic stance towards possibility and a challenging relationship to the limitations of any status quo. However, we need also to develop a degree of balanced pessimism. There are many limits to change and some of our clients will be wounded, scarred and disabled in ways which require acceptance and compassion when they present their difficulties to us in challenging and sometimes frustrating forms. This book is about retaining our creativity in the face of such difficulties without aggressively expecting more of others than they can bear.

2   Understanding Crises

Most people experience a crisis at some point in their lives: crises are ordinary, expectable and, in that sense, 'normal'. For any individual, however, crises are relatively uncommon, arising unexpectedly and taking us outside the range of our everyday experience. The word evokes a sense of threat and danger, of urgency and the need for immediate action: we are at risk. Psychologically, the experience is one of imminent or actual 'breakdown' – of our lives and ourselves 'falling apart'. Although most of us might go through a time which could be called a crisis, there may be limited prior experience to draw on to help us manage it. This can be true in the therapeutic role as well: we are faced, often suddenly, with someone in an extremity of distress where there is great pressure to act – but we may have had limited training and experience in specifically what to do, or even how to think about such an 'emergency'. Even with training we may feel ill-equipped to deal with the sudden extremes of pain and disorganization. Crises can create a sense of crisis in the therapist too.

Inherent in the idea of crisis, however, is something positive and forward-looking as well. The roots of the word are in the Greek verb, *Kritikos*, 'to decide' – related to our words 'critic', 'crux', 'crucial' and 'cross'. A crisis is a decisive moment – a crossroads, a time of judgement, a critical juncture. It is a turning point, a time when a new direction is taken – for better or for worse. Psychologically, there is an opportunity for growth. Within the personal disorganization of the crisis state, there is a chance for reorganization to take place and new structures to emerge. It has become almost a cliché to note that the Chinese character for crisis joins the terms for danger and opportunity. The balance of risk and opportunity depends on how the crisis is handled by the individual and responded to by those around her.

Defining crisis

There is some confusion around the use of the term 'crisis' and what falls within its scope. Clear thinking in the clinical situation is aided by a well-focused definition. A personal crisis is a state of *psychological disequilibrium* in which an individual's usual strategies for managing herself and the world are failing (Aguilera and Messick, 1982). Coping mechanisms and defences collapse in the face of an experience which is felt to be intolerable. Thus, a crisis is a state of mind – an experience of acute personal disorganization – not the circumstances which give rise to it. It is a psychological process rather than a specific event, although such occurrences as major loss, role changes and threats to self-image or health have a high likelihood of precipitating a crisis state.

In the crisis process, a threshold is reached at which a threat is experienced as beyond available resources – you no longer feel able to 'handle' it. This is, to some extent, a matter of degree and the intensity of a crisis state varies. The kinds of experience which characterize this phase of breakdown include: intense anxiety and panic; feeling emotionally overwhelmed; flooding with anger, guilt and shame; depression or numbness; major alteration of behavioural routines such as sleeping, eating or structuring time; inability to think clearly or formulate options; and taking impulsive action. This is a time-limited state. Crises have a rapid onset (or worsening of previous difficulties) and – although it is more than a momentary emotional outburst – it cannot be tolerated indefinitely and will usually resolve in some fashion in anything from a few days to a few weeks.

TABLE 2.1   *Characteristics of a crisis*

- A hazardous event or worsening of a vulnerable state causes a sudden onset of a crisis period.
- The nature or severity of the stress is such that the person fails to cope using their customary methods.
- They enter into a period of disequilibrium characterized by emotional, cognitive and behavioural disturbances.
- The period of the crisis is time-limited and typically lasts 1–6 weeks.

The variability in the intensity of a crisis and the involvement of common psychological processes means that there is overlap with other related states. While these distinctions are not clear-cut, it is important not to use the term crisis too loosely as if it applied to almost any emotional upset (Parry, 1990). It is not just unpleasant things happening or a *predicament* in which a choice has to be made between painful options. It is not only an *emergency* where urgent action has to be taken: the decisions or the actions required have to be felt to be beyond what the person can manage. Crises do often create emergencies for others, including therapists. The issue of 'stress' is of course closely related: pressure on the individual's coping processes are at the heart of both (Lazarus and Folkman, 1984). Adverse circumstances or heavy demands can be experienced by the person as a challenge in which they 'rise to the occasion' by giving extra effort; or as stress in which their resources and capabilities are severely taxed and they suffer an experience of sustained overload. This may lead into a crisis situation through eventual exhaustion or by leaving the person vulnerable to an event with which she might otherwise have dealt. However, as long as she feels able to manage the situation, albeit experiencing psychological or physical symptoms, such stressful times do not amount to a crisis.

It can sometimes be hard to distinguish a relatively short-lived flare-up of intense emotion and distress, occurring over a period of hours, from a true crisis. However, if this is a state likely to subside without need to adapt psychologically to changed circumstances, it is probably best to see this rather as a brief fluctuation in an ongoing state. It requires less concentrated intervention. This is particularly important in the case of what might be called 'furore' (Ratna, 1978), in which crisis-like reactions have become a chronic and repetitive pattern of response to any stress. People prone to present for help during such episodes require a different response from crisis intervention (as outlined in Chapter 5). Crisis is also not the same as *trauma* which is itself a complex and over-widely applied term. A traumatic event generally lies outside the normal course of a person's experience and expectations and is likely to produce intense fear, helplessness or horror in those who experience it. The reaction to such an event involves severe anxiety and hyper-arousal, together with shock or dissociation during or following it (Yule, 1999). This leads to a constellation of subsequent reactions – persistent re-experiencing, avoidance, arousal or numbness – indicating that the experience is difficult to process emotionally and accommodate cognitively. Such experiences may lead to an ongoing crisis state but they may not, and although crisis and response to trauma are closely linked, it is better to consider them separately. A *disaster* is an occasion in which so many people have collectively traumatic experiences that the coping capabilities of an entire community have been overwhelmed and the effects resonate throughout an extensive network of individuals and institutions (Hodgkinson and Stewart, 1998).

In the literature, a distinction is sometimes made between situational and developmental crises. We have been describing the former and believe the term is properly restricted to these. Developmental crises are occasions when maturation or other role transformations create wide-ranging demands for change and initiate a *transition state* (as described in Chapter 1). Transition states extend over a longer period of time with a lower emotional intensity. A crisis can find its resolution through being transformed into a transition state, initiating wider changes, and intervention may help to achieve this conversion.

Graeme was 45 when his business, manufacturing electrical components, ran into trouble due to a recession. He worked night and day to get contracts and increasingly found himself up at all hours trying to make the financial figures add up – he was under enormous stress. The obvious step was to lay off some workers, but the people who might go had been loyal employees and personal friends – the predicament seemed intolerable. Then he had a car accident. Graeme was uninjured but his passenger, a friend's son, was very badly hurt. He found himself reliving this trauma repeatedly; though on the surface he 'coped' surprisingly well, in fact he felt numb and found it hard to drive. The crisis when it came was triggered by something quite trivial: he read in a trade magazine that electrical components was a 'dying industry', that it was 'finished'. He felt in a total turmoil, almost overwhelmed by panic and by guilt, preoccupied with both the accident and the redundancies. When his wife found by accident that he had placed a hosepipe and a bottle of whisky in the boot of his car she recognized the gravity of the emergency with which she was faced. She called his best friend and they persuaded him to go with them to hospital where a psychiatrist admitted him for a few days. The firm was indeed taken into receivership and it was restructured, but Graeme took it surprisingly well. After a year, he had found a job running a programme to retrain the young unemployed. He told friends that the whole episode had given him a new perspective – he felt he had gone through some kind of transition after he left hospital and had rediscovered what was really important in life.

Models of crisis

The process of a crisis is not intuitively difficult to understand. However, various psychological models have been used to help articulate what is going on. Caplan (1964) employs the simple but helpful idea of 'homeostasis': people are constantly involved in maintaining an emotional balance in their transactions with the world; environmental demands and internal conflicts create pressures which can destabilize this; we respond using coping mechanisms in efforts to manage the demands and restore our equilibrium. Rebalancing maintains personal consistency, emotional stability and coherent expectations: life is usually managed within the bounds of our normal processes and routines. Hazardous events, however, can dramatically disturb this balance and tax our coping resources. A crisis arises when the demands go outside our ability to manage them and we sense that we do not have the resources to overcome or accommodate the hazard. This creates a serious disturbance to our emotional equilibrium and our normal ways of trying to maintain it.

Everyone is potentially vulnerable to this kind of disruption. People do vary significantly, however, in coping style and capability and so in their degree of vulnerability. The idea of coping mechanisms has been extensively researched in the stress literature (Lazarus and Folkman, 1984). People adopt different strategies and tactics in their efforts to manage the stress created by the demands of the situation as they interpret it. Broad *strategic approaches* to mastering, tolerating or reducing stress are:

- *problem-focused* activities designed to solve a conflict, reduce its intensity or proactively head off its escalation;
- *self-focused* work orientated towards redefining the problem and restructuring our perception of it to alter its felt demands or our desired goals;
- *effects-focused* self-management designed to reduce or control the emotionally disruptive impact of the stress.

The extent to which these are adaptive in any situation varies. Each approach has its place – and each can be used inappropriately:

- trying to anticipate events which are essentially unpredictable can lead to superstitious beliefs and behaviour;
- simply redefining a situation which could be changed by action may lead to giving up on important goals or denying the existence of a problem;
- trying merely to manage the effects of stress can result in inertia or regression – the classic case is substance misuse.

There is a continuum from effective reality focused strategies to more dysfunctional defensive ones. Under stress, it may be necessary to become more conscious and selective about what coping strategies to use, rather than remaining on the 'automatic pilot' we use in daily life. However, the greater the sense of psychological threat and personal vulnerability, the more we tend to resort to self-protective measures which may fail to address the needs of the situation. As a crisis deepens, the more chance there is that efforts to cope become ineffectual and may lead to the situation deteriorating.

When Jenny's husband announced that he was leaving her for another woman she couldn't really take it in, although she had known their relationship had been poor for several years. She threw herself into constant activity, particularly around the home: decorating the house, gardening and buying new things. When she did let herself think about what he'd said, she told herself that he didn't really mean it, or that he'd get over it. She found herself lost in daydreams about how things would be once he had tired of this 'fling'. A few days after he had left, in a sort of trance state she took all the pills she could find.

On finding a lump on her breast, Margaret went at once to her doctor. When tests showed that she had cancer it was hard to take in at first, but talking to her closest friends helped her to calm herself a little and collect her thoughts. By the time of her next appointment with the consultant, she had read two books about coping with cancer and joined an internet support group and so was able to discuss the options for treatment with him in an informed way.

Fundamentally, what may be at risk in a life crisis is the potential collapse of our sense of identity and belonging. A major life goal is felt to be under threat – something *essential* for personal fulfilment, safety or a meaningful life. In a sense, it is our understanding of ourselves, of who we are in relation to the world, which is threatened: our sense of identity no longer seems to be validated by our experience. There is a painful discrepancy; life is not working out within our current view of ourselves (Parry, 1990). In a crisis, people are no longer able to represent their experience coherently to themselves – to 'contain' it – or to sustain an adaptive way of dealing with this sense of violation. All the alternatives that present themselves are unacceptable within our current world view. This lack of options is a crucial feature of the crisis experience, giving a sense that there is no way out. The breakdown taking place within our understanding of the world also isolates us from other people since our usual ways of relating no longer seem to apply. The process of crisis is thus not merely a matter of failing to 'cope'; it is linked to psychological discontinuity, transition and change in general. In a sense, the crisis is created by our own 'resistance' – our difficulty, perhaps our reluctance, in finding a new understanding of ourselves which fits our experience better.

The process of crisis development

Crises develop over time in a patterned way. It is helpful to have a map of the probable overall course of a crisis even though in specific crisis situations individuals will show their own unique patterns of development and it is important not to overgeneralize. An important element of this is that the central experience of disorganization is time-limited. It is not a question of *whether* a crisis will be resolved but of *how* it will be resolved. The person's experience is often that 'this can't go on' or 'something has to give'. The clinical observation seems to be that this period extends from a few days up to four to six weeks maximum. Around this central period of disorganization, there are a number of possible phases in the development of the crisis which are summarized in Figure 2.1.

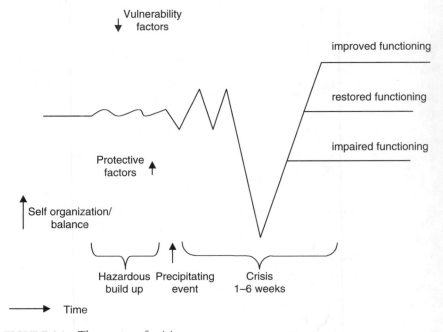

FIGURE 2.1   *The course of crisis*

Often there will be a 'hazardous build-up' to the crisis itself, a period during which the person is experiencing stress due to adverse life circumstances or is in a transition state. She may be managing this adequately using her normal coping repertoire for routine problem solving but her resources are somewhat depleted and vulnerability is increased. Indeed, there may be no very significant event which causes entry into the crisis state, in which case it may be called a 'crisis of exhaustion'. During this build-up phase, it may be possible to respond to early warning signs, foresee the potential for a crisis and act in anticipation. Improved understanding and responsiveness might prevent many crises.

Normally there is some clear event that precipitates a crisis, although the 'objective' severity of this may vary substantially depending on the individual's vulnerability, as well as on her unique perception of its meaning. This initiates a period in which routine coping mechanisms are deployed but felt to be ineffective. A sense of helplessness and increasing anxiety is created. This may result in the use of emergency coping mechanisms and defences but their effectiveness may be hindered by the increased disorganization. There may be outbursts of anger or distress and the apparent vulnerability may elicit help from other people.

Continued failure to avoid or resolve the threat is likely to cause the person to resort to 'desperate measures' – new or risky problem-solving measures, perhaps used in a trial and error fashion. This is 'make or break': it involves a major mobilization of both internal and external resources. During these phases of gradually increasing disorganization, the individual's psychological functioning in the realms of thinking, feeling and acting may all become radically affected in ways summarized in Table 2.2.

TABLE 2.2   *Psychological disorganization during crises*

Emotional	Cognitive
flooded	narrowed focus of attention
fluctuating	obsessive and catastrophizing
frozen	loss of concentration
somatizing	concrete (not abstract)
	confused
Behavioural	distorted time frame
regressive	magical thinking
dependent	excessive fantasy
suggestible	unable to formulate problem
susceptible to influence	isolated from feedback about actions
withdrawn	
impulsive	
pressure to act	

Overall: the person is not orientated to solving problems, but to escaping from them.

Solutions created during this phase of 'desperation' may well be incomplete or maladaptive, having ignored certain aspects of reality or distorted significant aspects of the person's identity or goals. However, failure to effect any solution leads to 'breaking point' through the exhaustion of all coping efforts. In such a breakdown, major personality disorganization occurs in a variety of ways: extreme distress; overtly disturbed behaviour; development of some neurotic symptomatology, anxiety state or depression; or for some vulnerable individuals, psychotic disintegration which may be transient or may initiate an episode of major mental illness.

These maladaptive 'solutions' – whether effected during the stage of disorganization or in the form of a breakdown – lead to a reorganization and restitution of greater stability. The crisis period ends but it may have resulted in some partially or significantly compromised level of functioning, with long-term deterioration and impairment or a persisting increased vulnerability to responding badly in future crisis situations. People may 'bear the scars' of past crises, perhaps in such a way that they relive them again when faced with future life events. It appears that quite a large proportion of people who have passed through significant life crises have a relatively poor outcome. For example, 30 per cent of bereaved women seem to be faring badly after two to four years (Parkes and Weiss, 1983). People do not just 'come out the other side' in a way that a simplistic reading of stage theories of transition might suggest. There may be persisting disruption and disorder which continues long after the end of the crisis episode.

Alternatively, however, the emergent organization may be a growth in the person's functioning and the restoration to a balance of coping at an improved level to that before the crisis. Thus, although this phase of disorganization carries real dangers, it is also an opportunity for growth. Because old habits are disturbed and known patterns failing, there is the possibility of learning new responses. The desperation, dependency and suggestibility make the person receptive to influence and help. This carries dangers of exploitation and abuse, but it can provide a route into receiving help which might otherwise be threatening. With internal boundaries between aspects of the self and external boundaries to other people both loosened, the individual is opened up emotionally to issues which are otherwise defended against. Although the impulse may be to suppress these issues, there is an opportunity for reworking them and reorganizing the self in significant ways. With this intensity of emotion compressed into a limited time, there is an opportunity for maximum impact with minimum intervention. In order to facilitate this, the therapist has to make the emotional pain and disequilibrium bearable, so that rather than resorting to desperate partial solutions, new learning and integration is made possible. Crisis intervention can be a demanding but rewarding role.

Understanding the individual in crisis

Each crisis situation is unique. It is important not to make assumptions that you understand it on the basis of general patterns. Each individual presenting in a crisis needs careful assessment of her particular situation and her own personal responses to it. Crises are the product of a complex sequence of interacting elements; Jacobson (1980) calls this the 'crisis matrix' – the interplay of internal and external elements, triggering and maintaining the state of disorganization. The factors influencing the development and outcome of a crisis fall into five broad categories:

- the hazardous event itself and its perceived implications;
- the background situation including vulnerabilities in the person and her life circumstances;
- the meaning and resonance which the event has uniquely for that individual in relation to her personal history;
- the coping efforts and responses to the developing crisis made by the person;
- the response of the individual's social network to the developing crisis.

The nature of the event, of course, has a significant influence on the person's response. Hazardous events vary considerably in their nature and consequently in their probable effects on those experiencing them. The main dimensions along which events differ are their controllability and the nature of the loss involved, but within these, a set of further issues has to be considered. These are summarized in Table 2.3. The degree of loss and how central it is to the person's sense of who they are, determines the extent of the personal change with which they are faced. Some changes will mean that the person is faced with some significant ongoing transition. Even positive events (such as marriage or promotion) can mean substantial change and be quite destabilizing. The degree of threat and of uncertainty are likely to impact on the level of anxiety experienced. The presence of danger, and particularly trauma, can influence fundamental perceptions about the safety and reliability of the world in which we are living. The presence of shame and humiliation have a great impact on an individual's ability to think about and emotionally process her experience. The presence of some warning which was not heeded increases the likelihood of feeling guilty. Sudden unanticipated accidents readily result in anger and a sense of injustice. Blame is always likely but is partly dependent on whether the event was in someone else's control. These are complex issues linked to the person's particular ways of perceiving the world but the characteristics of the event need to be considered as clues to guide an exploration of what the individual may be feeling.

There is often a 'last straw' which tipped the balance into a full-blown crisis state. This might be termed the 'precipitating' factor and it sometimes can seem relatively trivial. The question that might be asked is: 'What happened in the last day or two to upset you so much to cause you to seek help now?' Hazardous events standing in the background can occasionally be difficult to identify even though they are crucial. In assessing background factors, it can be helpful to explore 'when it all began'.

TABLE 2.3   *Dimensions of hazardous life events*

Issues of control		
Expectable	–	could be clearly anticipated
		were some warning signs
		chosen/created by individual
Preventable	–	with hindsight
		could be (realistically) avoided/mitigated
Controllable	–	influence event/subsequent developments
		realistic versus subjective wish
Uncertainty	–	period of continuing lack of clarity
Issues of threat and loss		
Personal Loss	–	relationship/role/belief
		what it meant to individual
Change	–	further role transition required
Threat	–	to personal integrity
		of potential loss
Danger	–	to physical safety/life
Trauma	–	massive, sudden threat to safety/integrity
Humiliation	–	creating personal shame
		loss of self-esteem
Negative Revelation	–	discovering pre-existing unwelcome information
		loss of trust

Background issues are those which provide a context for a crisis, enabling us to understand how the person was vulnerable at this time. This includes the stress from adverse circumstances in various spheres of the person's life in the recent past. Developmental transition states, both those connected to psychosocial role changes and those due to age-related growth may be a significant factor. There may have been multiple hazardous events which are related in complex ways to one another over a period of time. It may also be that the individual has chronically poor coping capacities, a deficit which renders her vulnerable to even moderately taxing life events. Indeed, the present crisis may be one in a long series which constitutes a repetitive pattern of stress response.

Life events have unique meanings for each individual. These arise from the particular interpretations, resonances and links which the event triggers for an individual in relation to her own history. The acceptability of different courses of action which could be taken is greatly influenced by an individual's cultural context and belief system. To take a simple example, opting to get divorced has very different meanings in different sections of our society today. Equally, habitual irrational assumptions may distort how an event is interpreted. People may berate themselves for not coping or doing more; they may generalize their difficulties in coping to hopelessness about their ability to manage life generally. Grieving may be inhibited by a belief that it is weak to show feelings or by an irrational guilt produced by an excessive sense of responsibility. Therapists may fail to explore adequately distress which seems to them 'understandable' in terms of what has happened to the person; but it is essential to search for the personal meanings which affect the individual's reaction and not to assume that you know what an event means.

Memories of past experiences, particularly those which were traumatic or unresolved, are often rekindled by the current crisis. Painful feelings start to break through but may then be feared and avoided. The maladaptive response which results from this hidden conflict often underlies the person's inability to cope well with the current situation. To understand the present crisis fully, it is essential to explore the resonances which the event evokes and so understand the symbolic and interpersonal meanings which it has for the individual. It may be linked to long-term, fundamental existential issues for her. Core conflicts and beliefs can become accessible to exploration and challenge. It is often this feature of a crisis situation – the relatively open access to past emotional pain – which can make it possible for dramatic positive change to occur in a short period of time.

Maya's father was almost 80 and had been ill and in pain for two years. She was prepared for his death and though intensely sad, thought it for the best. When the end came however, it hit her with overwhelming force: she felt utterly abandoned and unsafe. Talking with her sister three inconsolable weeks later, she realized that these feelings were somehow linked to when she was five years old and her parents went abroad to start their new life. She had been left with an aunt whom she didn't like – the loneliness and fear she felt then had somehow all come rushing back.

Andrea's new house – purchased on the basis of a large bonus and a promotion at work – was everything she had ever dreamed of. She felt that she had finally 'arrived'. On the day of moving however, her excitement turned to unease and when the movers left, she found herself prey to a deepening sense of emptiness and dismay. She wandered around feeling lonely and increasingly frightened and decided that she could not spend the night there. The mood did not lift and she spent several nights in a hotel, almost unable to bear visiting her new home, alternately weeping and feeling numb. She had fought her way up the career ladder and left her emotionally distant family behind. It was as though in achieving success, a large area of emptiness and yearning in her personality had suddenly opened up, leaving her disorientated and deeply depressed.

A crisis is often intensified by the individual's attempts at managing it proving to be unhelpful. To understand the development of a crisis you need to know what the individual has done to deal with it at different stages in the process. Clarifying coping strategies and reviewing their effectiveness allows you to track the process by which subsequent events – particularly deterioration in the situation – have been the result of actions that the individual has (or has not) taken. Equally, it may highlight ways of responding that are working effectively, identifying solutions and capabilities in a situation which can seem to be dominated by the lack of alternatives. It is also essential to make an assessment of the person's ability to be helped – whether she can co-operate actively or is only able to respond passively; or whether she might be suspicious or resistant or uninterested in other people's efforts on her behalf.

As important in understanding the development of a crisis as the person's own responses to it are those of her social context. Some people who present in crisis are socially isolated and have virtually no networks of support upon which to draw. They are more likely to be dependent on professional and general community resources. For most however, inter-action with family and wider social networks will have been crucial in the process of the crisis developing. Social relationships provide both support and an implicit control over impulsive actions. They can be a channel for the expression of feelings as well as providing practical help, information and companionship. However, if the network is strained, these resources may become weakened or absent. Indeed, at some point social networks may start to reject the person who is the focus of the disturbance. In a sense, crises – in terms of those which present to professional services – always constitute a breakdown in the framework of natural helping pro-cesses: it is the whole social network that is faced with a crisis which it is unable to handle without calling in outside assistance.

Crisis assessment

There are two major aspects of the clinical assessment of a person in crisis. One is that of *risk assessment*: making an appraisal of the degree to which there may be some significant threat to safety, either that of the client or of other people. Such an assessment is a priority although it is not always the first thing that can be done. It may take more or less prominence in different cases and sometimes 'risk' may be quickly 'screened out' as largely irrelevant. It is nonetheless very important for any therapist to know the elements of risk assessment and we devote much of the next chapter to it. The second level of assessment, *understanding the person in crisis*, depends on the therapist's ability to explore and integrate all of the kinds of infor-mation outlined in the section above – summarized in Table 2.4. The therapist needs to arrive at a view of the intensity and extensiveness of the disruption that person is experiencing and the degree to which she is unable to function in her usual life role. Eventually, she should be able to under-stand the primary sources of vulnerability and maladaptive response that have led to the crisis and to formulate an overall picture of what is inevitably a complex, multifaceted situation. This understanding can then shape the formation of a *crisis intervention plan* – including what assistance to call in, what concrete help and guidance to provide and what subsequent therapeutic focus may be adopted.

In making a clinical assessment of an individual in crisis, it is doubtful that there can be any useful 'protocol' for conducting it in detail. So varied

TABLE 2.4 *Crisis assessment – issues to investigate*

- Nature of trigger event
  - what has happened to precipitate crisis
- Individual meanings of the event
  - characteristics and emotional impact (see Table 2.3)
  - personal meanings and resonances (individual's history)
- Background life demands
  - ongoing life stresses
  - transition states
- Degree of disruption/disintegration
  - to emotional stability
  - to daily routines
  - to ability to care for self
  - to cognitive functioning/perception of reality
- Nature of coping strategies
  - main coping mechanisms
  - effectiveness: making situation worse or better
  - normal coping style and abilities
- Resources
  - personal strengths and achievements
  - employment/financial/accommodation stability
  - social networks/support
- Involvement/attitude of others
  - willing/able to help
  - absent/exhausted
  - hostile/rejecting
- Amenability to help
  - collaborative with therapist
  - willing but passive
  - disengaged/rejecting
- Level of risk (Chapter 3)
  - to self: suicide, self-harm, self-neglect, exploitation
  - to others: homicide, violence, abuse/neglect of dependants
- Resources of therapist/agency
  - willingness to respond
  - actual ability to provide required support

and, on occasion, so demanding are the ways individuals present in a crisis state that each initial contact has to be handled differently. Even more than with most therapy, the immediate need is to make an emotional connection with the person. This may require some form of practical action to contain the situation before any more thorough assessment can be conducted. However, this must not obscure the vital need to make an assessment which guides decisions about the way forward. It is important not to rush to active intervention which may be unnecessary or make the situation worse. The therapist generally needs to stay focused on the present situation and what seems directly relevant to that, but of course what is relevant cannot be known in advance. Information often emerges in an idiosyncratic order. It is important to be able to be active and direct, asking simple questions in a straightforward manner as well as to be empathic and reflect feelings. By ensuring that there is some order in the process of the interview, a sense of safety and containment is provided to the client. For example, it is extremely helpful to identify hazardous and precipitating events which may well be quite unclear to the client in her confused and overwhelmed state of mind. Discovering the upsetting event can introduce a degree of clarity and perspective and a sense of potential control which had been lacking in the situation. In this sense, the process of assessment is very much part of the process of intervention in a crisis situation.

Conclusion

Clients often present for help in the midst of a crisis. This is, of course, particularly the case in relatively accessible frontline services – GP surgeries, student and employee counselling services, walk-in help centres or telephone hot-lines – but it can also be so in services with longer response times or more specialist referral routes and for therapists in independent practice. These helping contexts are themselves important in terms of the message they give about the meaning of a crisis, as well as what kind of response can realistically be offered. Therapists should plan for – and communicate a clear message about – how they respond to crises in a way that is appropriate to the setting within which they work. Crises can, and often do, occur in the midst of an ongoing therapy; this situation has some significant differences from crises presenting at an entry point for help and these specific issues will be dealt with in Chapter 5.

3   Assessing and Responding to Risk

Risk is inherent in a crisis: things could end badly. The client may see only disaster while the therapist is trying to help her discover a better outcome. Of course, any situation and every action involves an element of risk – we cannot be sure of the consequences. Crises are times when safety is reduced and the sense of risk dramatically heightened. One way of seeing the task of crisis intervention is as maximizing the chances of a good outcome and minimizing the risks of a bad one. This means that risks have to be assessed and that interventions should be intended to keep risks at an acceptable level.

Taking responsible decisions

Risk is something that we *take* – it should involve weighing pros and cons, making a judgement and taking responsibility for it. Risk assessment is sometimes portrayed as an objective – even quantifiable – exercise. It is not. Our perception of the nature of a risk, its acceptability and who is responsible for what, is always socially constructed. In recent years, risk seems to be less acceptable in our culture and public opinion has often moved towards a position of holding professionals responsible for ensuring safe outcomes of situations that are both dangerous and uncertain, such as child abuse within unstable families or violence by the mentally ill (Beck, 1992; Douglas, 1992). Assessing risk always means making a judgement both about the level of *probability* of a particular outcome and its *severity* and taking a view about the *acceptability* of that level. Even for outcomes such as death or serious harm to others or to the client herself, it is unhelpful and unrealistic to expect that *risk elimination* is an appropriate goal.

In crises, therapists are naturally prone to feeling anxious. This is increased when the therapist herself may be at risk of being held accountable for failing to prevent violence or suicide. This added anxiety can interfere with the thinking needed to assess the risk accurately. A climate of blame can result in defensive practice in which the main concern is to cover your back rather than do what is right for the client. This generally means over-estimating the possibility and seriousness of harm. Anxiety may operate at a subtle level to bias judgement leading to an artificial sense of certainty: suspicions become theories, anecdotes are evidence and prejudices used as indicators (Morgan, 1998). Therapists may feel impelled to be over-confident in their attitude, failing to think through the whole situation and taking impulsive action.

However, biases can work in the other direction, with therapists denying the implications of indicators of risk: it is easy to become over-involved in the client 'doing well', or over-invested in the success of your own interventions. What is needed is the capacity to tolerate doubt and to continue to think about what is realistically achievable. It is important to be aware of our own potential biases and to take account of the full range of factors involved – both those internal to the client (to which therapists often attend exclusively) and also those in the external situation which can be very influential in determining outcome.

It is important to be realistic about the risks to the therapist in these situations. Therapists do have a 'duty of care' which means that you should have taken steps to actively assess and manage a risk which could reasonably be foreseen. However, you are not liable (in law or anywhere else) for an error of judgement. The issue is: is the decision justifiable and based on a formulation of the client and her circumstances? Following appropriate procedures and taking measures which would be regarded as reasonable by professional peers is all that is required. In a sense, the law is sympathetic to professionals in these circumstances (Jenkins, 1997). It is important that the agencies within which therapists practise should also be supportive, both by outlining realistic procedures to follow and by avoiding a culture of blame when incidents occur. We outline below guidelines for assessing and responding to risk which are realistic and applicable to the situations which psychotherapists and counsellors might expect to face. The keys are:

- to undertake an assessment that incorporates the range of relevant issues;
- to consult with colleagues about any tricky decision;
- to involve the client appropriately;
- to record carefully your thinking and your plan for the way forward.

The major risk events which therapists encounter are the possibility of suicide and self-harm and the possibility of violence and harm to others. We will address these in detail, together with a number of other situations including the consequences of mental breakdown and specific dangers to children.

Major risk events are relatively rare and, being the product of many interacting factors, each one is unique – consequently, each therapist's experience provides limited guidance. Our ability to predict such events is also limited. The predictors derived from research are often crude and not particularly helpful in an individual case. Agreement between individual practitioners may not be high. Efforts to improve prediction by creating standardized systems to estimate probable risk tend to be limited in scope and inapplicable to the complex patterns of different risk situations. Whilst it is useful to have some format to aid decision-making, structured assessment schedules and tests tend not to be useful for therapists who do not typically employ these in their usual practice. Checklists of risk factors help by drawing attention to important features of a situation but if they lack a meaningful rationale are hard to remember and do not aid in thinking things through to arrive at a formulation which leads to robust decisions about the best way forward.

Outlined below is a practical, clinically oriented structure for drawing together the most relevant information in assessing major risk situations. It is simple enough to be kept in mind in the therapeutic situation but is an aid to thinking rather than an interview protocol. It provides a reminder to enquire into relevant areas and a way to assemble information into a useable formulation. This structure can be applied to both suicide and violence risk assessments by modifying only the content of the sub-issues. There are three broad areas, each containing a set of important issues to be considered:

- Current Personal State
  - current psychological state
  - ideas and plans about acting
  - current life difficulties
  - personal/social resources
- History and Personality
  - history/context/seriousness of relevant previous behaviour
  - psychological characteristics
  - other warning signs
- Background Risk Indicators
  - medical/psychiatric factors
  - socio-demographic factors

Much of this information will be gathered in the course of assessing a life crisis generally (see Table 2.4, p. 25). Some of it, however, must be sought through active enquiry with the client. If it is decided that risk of harm is a significant issue, then the therapist must move into a phase of formal risk assessment at some point. Typically, this should come after establishing an understanding of the current situation and creating enough trust to manage the risk assessment effectively. In the process of making this kind of assessment, the therapist must try to maintain a balance between tact which elicits the client's co-operation, and being explicit and direct in order to obtain the information needed and to allow the issues of risk to be raised and openly addressed.

Risk assessment in a crisis is, of course, about making decisions for the short-term. The information about current personal state is highly relevant to this but takes on meaning in the context of the background issues of the individual's history, personality and risk factors. These latter categories of information are relevant to assessing long-term risk, an even more difficult undertaking. Where a client seems to be at long-term risk, it is wise to have a specialist assessment from someone experienced in the relevant field, or at least to seek consultation from them. People assessed to be at significant long-term risk should probably receive care from an agency with the resources to respond adequately to it. Particularly for violence, specialist practitioners seem better equipped to respond to it (Manley and Leiper, 1999). Because concerns about suicide are so common in therapeutic practice we outline the issues in working with them in a later section. Therapeutic work with people who are at risk of presenting repeatedly in crisis during the therapy is addressed in Chapter 5.

Good practice in assessing risk also involves obtaining information from others in addition to that provided by the client, both from relatives and friends and from other professionals who are involved. This kind of shared knowledge provides a more comprehensive and accurate view of what is going on. In crisis situations where the person is presenting for the first time, there is limited background and a lack of corroborating information from other sources, and so accurate predictions are more difficult. Because risk is fluctuating (sometimes rapidly in a crisis), only short-term predictions are likely to be accurate. The conclusion must be that risk assessment should be an ongoing matter throughout a crisis period and subject to regular review for people considered to be at high, long-term risk.

Assessing risk of suicide

Suicide is a significant cause of death at a population level with an incidence of 1 per cent of all deaths annually (O'Connor and Sheehy, 2000). Recognizing suicide risk is a vital contribution to saving some of these lives. A significant proportion of those who go on to complete suicide have had some contact with a helping professional in the month before making their attempt; for example, about half saw their GP. Ambivalence is almost always present and these professional contacts are an opportunity to tip the balance, rekindle hope or reduce mistrust (Williams and Morgan, 1994). Such opportunities can be missed even in an explicit crisis presentation because the practitioner feels uneasy about broaching the topic. They may fear that raising the issue of suicide may make it more of a real option: this is not the case and talking frankly is likely in itself to be preventative. There may also be an underlying fear of taking responsibility in a situation which is hard to handle, but it is extremely helpful to offer concerned availability. It may be useful to bear in mind that most people with suicidal feelings are not at immediate high risk; that most who think about suicide, do not act; and that most who make an attempt, do not die. Indeed, it is not at all uncommon for people to experience occasional wishes to die: it may be understood as an expression of intense feeling and not generally as an emergency. Some anxiety in the therapist is inevitable but it should not be allowed to become excessive or disabling.

All indications of suicidal feelings should be taken seriously. Comments such as 'I can't stand it'; 'I can't go on like this'; 'I can't live without X'; 'I'd be better off dead' require exploration. The topic can be opened up with general open-ended questions such as 'How do you feel about the future?'; 'What has passed through your mind about what to do about all this?'. Tactful and sensitive questioning is needed, especially when it is not clear whether suicide is a significant issue for the client. It is useful to bear in mind a sequence of topics which can be explored through various forms of open-ended enquiry, such as:

- Hope – Are you feeling hopeful about things? Can you see a point to living?
- Despair – Do you feel it is impossible to face the future? Does life feel like a burden?
- Death – Have you wished it would all end? Have you had thoughts of ending your life?
- Means/Plan – Have you thought of how you might do it? Have you made any preparations?
- Safety – Do you feel able to resist these urges? Are you able to reassure me you will be safe? Do you feel able to ask for help if things get worse?

Once the issue has been opened up in this way, the need to follow up with a fuller enquiry is clearer. The structure of the information needed to assess the current and future risk is presented in Table 3.1. Therapists need to understand the *relevance of all the factors* suggested in this table (see also Bongar, 1992).

In the enquiry, the specificity and detail of any suicidal plan is a vital clue to immediate risk. Availability of means is also crucial, since impulse is an important element in suicidal acts which often stem from the transient worsening of distress. The willingness of the client to hand over, dispense with or avoid the proposed means has both symbolic and practical significance for ensuring safety. There are two stereotyped versions of the suicidal individual: they are either viewed as despairing of life with a commitment to end it; or as deeply discontented people who are trying to command others' attention but are not serious about dying. Although these pictures have some degree of truth, the great majority of people fall between these extremes and may in fact fluctuate between them. Hopelessness is the most consistent single risk factor; it may be more obvious alongside depression and despair, but is likely also to be present in bitterness or rage. There is potentially serious risk in both types of presentation. Although depression is not universally present, the symptoms should be carefully enquired about. Lack of reasons for living and social isolation, whether or not associated with depression, put the person substantially more at risk. Impulsive personality traits and poor coping skills (especially a tendency to avoid tackling problems) lead people to resort to suicide as a response to difficult situations. Abuse of alcohol or other drugs increases impulsivity as well as forming part of a poor pattern of coping: it is a very significant risk factor.

TABLE 3.1 *Structure for clinical assessment of suicide*

I Current personal state

1 Current psychological state
   (a) hopelessness – pessimism about situation/recovery
   (b) helplessness – inability to act/make impact
   (c) hostility – frustration/rage towards situation/others
   (d) unexplained changes in behaviour e.g. giving away possessions, impulsive risk taking, recklessness, stopping eating
   (e) withdrawal – from others into self, loss of concern/engagement

2 Suicidal ideation/plan
   (a) attitude to living – wish to live versus to die; reasons for living versus dying; desire to make active suicide attempt and to passively take risks
   (b) suicidal wishes – fleeting versus continuous; frequency; accepting versus rejecting of wish; sense of control; concern about deterents to attempts (children, family, religion, fear of pain/injury)
   (c) reasons for attempt – manipulate environment (attention, revenge, create guilt) versus escape, release from life, solve problem
   (d) plan – specificity of method (means, time, place); availability/opportunity of means; preparation for attempt; suicide note; final acts (will, putting affairs in order); deception/concealment
   (e) lethality of plan – likelihood of death by these means; prevention: discovery/ intervention in situation; how equivocal is probable/presumed outcome? calculated risk?

3 Current life difficulties
   (a) current crisis/stressful life events
   (b) recent losses (or anniversaries)
   (c) removal of safety factors e.g. disruptions in therapeutic relationship; time of hospital discharge

4 Personal/social resources
   (a) absence of supportive social networks – family, friends, therapist; collusion or loss of concern by others
   (b) lack of stability and 'prospects' – security, finances, skills, personal goals: contributors to sense of hope
   (c) no alternative strategies to deal with intolerable emotions
   (d) minimal openness to collaboration with therapist

II History and personality

1 Seriousness of previous suicide attempt(s)
   (a) Prevention of discovery – isolation, avoidance of intervention, action to get help during/after
   (b) Concepts of fatality – expectations of lethality of method; concept of medical reversibility; current belief about seriousness of attempt to end life
   (c) Planning – final acts in anticipation of death; planning/preparation of attempt; degree of premeditation; suicide note; communication before attempt
   (d) Purpose/intent – degree of ambivalence towards living/dying; aim to change environment versus remove self
   (e) Context/circumstances – nature of precipitants; pattern/similarity to current events

2 Psychological characteristics
   (a) impulsiveness – difficulties in self-control, risk-taking
   (b) aggression – history of violence

(continues)

TABLE 3.1   *(continued)*

   (c)   isolation – poor social/communication skills; tendency to withdraw
   (d)   poor coping skills – lack of assertion, problem-solving abilities
   (e)   depression
   (f)   lability of mood
3   Warning signs
   (a)   history of misuse of drugs or alcohol
   (b)   family history of suicide
   (c)   childhood bereavement
   (d)   therapist's hunches/gut feelings

III   Background risk indicators

1   Medical/psychiatric
   (a)   chronic disabling/painful illness
   (b)   terminal illness
   (c)   psychiatric diagnosis of
      –   schizophrenia (10% lifetime risk)
      –   depression (15% lifetime risk)
      –   alcohol/drug addiction (15% lifetime risk)
   (d)   personality disorder: borderline; antisocial; avoidant; dependent

2   Socio-demographic
   (a)   male
   (b)   elderly/young
   (c)   divorced/widowed/single
   (d)   living alone/socially isolated
   (e)   unemployed/retired
   (f)   social classes I and V

Of those who make a suicide attempt, 40 per cent repeat it within two years; 1 per cent kill themselves during the next year; and 10 per cent do so eventually (Appleby, 1992). There may be an escalating pattern of seriousness in successive suicide attempts. Understanding the seriousness of past attempts requires cool and detached questioning about the circumstances and the client's intent and beliefs about risks. It is helpful to know about the lethality of different means (Linehan, 1993): hanging and carbon monoxide are very dangerous; jumping (from buildings, in front of vehicles, etc.) depends more upon the detailed circumstances; cutting relatively seldom leads to death. It can be helpful to have a knowledge of drug dosage lethality but non-medical professionals should be very cautious since many factors influence actual risk and the client's intent must be considered in the light of her own knowledge.

There may be major difficulties in the process of assessing suicidal risk. A person in a severe pre-suicidal state may appear calm and deliberately deny intent. It is important to consider circumstantial information and wider changes in behaviour such as giving away personal possessions. The therapist should be alert for signs of the person withdrawing into herself. The rapid fluctuation in degree of suicidal feelings is another common problem which can mislead the therapist – the situation might quickly become more dangerous. Being misled by the false improvement produced by temporary withdrawal from a problem situation during crisis intervention is a common danger. People who are angry and unco-operative in their way of presenting distress while suggesting a risk of violence, may equally be potential suicides. This is particularly likely when the behaviour results in criticism, rejection and loss of support from those around. The collusion of significant others with the client's wish to die is a very significant danger. Experienced therapists may need to trust any hunches or gut feelings as an additional indicator which will alert them to any of these problematic, often hidden risks.

Putting all the information together should allow the therapist to arrive at a formulation of the individual in the context of her current circumstances and her typical patterns of responding. Although it can seem somewhat artificial, it is a useful discipline to attempt to arrive at an estimated risk level which acts as a summary of the urgency of an intervention plan. A suicide risk rating scale is provided in Table 3.2.

TABLE 3.2   *Rating suicide risk*

---

0 – No predictable risk of suicide now:
      no or fleeting suicide ideation
      no history of attempts
      has satisfactory social support

1 – Low risk of suicide now:
      has suicidal ideation with low lethal method
      no history of attempts
      wishes and is able to control behaviour
      no recent serious loss
      has satisfactory social support

2 – Moderate risk of suicide now:
      has suicidal ideation with high lethal method – but no plan or threats or clearly
            ambivalent about expression
   or   has plan with low lethal method – and/or history of low lethal attempts and/or
            other problems with impulse control

3 – High suicide risk now:
      expresses intent but some degree of ambivalence and no current signs of action
      has current high lethal plan
      obtainable means
      history of previous attempts/impulsive behaviour
      unable to communicate with significant other

4 – Very high risk of suicide now:
      expresses/hallucinates current intent or has made recent serious attempt
      has current high lethal plan
      available means
      history of suicide attempts/unpredictable impulsiveness
      cut off from resources

Source: Adapted from Hoff, 1978

Assessing risk of violence

Therapists should be aware of the real possibility of violence as an expression of frustration and defensiveness in crisis situations. Of course, the most likely clue to this possibility will be the client's presenting in a tense, agitated state with signs of frustration and the sense of a potential explosion of rage. However, what should be striking in the accompanying Table 3.3, which details factors contributing to an assessment of violence risk, is the many points of similarity in content to the risk factors for suicide. A basic pattern of poor coping capabilities, low self-esteem and difficulties with impulse control are common to many people exhibiting both kinds of risk. Consequently, there is the danger of a client seeming to be at one kind of risk, also exhibiting signs of the other – both possibilities may need to be kept in mind. This is particularly serious where someone in a suicidal frame of mind also has violent or vengeful fantasies towards others, since the possibility of suicide frees them from the usual social and legal consequences.

TABLE 3.3 *Structure of clinical risk assessment of violence*

I Current personal state

1 Current psychological state
   (a) hostile – threatening, suspicious, challenging, abusive, angry
   (b) irritable – overactive, aroused, tense, agitated
   (c) sense of grievance or humiliation; firm wish to get even
   (d) control-override symptoms – firmly held beliefs of persecution; delusions of mind/body being controlled

2 Violent threats/plan
   (a) threats (actual or implied) – to harm or seek revenge: presence of violent fantasies; information from others about their concerns
   (b) identified targets – people experienced as responsible, especially named individuals or relatives; scapegoated groups; others experienced as potential victims
   (c) plan – existence of specific, elaborated method of attack; availability of means/possession of weapon
   (d) triggers – identified circumstances in which violence is liable to occur; likelihood of encountering trigger situations
   (e) attitude to violence – believes aggression is/not acceptable, and wishes or not to control; believes has degree of control; recognizes trigger situations; can identify own experience during trigger situations; wishes to collaborate with therapist

3 Current life difficulties
   (a) current crisis/stressful life events
   (b) threats to self-image/sense of control
   (c) removal of safety factors – changes in medication; disruptions in therapeutic relationship

4 Personal/social resources
   (a) supportive social networks – family, friends, therapist
   (b) stability and 'prospects' – contributors to sense of control
   (c) alternative strategies to control reaction to trigger situations
   (d) openness to collaboration with therapist

(continues)

TABLE 3.3 *(continued)*

II History and personality

1 History of violent/dangerous acts
  (a) record of previous violent action (not only convictions) – youthfulness when started; frequency; recency of last; seriousness of act; previous use of weapons; any sexual offence; cruelty to animals
  (b) general fascination with violence – possession of books/videos/militaria; involvement in martial arts; fantasizes about violence; sexually aroused by violence/sadism
  (c) circumstances of violence – commonness of trigger situations; bizarre act; alone rather than group; not in course of other criminal activity; similarity to current context/circumstances

2 Psychological characteristics
  (a) impulsiveness – difficulties in self-control, risk-taking
  (b) aggression – angry outbursts
  (c) isolation – poor social/communication skills
  (d) poor coping skills – lack of assertion/problem-solving activities
  (e) lack of guilt – unconcerned about others, no remorse
  (f) feelings of inferiority – hostility to authority, takes offence easily

3 Warning signs
  (a) history of misuse of drugs or alcohol
  (b) social background/sub-culture exposes to/promotes/supports violence
  (c) poor compliance/engagement with prior therapy
  (d) therapist's hunches/gut feelings

III Background risk indicators

1 Medical/psychiatric
  (a) psychotic symptoms – delusions focused on individual, violent theme/preoccupation; delusions of passivity (being controlled); delusions of persecution; command hallucinations; morbid jealousy
  (b) alcohol/drug addiction
  (c) personality disorder – antisocial; paranoid
  (d) medical conditions destabilizing mood e.g. diabetes

2 Socio-demographic
  (a) male
  (b) young
  (c) low educational achievement
  (d) rootless/socially unstable/frequent changes of employment or address
  (e) experience of institutions

In spite of the similarities, risk of violent acting out may be even more difficult than suicide to predict confidently (Blumenthal and Lavender, 2000). Violence is probably controlled to an even greater extent by impulsive responses to trigger situations. This makes it more fluid. There is a possibility of displacement of violence from the original object of resentment to another victim. It is therefore essential to make an assessment of both potential targets and trigger situations and the likelihood of encountering them. The best predictor of violence risk is a history of previous violence, convictions and dangerous actions. It is essential to investigate in detail what the circumstances of such previous incidents were. The client's inability to identify trigger factors clearly, or to recall the state of mind which led up to the incident, makes her a higher risk and more difficult to help. It is prudent to be alert also for the possibility of 'special' forms of violence such as arson, sexual assault and stalking or harassment.

As with suicide, violence is a sensitive topic which should be explored carefully and tactfully. Some clients may harbour intense fantasies of vengeance or have elaborated specific plans against someone but be exceedingly cautious and suspicious about revealing them. Nonetheless, ambivalence about acting on these thoughts is likely to be present. The client's attitude towards the possible violence is crucial: whether it is recognized as a problem and something which may be later regretted. Many forms of violence may be encouraged in certain sub-cultures as a legitimate way of dealing with situations. Difficulties in accepting help may be particularly pronounced for clients presenting in a violent frame of mind: it may be seen as creating a situation of weakness or passivity. Again it is useful to summarize a risk assessment with an overall estimation of the level of risk. This may be done using a 5-point scale, similar to that for suicide risk.

Interviewing people at high risk of violent acting out may of course place the therapist herself at some risk (Breakwell, 1995). You should be aware of any imminent verbal and non-verbal signs of rage building up and attempt to deflect it by addressing the feelings calmly. You should have the means of ensuring your own safety and should not feel obliged to continue an interaction in which you feel at personal risk. The interviewer's manner has a great effect on this situation: being assertive but not confrontational and letting the client know you are in control of yourself provides her with a sense of safety; it is essential to show the client you can hear the strength of her feelings and to avoid accusation. Trigger situations for violence tend to be such things as refusing requests or giving bad news. Although many helping professionals do become the victims of violence, it is less common for psychotherapists and counsellors to be attacked, since they are not typically in a position of control over resources.

Assessing other risks

There are certain other types of risk which therapists should be alert to but which are in general less likely to occur in the contexts in which most of them work. If the risk is high, other agencies ought to be involved (if they are not already). Specialist assessment and resources are usually needed.

Firstly, there is severe *vulnerability*, typically as a result of significant mental illness or impairment. This may take the form of serious self-neglect, such as failing to eat or drink adequately, to maintain a healthy living environment or otherwise care adequately for one's own health and well-being (Morgan, 1998). Clients vulnerable in this way often have ongoing mental health problems which have isolated them socially but they should be in contact with statutory services. They require assertive intervention and advocacy to secure their social welfare. Exceptionally, some people in severely regressed states, during or after a life crisis, may be neglecting themselves in this way; the response should be equally vigorous. The people who are liable to be vulnerable in these ways are also sometimes subject to violence, harassment and exploitation. Crisis states do leave people in danger of being taken advantage of in various ways – financially, sexually or emotionally – and crisis assessment and intervention should attempt to offer protection.

The other main area of risk is *abuse or neglect* of vulnerable others, particularly children. It is easy for therapists accustomed to dealing with individual adult clients to overlook possible harmful effects of their client's behaviour on other people. We might say that this cannot be our responsibility. However, in the case of children and other people whose ability to care for themselves is limited (such as the mentally or physically frail elderly, or people with intellectual disabilities), complex issues of responsibility are raised. Risks of abuse or neglect may be increased during a crisis: uncovering such problems at any point is likely to create a predicament for the therapist concerning the extent of her involvement. Some effort to assess the seriousness of the risk must be made. The client may be willing and able to collaborate in such an assessment but she may not.

Therapists working in agencies – and certainly in statutory agencies – are likely to have an obligation placed on them by their employer's policies to report evidence that a child has suffered, or is at risk of suffering, significant harm, whether through serious neglect or through physical, sexual or emotional abuse. The legal obligations of independent practitioners are less clear-cut but they would normally be expected to place a very high priority on the protection of a child (Bond, 1993). Harm is where there is ill-treatment or an impairment of health or development; concern should be triggered when this impairment is significant compared to the health or development of another similar child (Herbert, 1993). Therapists do not have to – indeed they should not – make these decisions unaided. The local Social Services Department provides facilities for telephone consultation with a specialist who can advise whether any particular situation warrants a formal referral for investigation and assessment of the risk to the child. Such consultation can be sought without providing details of the client. For independent practitioners, indeed, it is possible to seek such consultation as a 'member of the public' and to do so on an entirely anonymous basis where concerns about breaking confidentiality are strong.

Responding to assessed risk

In concluding an assessment of someone presenting in crisis, particularly where there is a significant level of assessed risk, a number of steps should be followed to ensure that all the relevant issues have been addressed.

Firstly, *consultation with colleagues* is a vital part of risk assessment. Good decisions are informed by detailed discussion which can counteract biases and blind spots and help the therapist deal realistically with her anxiety. If immediate action needs to be taken and there is no opportunity for consultation, this should be recorded and time made to review the assessment as soon as possible.

Good practice requires a thorough *record* of a crisis assessment which not only allows the therapist to marshal her thoughts but also provides an explanation of the decisions made, should that become necessary. Good recording is one piece of 'defensive' practice which we would endorse. Included in the record should be all the relevant risk assessment information; it can usefully be summarized using the assessment structure above (p. 29) – current presentation and context, individual history and personality and further background risk indicators. It should conclude with a summary formulation of the nature of the risk – what might happen to whom, how, in what circumstances and on what time-scale – together with a judgement on what the current level of risk is estimated to be. The record should include any consultations which have taken place, other communications being made and provide an account of what plan of action has been agreed.

It is particularly important following a risk assessment to outline a written *plan* of how the risk will be 'managed'. It should include a rationale for the decisions made and a note of any limitations in implementing it fully. The focus is on the short-term risk – making the situation safe for *now*. The plan should include the provisions for future contact and who else – professionals or friends and relatives – will be involved (see Chapter 4). Decisions about 'fail safe' measures if the plan goes wrong should be made; for example, if the client does not attend an appointment or if the therapist is unavoidably absent.

A practical aspect of the intervention plan is for the therapist to play for time while she works to diffuse the crisis. Keeping things safe in the short term allows the situation to change. Because much of the risk arises from impulsive action, offering to remove the means of self-harm or of attack offers the client a degree of protection. Other ways of providing external controls such as taking the person away from the problematic situation, providing respite or psychiatric admission, helps with this. Enlisting the client's social network counters the sense of isolation and rejection that she feels. The frequency of contact and the number of professionals and others involved can be adjusted to the level of protection needed. Contracting with the client to telephone the therapist between appointments if she feels like carrying out her threat of suicide or violence offers some reassurance to both parties. A reliable telephone helpline should be suggested as the alternative for when the therapist is not available. The therapist may need, in an emergency, to escort a suicidal client to her GP or the casualty department of the nearest hospital, although of course it is better that a friend or a family member do so if the client is not safe alone.

The client should be as *informed* and *involved* as possible. She needs to understand what the therapist is thinking and planning to do. The client should be involved in estimating her level of risk and in agreeing a way forward. The client's collaboration is, of course, crucial in the success of the intervention. Informing a client that her difficulties and/or her safety are being taken seriously is itself one of the most significant interventions that can be made to contain a crisis. It may be important for the therapist to make a decisive statement about this: for example, 'I'm here to help'; 'I don't want you to kill yourself'. This kind of positive commitment can change the balance of the client's ambivalence and increase her sense of safety. Normally, the client can be assisted to actively manage her own risk through identifying trigger situations, patterns and early signs together with agreed actions and support to be utilized. The only exceptions to keeping the client fully involved are if her physical state precludes it (for example, she is intoxicated), or if this would seriously escalate a dangerous situation, or perhaps if it might lead to the destruction of evidence needed for prosecution in a case of child abuse.

Crisis situations can mean extending the boundary of communication further than most therapists are accustomed to dealing with. This can create unease but it is unhelpful for the therapist to feel trapped by an excessive need for confidentiality. Clearly the normal and desirable approach to communication with others is for the client to give her explicit consent and a careful effort should be made to obtain this, clarifying the consequences of disclosure. The greater the risk, the more justification there is for overriding lack of consent if necessary. The client should be told what is being said to whom. Within an agency, information should be shared with others involved in the client's care on a 'need to know' basis: colleagues have to have the information to perform their roles and (where relevant) to do so safely. It is rarely necessary to inform an outside agency of a risk but the protection of the public or the client may make this essential. The threat of serious violence poses particular problems. If there is an immediate and specific threat, it may be necessary to inform the police, who may then warn the client that they know about the situation and assist the potential victim to take safety precautions. Informing the potential victim oneself is a very serious breach of confidentiality and should be avoided if possible. Where threats of violence are more generalized, a decision may still need to be made to inform the police but in reality there is often very little that they can do to prevent a threat being carried out.

Responding therapeutically to suicidal states

The emergence of a real possibility of suicide in a client – especially one whom the therapist knows and is committed to – is amongst the most alarming and distressing kinds of crisis. It can be a sudden eruption in an ongoing therapy, but is often an issue extending over a longer period, its emergence often predictable from the client's history and quite possibly the reason for seeking therapy. This doesn't make it any easier. Of course, the therapist needs to make an assessment of immediate risk and if need be a crisis plan to manage it, as covered above and in Chapters 4 and 5. However, it may also often be necessary to work with the issue in ongoing therapy. It is probably the commonest and the most difficult crisis issue which therapists routinely face so we explore it in detail here. It can be hard to maintain your ability to think when confronted with this disturbing situation.

Ambivalence is generally at the heart of suicidal feelings and acts. Although there is a stereotype of suicide attempts as arising either from depression and despair ('wanting to die'), or else from 'a cry for help' and manipulation of others, the psychology of suicidal people is better thought of as a complex and shifting combination of motivations. The person both does and does not want to die. 'Rational' suicides seem to be relatively rare (Fairbairn, 1995). Suicide attempts appear on analysis to arise principally not from a wish to die, but as a way to deal with and express desperation in psychologically intolerable circumstances. The therapist might accurately say: 'You don't really want to be dead – you just don't want to hurt so much' (Williams and Morgan, 1994).

The many factors which can underlie a person reaching a suicidal state of mind (see Table 3.1) point to the complex, overlapping processes and motivations involved (Schneidman et al., 1994). The therapeutic approach depends on the formulation of which factors are most influential for a particular individual – it may well be appropriate to use several strategies at once. All approaches emphasize the value of exploring frankly and in detail the circumstances, beliefs and wishes surrounding suicidal thoughts and actions: this robs the idea of suicide of its mystique and enables it to be viewed more objectively. The therapist has to offer a calm acceptance of the seriousness of the risk and then make it a topic for exploration. This conveys respect for the client's capacity for self-determination but promotes the value of exploring alternatives and so implicitly stands for a sense of hope.

A good starting point is to see suicidal behaviour and feelings as mal-adaptive solutions to personal problems which the client feels ill-equipped to meet. This perspective provides a basis for a problem-orientated approach to therapy. It is a specific application of the general crisis model and is outlined in Figure 3.1. When the client's problem-solving efforts fail, hope-lessness and helplessness take over and suicide becomes seen as a viable alternative solution: it is a way out of the 'grid-lock'. When this happens repeatedly, it can become a fixed, self-limiting pattern of response (either as a long-term way of functioning or during periods of depressed mood). The client's fundamental difficulty is her inability to generate alternative per-spectives or feel capable of effectively implementing other solutions due to poor coping skills and a range of 'cognitive distortions' – that is, skewed perceptions and inferences (Weishaar, 1996). The client's core beliefs reflect themes of loss, deprivation, defeat and worthlessness. She has difficulties tolerating both emotional distress and the anxiety inherent in problem-solving. The thought or the act of suicide comes to function as a comfort; it sometimes seems to have an addictive, drug-like quality in this respect.

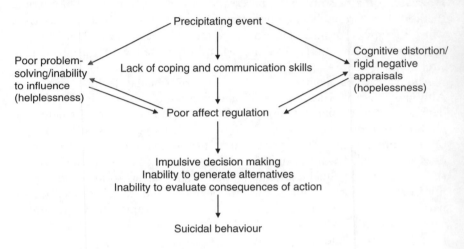

FIGURE 3.1   *Model of suicidal behaviour*

The therapeutic approach is to identify and gently challenge each of the components which supports suicide as a solution. It is vital to identify the particular life situations which provoke an increase in suicidal ideation and to improve the person's tolerance of distress and the effectiveness of her problem-solving in them. Helping the client to attain some distance from her hopelessness and to see it as a problem in itself rather than a reflection of reality provides a basis to challenge the cognitive distortions inherent in her hopeless and helpless view of the situation and opens up the possibility of finding alternatives. A tendency to focus on any negative aspect of possible solutions – a 'Yes but . . .' attitude – must be tackled as a self-defeating distortion in its own right.

It is also crucial to tackle the belief that suicide is a desirable 'option'. The therapist may say that while suicide seems to present a way out of the difficulty, it cannot be undone; other solutions not now apparent may later emerge, while suicide always remains as a possibility. Surfacing and challenging beliefs that support suicide without getting into a fight about them is the best approach – arguing is generally useless. One way to do this is to calmly facilitate the client to identify reasons for living and for dying and to make an appraisal of them. The therapist should be able coolly and explicitly to consider the pros and cons of suicide. Doing this enables distortions about the advantages of dying to be addressed and the balance shifted in the direction of life. Simply undertaking this in a dispassionate way, in itself opens up the possibility of choice and unlocks what can otherwise seem to be a closed system of thinking about suicide. Beliefs about 'another life' are generally best circumvented by emphasizing that this remains unknown and that it is best to stay with what we do know about this life.

A very common feature of suicidal states of mind is the existence of a suicide 'fantasy' in which, although the body is dead, the person continues her existence and experiences the consequences of her death (Morse, 1973). In a sense, it is as if the person kills her body in order for her 'self' to survive. These suicidal fantasies concerning the meaning of death have a limited number of themes which are identified in Table 3.4. Suicide thus combines a sense of hopelessness about reality and an idea that death is better: it is this which motivates the suicide. It is essential to explore the suicide fantasy, acknowledging the magical thinking on which it is based by taking the psychological realities seriously. This element of 'cognitive distortion' involves a serious breach in the client's contact with consensual reality – suicide is based in a deeply confused and fragmented mental state in which the client is in danger of translating fantasy into action (Campbell and Hale, 1991).

TABLE 3.4 *Suicidal fantasies*

Leading to wish for death:

Revenge	– Attack on others, hateful, sadistic, murderous feelings
	Impact death will have: 'they will be sorry'
	Sense of triumph
	Surviving self as invisible observer of others suffering
Atonement	– Expiate guilt and express self-hatred
	Punishment deserved
	Masochistic gratification/eroticization of pain
	Escape – end pain caused by guilt
Merger	– Return to nature – nirvana
	Blissful, dreamless sleep; permanent peace
	Fusion with mother – like infant
	Reunion with dead love object
Transcendence	– Rebirth – new self as wish to be
	Elimination of pain
	Escape from body (source of adolescent disturbance)
	Immortality – omnipotent mastery over fear of death

Leading to wish to take risks:

Rescue	– Wish to be found and prevented
	Test of other's love
Gamble	– Dicing with death
	Test own omnipotence
	Survival proves specialness

A problem-solving therapeutic style emphasizes collaboration and so implicitly counters the client's helplessness by fostering her independence and sense of worth and control. An element of this is to have her participate in setting her own limits in ensuring that she remains safe. One way can be to construct an explicit contract around the issue of suicidal actions. This functions as a symbol of her commitment to continue to live and to work on her problems, promotes discussion of the issues around safety and provides a degree of felt security for both client and therapist. Such contracts generally include the client's commitment to attend sessions and not to harm herself for a given period which the client feels she can realistically commit herself to. There should be some default 'options': what alternative actions are available if she is feeling suicidal and how to contact the therapist to discuss changing their agreement – taking care to be clear that inability to fulfil it is not to be regarded as a failure. There are real potential dangers in such 'no suicide' contracts: if carelessly handled, the client might be provoked into a decision finally to kill herself rather than break the contract by making a suicidal gesture. They can amount to inappropriate and ineffective efforts to control the client rather than to foster her sense of self-control. Much of their value lies in creating a detailed discussion of the issues, so bolstering engagement with the thera-peutic process and curiosity about the possibility of change and so deferring acting on impulse. These are elements of any good therapy in a suicidal situation.

Responding to trauma in suicidal acts

In suicidal states of mind, clients are attempting to manage extremes of emotional pain. There is a failure to contain intolerable thoughts and feelings and an effort to escape from experiencing them. Suicide attempts are actions designed to relieve psychological tension and to express emo-tional experiences which cannot be represented in any other way. In particular, psychodynamic therapists draw attention to the hostility and rage which are a crucial aspect of suicide. The *effect* of suicide is to destroy the person's life and to torment the minds of others (Campbell and Hale, 1991). It is vital to grasp the fact that this is also its *aim*, though not necessarily a conscious one. Violence is inherent in the act even though the aggression involved may be unacceptable and cannot necessarily be immediately interpreted to the client. This is an old idea – directing hostility towards the self and perhaps, implicitly, towards an 'internalized other'. It is quite common for therapists to overlook this aggressive intent and to focus only on the sense of despair or the appeal for help. Because the client is not necessarily aware of the aggression, it may be necessary to work with the more 'victimized' role in the early stages of the work – but in the longer term it is necessary to address the implicit violence and cruelty: the therapist has to grasp the nettle of the client's rage.

Suicide often occurs in the context of a breakdown of close interpersonal relationships. The separation from the other is experienced as equivalent to a death, something which cannot be tolerated or represented other than by taking action. Those prone to such an experience frequently have intense unstable relationships in which experiences of merging and being engulfed alternate with the experience of abandonment. Relationships are in a fragile equilibrium and any conflict or disappointment can be experienced as a catastrophe: there is a 'narrow corridor of safety' (Glaser, 1992). The response is rage which can be expressed as either violence to the partner or to the self. It is for this reason that breaks or disruptions in the therapy itself are times of increased risk for vulnerable clients and must be treated with great care, with attention paid to preparation or the provision of alternative sources of contact.

A suicide *attempt* is in a sense a 'traumatic' event, a violent attack in which the client is both victim and perpetrator. Clients who have made a suicide attempt frequently engage in a variety of defensive manoeuvres to obscure from themselves the frightening and violent nature of the thoughts and actions which have been part of them. There is a 'sealing over' of awareness following an attempt:

- Rationalization which fails to convey the sense of compulsion and desperate need to rid the self of unmanageable experiences.
- Denial and dissociation so that the client appears oddly calm and the reality of what happened is lost.
- Splitting and projection which result in the sense of persecution being externalized as belonging to others, with the client's own hostility denied.
- A focus on surrounding circumstances or even past history rather than on the reality of the suicidal act which permits the client to identify with the victim role and to disengage from her own responsibility for perpetrating violence on herself.

The therapist should examine closely and in detail the client's state of mind leading up to any suicide attempt in order to bring this into sharper focus and to help her reclaim responsibility for it. It can be shocking to the client to be aware of what she has done, both in terms of its violence and the damage to her psychological integrity and she resists thinking about it. She is likely to be frightened, humiliated and fearful that she will be overwhelmed again. She may also expect to be attacked and vilified for what she has done and it can be helpful to address her expectations of the therapist in this regard. Combined with the more general pessimism, sensitivity to humiliation and suspicion of others common to such clients, this can result in negation of offers of help in spite of continuing distress. Sensitive and concerned initial contact shortly after a suicide attempt is vital to prevent withdrawal.

The intensity of these conflicting emotions in the client means that therapists almost inevitably become involved and identified at some level with the client's struggles. The therapist may be caught up in the excitement of the crisis and overly ready to take responsibility, thereby reinforcing the client's passivity. The affirmation of the value of life is at stake in the face of the client's terror and despair and under great pressure from the pervasive sense of futility. The therapist has to cope with the hostility and aggression implicit in the suicidal feelings which attack her wish to make things better for the client and her sense that she has the capacity to do so. It is quite common for practitioners to feel frightened by suicide and so immobilized, uncertain of the value of their usual skills. They may react to this by moving into over-managing and controlling the situation. It is also commonplace to deal with the difficulties by ignoring them. Therapists and others may fail to notice or acknowledge the significance of indicators of risk or the client's communications about it. Therapeutically, this often manifests as a failure to obtain relevant details or to document or com-municate these when others are involved. It can sometimes seem as if there is a conspiracy 'not to know'. The conflicting feelings in the client can result equally in splitting and confusion on the part of the therapist, with a variety of partial and contradictory reactions taking the place of balanced therapeutic work. There will often be a passionate wish to rescue the client, fuelled by pity for her isolation and despair, which views the client entirely as a victim and overlooks her own violence and her responsibility for it. In a sense, the client has projected her own wish to live onto the therapist and may then be inclined to disparage and mock that wish. If the therapist responds by trying harder and giving more, her efforts will eventually break down into exhaustion or angry rejection.

When the therapist gives up, either partially or overtly, from working with the threat of suicide, she conveys her discouragement and behaves in a more or less subtly rejecting manner (Modestin, 1987). Throughout a suicidal situation, the client is liable to provoke rejection and hostility from those around her. By withdrawing both from the hostility and the intense dependency, the therapist may collude with the client and implicitly sanc-tion the client's wish to die. The therapist may betray the client by switch-ing loyalty and sympathy to her family, supporting them instead. Suicidal people often find themselves very badly treated – rejected, dismissed and punished. They are frequently told: 'If you want to kill yourself, do it properly.' In emergency rooms they may be treated medically with deliber-ately painful interventions. Therapists easily become confrontational, even contemptuous, or more subtly, demand levels of responsibility which the client cannot manage. All of this is an aggressive retaliation for the provocation and implicit hostility of the suicidal act.

Jim felt beside himself with rage when his wife left him for another man – he was almost murderous. As he 'accepted' the situation he became quite depressed. His work as an electrician became erratic; he grew more isolated; and his drinking got worse. When he was referred to the mental health service he was assessed as a moderately severe suicide risk and passed to a therapist who focused on his loss and sense of shame and tried to help him come to terms with it. She felt very concerned for Jim, trying to support him and to motivate him 'to start a new life'. His attendance at sessions was irregular and he often did not do 'homework' assignments they had agreed. In sessions he was often suspicious and put blocks in the way of most alternatives. He talked about 'ending it' and how pointless life was. The therapist felt frustrated but persisted in trying to be helpful and positive. She did not feel able to tackle his anger generally or his resentment of the therapeutic work. As this persisted over many months, the therapist began to feel isolated with the case and resentful towards colleagues who had 'dumped' Jim on her. She began to feel convinced that Jim was incapable of changing and had thoughts that if this is how life was going to be for him, perhaps he would be better off dead. She forgot about a session and when she realized, was slow to make contact and rearrange. Three days later, Jim only just survived a serious car crash.

These reactions can occur both in therapists and in other care staff working with suicidal people and amongst significant others in the person's life (Watts and Morgan, 1994). An important contribution that a therapist can make is to help others be aware of and manage their own conflicting feelings so as to respond more constructively. However, the intensity of the therapist's own feelings can go unrecognized and in the midst of crises there may be no space to reflect. The therapist needs to scrutinize her work constantly for signs of counter-transference reactions. She needs to tolerate the experience of being attacked and of feeling useless and unable to help, acknowledging the reality of the client's desire to die without condoning it. She needs to hold onto hope and her sense of responsibility rather than too readily putting it onto others (such as psychiatrists). She needs to know that she cannot keep the client alive but can maintain in view and respond to the part of the client that wishes to live. In working with the possibility of suicide, the therapist needs to be able to sustain her positive commitment to the client, her sense that the client's life is worth preserving and a conviction that this is feasible – but to do so in a calm and clear-sighted way.

Success is never guaranteed, however. Amongst the most painful situations for a therapist to deal with is the completed suicide of someone with whom they have worked (Litman, 1994). A sense of defeat, hopelessness and inadequacy are almost inevitable in the face of such a final blow to the wish to be a healer, which is central to the identity of any therapist. The biggest problem is guilt and self-blame. Self-recrimination about what we might have done differently can become corrosive. Reversing this into anger with the client is also likely, as we hold her responsible for our distress. Anyone closely involved with someone who commits suicide – friends and relatives – also suffers from guilt and anger which are particularly difficult to bear when, as so commonly will be the case, there has been an ambivalent relationship with the person. It is necessary, but very difficult and painful, to work through this kind of grief. It is not usually wise for the ex-client's therapist to be the one to help with that. She may need to meet with her former client's family – but on the basis of providing information within such boundaries of confidentiality as seems appropriate, not on the basis of being their therapist when there are likely to be so many competing feelings and agendas on both sides. Therapists inevitably fear criticism and reproach and worry about the possibility of being sued in a case of suicide. This is unusual in reality and only at all likely if there has been actual negligence. It can be an extremely helpful process to convert this anxiety into a real attempt to review the case with supervisors, peers and with any other professionals involved, trying to understand what happened and what can be learned. Especially with a supportive institutional context, this has the potential to be of enormous value in enabling the therapist to work through an experience which can be shocking and undermining and even lead to a crisis of professional confidence.

Conclusion

In deciding on how best to respond to a crisis situation which contains an element of risk, the right level of input needs to be chosen: this involves appropriate, responsible risk-taking. It has to be borne in mind that interventions can increase as well as decrease the level of risk to the client. This is especially true where over-assertive intervention might damage the therapeutic relationship – normally a major protective factor. Whilst promoting choice and independence is a normal therapeutic goal, crisis situations may tempt the therapist to ignore this. It is risky and damaging for the future if this happens; for example, compulsory psychiatric involvement may make it less likely that the client seeks out appropriate help in the longer term. It is vital to weigh up the pros and cons of intervention in a responsible manner, rather than always opting to 'play safe'. In the following chapter, we outline the therapeutic approach which can be used to respond flexibly to crises, including situations where the risk is high.

4   Crisis Intervention

Every therapist needs to know how to respond effectively in a crisis. While some agencies specialize in this work, for most of us crises do not happen frequently and so are not a routine part of our practice – but they do happen: there is no certain way to avoid them, even if you would prefer a quiet life! Yet many therapists remain somewhat ill-equipped to deal with crisis situations. A crisis is an important and potentially productive time to intervene (as reviewed in Table 4.1) but our style of therapeutic work may need to be adapted to the different demands. 'Crisis intervention' is not a clearly delimited therapeutic theory or technique, but an approach designed to stabilize crises and resolve them as productively as possible (Aguilera and Messick, 1982; Gilliland and James, 1997; Hoff, 1978). The principles of this way of working are an important – even essential – element in the repertoire of skills of the competent therapist. It involves a more active, problem-solving stance and a willingness to extend boundaries to involve others when necessary.

TABLE 4.1 *Characteristics of crises and implications for intervention*

- Crises are brief and self-limiting in time.
  'Resolutions' are achieved fairly quickly but vary in adaptiveness.
  ⟶   Intervention should be available as early as possible.
- Psychological disorganization results in increased dependency needs.
  Requests for help may be indirect or disguised.
  ⟶   Intervention should be active and accessible.
- Crises involve disruption of a network of relationships.
  ⟶   Intervention should involve the family and wider network.
- Crises are not pathological.
  The disruption can be an opportunity for learning and growth.
  ⟶   Intervention should support and normalize this process.
- Disorganization may open up old conflicts.
  Past difficulties are more accessible.
  ⟶   Intervention can achieve more change in a short period of time.

The essential goal of crisis intervention is to facilitate a return to at least the person's pre-crisis level of functioning as quickly as possible. There may be an opportunity for additional gains but that is a bonus! It is essentially a process of remobilizing the individual's own adaptive coping capacities. The priority is to defuse the worst possible outcome and create a facilitative context to initiate further change. This aim guides the therapist's intervention strategy which endeavours to:

- manage overwhelming affect creating an experience of safety and helping the client regain a sense of personal balance;
- correct cognitive distortions, decreasing the sense of chaos and loss of control, fostering effectiveness by finding new coping mechanisms and resuming a problem-solving approach to the difficulties;
- use available help and connect with social networks and resources without fostering dependency;
- integrate the whole experience to improve future capability by coming to terms with the experience of losing control and perhaps being more aware of the underlying conflicts; consolidating the learning of better coping patterns; building future support in order to prevent recurrence.

How such goals can be attained in any specific crisis will vary and appropriate intervention depends on accurate assessment (Baldwin, 1979). In some cases, encouraging informal emotional support or simply providing information, guidance or reassurance is sufficient and doing more may be 'overkill' which could be detrimental in the longer term. If a process of emotional change is underway and there are no significant cognitive distortions or maladaptive forms of coping, a problem-focused therapeutic intervention might interrupt the individual's own attempts at emotional processing and interfere with the natural adjustment process. If the crisis is reasonably well contained, but development would be helped by therapeutic work, moving directly into a brief therapy or providing a consultation to set up a longer-term psychotherapy is the best response – not a crisis-orientated intervention. At the other end of the spectrum of difficulties, if the person has had severe long-term problems, it is appropriate simply to stabilize the situation with the minimum possible intervention and to connect her to appropriate forms of long-term support or therapeutic help. Otherwise, there is a danger of fostering dependency and reinforcing crisis-like behaviour as a means of seeking help. Intervention must seek to limit a maladaptive pattern of repeated crisis presentations and not amplify it. A crisis which has already passed and has reached some form of 'closure' is also unlikely to be helped by crisis intervention: both the urgency and the openness to change are no longer present and a general therapeutic assessment is needed to consider the best way forward.

In general, the approach to intervention outlined has been developed in specialist contexts and is designed to deal with people initially presenting to an agency or individual therapist in a state of immediate crisis. While most of the issues and many of the techniques are also relevant to crises occurring in the context of an ongoing therapy, a number of different considerations are relevant and a crisis intervention strategy should not automatically be implemented in an identical fashion (see Chapter 5). The main principles of crisis intervention are summarized in Table 4.2 and are elaborated in subsequent sections.

TABLE 4.2 *Principles of crisis intervention*

Rapidly make emotional contact and form a containing relationship Adopt an active, directive stance Maintain a focus on present realities Facilitate expression of emotion	active structuring relationship
Provide alternative perceptions of situation Support a problem-solving attitude Enhance coping skills	structuring cognitive/didactic interventions
Involve family and social network Adapt the environment and mobilize resources Develop a plan of action Ensure follow-up	active case-management approach

Rapidly establish a containing relationship

Someone in crisis is greatly supported simply by the presence and involvement of a calm other person. Almost any involvement has some benefit – emotional contact, companionship, advice and guidance, practical help and physical care-taking – the ways of expressing concern which are provided by naturally occurring support networks in crisis situations (Parry, 1990). They provide a sense of safety and a stable reality. A crisis therapist can provide this simply through her presence and availability through active listening. However, in order to make emotional contact, such listening may need to be more 'active' than in other circumstances. The client's withdrawal and possible sense of shame may cause her to feel cut off from others. Her emotional and cognitive disorganization may keep the therapist at a distance and diffuse the experience of the therapist's presence. It may be necessary to reach out to counteract these features of a crisis state which act as resistances to the experience of being helped. For example, a stance of active enquiry, with more questions and greater structure to the interview may be helpful. Sometimes shorter and more frequent contacts in the early stages can be a useful supportive strategy.

In this contact, the therapist needs to manifest a containing calmness. Overall, the guiding principle must be – 'Don't Panic!' The therapist needs to be both emotionally available and attentive to the wider picture: each requires calmness and the ability to communicate a combination of detachment and concern. A confident manner, unforced warmth and occasional humour can provide a basic sense of safety in the relationship. However, there are intense pressures on the therapist which can disrupt these capacities (especially if she is inexperienced or tends to adopt a rigid approach to her work). An excessive need to rescue, impose control or 'put the world right again' will cause the therapist to block the process when she needs to stay with it. Alternatively, the fear of creating dependency may prevent some therapists recognizing and responding to the temporary need for nurturance which is inherent in a state of disorganization. The capacity to manage these 'counter-reactions' and remain emotionally present is the foundation of intervention in a crisis.

An active directive stance

A crucial difference between crisis intervention and many other therapeutic styles is the need for the therapist to be able and willing to shift pace and to take a direct and active approach to the client's current situation. This is linked to the issue of actively establishing emotional contact, but goes further. It means accepting a degree of responsibility for the resolution of the crisis and specifically working towards this. It may mean going beyond what a non-directive, exploratory therapist feels is the normally appropriate therapeutic role, by giving advice and guidance about appropriate actions; making suggestions about what to do; providing information about available services or about social norms; educating the client about what experiences can be expected over the course of the crisis; giving professional feedback about how the therapist sees the situation; or actively 'case-managing' the person's need to be connected to other resources. The therapist may provide reassurance (whilst guarding against doing so falsely); maintain the client's sense of hope and enhance her self-esteem; state positively that it is 'alright to accept help'; and capitalize on the client's expectation of being helped by someone in a professional role. Since the confusion of the crisis state impairs the client's capacity to think abstractly, concrete simple communication and decisiveness on the part of the therapist is vital. This helps to re-establish the client's sense of safety and security and responds to her wish to feel nurtured and cared for. It may sometimes be appropriate to use some physical contact to calm, comfort or reassure, but obviously this needs to be done with great discretion and an awareness of both the therapist's and the client's needs and cultural norms: a hand on the person's elbow or shoulder should be all that is required. Explicit reassurance can increase the client's confidence, mobilize strengths and reduce anxiety to manageable levels. It may be given through approval of the client's statements or actions, or by providing factual information – that there is a solution; that crises are time limited; that people do 'make it through' such times; that there are some common patterns and she is going through what others have experienced. This should be used sparingly, ensuring that the therapist does not appear to be minimizing the client's distress or being careless of aspects of her culture and values.

It is important on the one hand not to be overly nurturing (which can deepen a state of regression or add to the client's confusion and sense of helplessness), and on the other not to be controlling or more active than is needed. The preferred stance is to be a 'consultant', assisting the person to review options and make decisions. Sometimes, however, the client simply does not know what to do and it is appropriate to become an 'auxiliary ego'. It is vital to assess the client's capability for active decision-making and to respect her limitations, rather than seeing passivity simply as 'resistance'. By attending to this, it should be possible to avoid creating unnecessary dependency and to reinforce client choice by making it explicit (in whatever terms are appropriate for the client's state of mind) in a therapeutic contract. This contract will spell out goals and time limits and make clear the expectation that the person continues to be in charge of her own life and will be helped to make all the decisions that she feels able to.

Focus on the present situation

It is essential, especially in the early stages of crisis intervention, to stay at the conscious level and to help the client identify the major problems which she is struggling with in her present life situation. It is easy to be led into elaborating issues which may be only tenuously linked to the immediate problems. This can happen when the therapist's normal therapeutic style seeks to find patterns of difficulty or underlying problems that are at the root of the distress – this may be useful but only at a later stage. Equally, in the distress and disorganization of the crisis state, clients often switch from one topic to another, invoke former difficulties and list all the areas of pain or dissatisfaction in their life: the therapist may be drawn into trying to follow the client (non-directively) through the maze of her confusion and become overwhelmed along with her. The client should be discouraged from invoking former problems; her difficulties are best responded to selectively, in order to identify the major current issues. Focusing on the present problem and clarifying it leads to its reformulation. This restores the person's sense of equilibrium and control, overcomes the experience of 'falling apart', and helps her maintain a focus on her present reality.

As it is often not clear from what the client is initially saying, the therapist may need to seek out the 'trigger' event which precipitated the crisis. For example, it can be helpful to track certain elements of the client's emotional response – her sense of shock or of shame, her wish to retreat from the world and so on – and try to discover when this began: the experience or incident which precipitated this difficulty. For some clients, this process of connecting the crisis to specific events greatly clarifies their experience of the crisis situation. It can take considerable persistence and care on the part of the therapist but forms the basis for linking the overwhelming affect experienced to its source.

Elaine phoned the student counselling service in a desperate state. She was sobbing and confused and it was hard to make out quite what the problem was – but she did say she was thinking of taking some pills. Roger, the counsellor who took the call, felt concerned by the confusion and panic. He established where she was (in case she rang off) and that she did have paracetamol tablets with her and that she was on her own. In listening to her distress and desperation, he felt he had established some degree of trust and told her that he thought what she really needed was to talk more but that it would be most helpful if she came into the centre to do that – she agreed quite readily. Elaine did come in about 45 minutes later and did not have to wait long to see Roger. He listened quietly for a few minutes but it was still difficult to make a coherent story out of the scraps of the different things she was saying. He intervened saying that he thought she felt as though there were so many problems and they were all too much for her so that it felt impossible to put it all together by herself at the moment – he would like to ask some questions to help them both look at the whole picture. She agreed and he asked her when it had started to feel as desperate as this, after which he enquired gently about the various events which had led up to the previous night when things seemed to fall apart. A story started to emerge. Three weeks ago she had broken up with her boyfriend when he had slept with her flatmate. She hadn't been able to go back to her flat since and had been sleeping on her best friend's floor. Last night this friend had invited her out to the pub but when she was reluctant had said 'You can't mope around forever, or no one will ever want to know you' and had gone out. At that point she felt as though her world had caved in. As Roger pursued his enquiry, Elaine talked, still in rather a mixed-up way, about her home background: her parents had split up earlier that year and Roger sensed that this had always been an unhappy and conflicted family, but he didn't pursue any of that. Elaine also talked about feeling ugly, feeling shy around people and as though she just didn't fit in. She also saw herself as failing at college – her last essay had received a poor mark and she was late with the next two. Roger fed back all of the problems that Elaine had poured out, listing them, grouping them together and making some tentative links about Elaine's sense of rejection and worthlessness. She had become calmer as she explained things in response to questions and was able to listen and looked thoughtful as Roger asked her if she had any ideas about what she needed to do next.

Encourage the expression of emotion

Maintaining a reality focus should not be used as an escape for the therapist from staying with the client's painful feelings. It is important to *start* by attending to emotion more than to the content of what the client is saying. It may be necessary to push for the discharge of feelings which are being held back. It can sometimes be helpful to ask a client to describe in detail her 'reactions' to an event, rather than her 'feelings', which for some people can be alarming or too unfamiliar. Ventilation of affect can allow movement in a stuck situation and be the beginning of greater clarity.

Where the events leading to the crisis have a traumatic quality, the facilitation of emotional expression may have particular importance since shock or dissociative reactions may have psychologically numbed or isolated the experience. The use of a 'debriefing' approach may be appropriate in these circumstances (Hodgkinson and Stewart, 1998; Raphael, 1986), setting up the session to go through the client's memories and experience of the event in a structured and detailed fashion – see Table 4.3. The emphasis is on enabling recall, facilitating emotional experiencing and processing and providing a cognitive framework which 'makes sense' of what the person has gone through. Single-session models of debriefing have been developed out of group methods to process reactions to disasters and critical incidents with the aim of preventing the development of post-traumatic disorders. There has been concern that if routinely applied, these may risk making things worse rather than better by retraumatizing clients or encouraging them to see themselves as likely to become psychologically ill (Wessely et al., 1998). These dangers are minimized by undertaking such debriefings in the context of a crisis counselling which extends over several sessions; where attention has been paid to establishing a safe relationship which is both normalizing and responsive to the needs and pacing of each individual; and where there are other supportive interventions including a focus on the meaning of the crisis and ways to cope with it. The persistence of emotional blocking around a significant incident might alert the therapist that there is a high risk of continuing disorder and the need for follow-up and ongoing work (Scott and Stradling, 1992).

In any crisis situation, by accepting the client's feelings and communicating their validity, the therapist normalizes the experience of distress and assists her to see it as acceptable. It may be necessary in this to help the client tolerate these feelings, rather than to suppress or escape from them. The therapist may need to support her 'going through the pain', repeatedly empathizing with the difficulty of this but pointing out that it cannot be simply 'fixed' or made better (Linehan, 1993). The distress should be viewed as necessary – difficult but manageable. In addition to facilitating and supporting the expression of feelings, the therapist can provide simple statements which clarify the often complex and competing emotions generated by the situation. For example, pointing out to a belligerent client that she may be feeling frightened and helpless can sometimes create a dramatic shift in her sense of safety and accessibility. This enables the client to begin to place her emotional confusion in a more manageable context.

Explore alternative perceptions

Emotional disorganization disrupts the ability to maintain a perspective on the reality of the situation. Enabling the client to gain understanding and achieve some cognitive control can be achieved by offering alternative perceptions of the crisis events and by examining the totality of the problem situation, summarizing and formulating the problem in new ways. The therapist should attempt to work towards shared understanding of the nature of the difficulties. This enables the client to put some order into her chaotic thoughts and feelings, to search for boundaries to her dilemma and to appraise the meaning of the situation for her, in order to move towards problem-solving.

TABLE 4.3 *Structured debriefing for traumatic incidents*

- Introduction and Contract
    outline what you intend to do
    provide rationale: value of talking experiences through
    no one has to say more than seems right to them
    ⟶   Seek agreement

- Review facts of events
    what led up to the incident?
    when and where did it happen?
    how did it start: what were you aware of first of all?
    what happened: go through in sequence and in detail
    ⟶   Gain cognitive organization of confused events

- Recall thoughts
    thinking during/around the incident
    first impressions
    uncover decisions made about what to do
    ⟶   Reveal personal meanings

- Re-experience emotions
    what feelings/personal reactions are associated with the event: during incident or
        subsequently?
    what is the worst thing about the incident for you?
    focus on: fear/helplessness
                anger/self-reproach
                unexpected/unacceptable feelings
    gently seek cathartic expression
    ⟶   Release and validate emotions

Possibly

- Repeat review
    repeat over further sessions if:
                lack of 'closure' to experience
                client remains troubled
                client is willing to work it through
    check for connection to past events
    ⟶   Promote emotional processing

*In incident debriefing, two further stages conclude the process – however, these are typically
included in further stages of crisis intervention (below) –*

- Review stress symptoms
    during/following the incident and remaining currently
    look for PTSD responses: re-experiencing, avoidance, numbering, arousal
    check impact of incident on other relationships
    ⟶   Uncover potential impact

- Inform/teach
    provide normalizing information/models of stress
    advise about coping skills
    plan for future support
    ⟶   Integrate experience and problem-solve

The therapist helps the client accept reality and should advocate facing the crisis rather than becoming trapped in ways of avoiding it. This means discouraging denial or evasion, including anything from over-sedation (by medication, alcohol etc.) to a geographical 'escape' (through a holiday or relocation) – tactics which may sometimes be supported by others in the environment. A client may need assistance to find rest but should be supported in returning to face the problem. Distorted patterns of thinking and coping should be identified and gently challenged. Meaningless activities, scapegoating and blaming others, self-deprecation or self-pity and 'magical thinking' are all ways in which people avoid accepting the reality of what is happening to them. It can be difficult not to collude with this kind of avoidance where the situation which faces the client is genuinely cruel or unfair, but it is important to help her take appropriate responsibility for her own future.

It can also be helpful in the middle phases of crisis intervention to look for beliefs which amplify the perception of the crisis or interfere with processing it. For example, a fear of expressing emotion, a sense of guilt or disloyalty, feelings of shame or rage may all distort perceptions of the situation. The particular meaning of the events for each individual has to be understood. It is not enough to assume that the distress is 'understandable'; its particular implications and resonances have to be identified. Depending on the therapist's orientation, this might mean looking at basic assumptions and automatic patterns of thinking or it might be conceptualized as seeking the out-of-awareness resonance of an event, the ways it echoes significant aspects of the client's previous history or major personal or interpersonal issues. For example, a failure to get promotion may be responded to with typically perfectionistic or self-condemning assumptions, perhaps echoing crucial school failures; or it could stir rivalrous feelings with a more favoured sibling. A lover's infidelity may set off old doubts about self-worth or touch memories of disappointment or abandonment by a parent. It is frequently these underlying personal meanings which function as amplifying and distorting features of the crisis situation and which have made it difficult to cope with. Helping the client to make links to such unresolved developmental issues and to conceptualize them can be a source of major growth potential in crisis situations. Where crises occur in the course of ongoing therapy, the experience of the crisis should be linked to the therapeutic work which is taking place, enabling the client to see these events in a wider context and as part of the continuing process of growth and learning.

Facilitate problem-solving

The process of formulating potential solutions in the crisis situation emerges directly out of the work of clarifying the problem itself. It can be helpful to work with the client to identify, say, the three most critical difficulties out of a complex array that she is facing, taking each area of difficulty and breaking it down into different parts so as to focus on them one at a time. This only works with real problems: clients sometimes present as 'problems', actions which are better seen as ineffective 'solutions' – such as suicidal impulses, or the wish to drink. The therapist should not be led into attempting to solve these directly, but should trace them back to the problematic situations and feelings to which they are a maladaptive coping response. The client should be encouraged to explore alternatives for dealing with the issues and so helped to discover new ways of coping. She might be helped to list the possibilities and then to evaluate them in terms of their likelihood of achieving her goals. This kind of thinking avoids the dangers of impulsiveness, promotes mastery of the situation and models the therapist's belief in the possibility of positive alternatives.

In evaluating the options, it is important to encourage the client to think through the likely consequences of her actions, particularly on her relationships and her self-esteem. Clients are likely to focus on short-term benefits and it may be essential for the therapist to keep attention focused on the longer-term issues. Where it is difficult for the client to examine the pros and cons realistically and the therapist believes that her proposed coping strategy is likely to be detrimental, the therapist should not be afraid to confront this directly. Of course, this is also an opportunity to help draw attention to distorted patterns of thinking, unrealistic beliefs and ineffective coping habits. People are often fixed on one solution which may amount to a fantasy of undoing what has happened and restoring the situation which existed previously; this can reduce both therapist and client to a state of helplessness. In steering the client towards positive solutions, the therapist also needs to clarify and reinforce adaptive responses when they are generated by attending to them and referring back to them at a later stage.

Teach new coping strategies

The client's sense of self-efficacy can be promoted through encouraging her to take simple actions 'one step at a time', thus countering the sense of loss of control. One of the potentially positive outcomes of a crisis is that the client learns new and more effective ways of coping which can be applied to the rest of her life. Sometimes all that may be necessary is to give permission for the client to act on her own ideas. For others, it may be helpful to give authoritative suggestions about what to do. The therapist should help the client actively plan strategies to respond to her situation as an outcome of the problem-solving work. This may mean providing information and assisting the client to learn new skills, actively instructing, providing opportunities for rehearsal within sessions and planning situations for practice. This cognitive-behavioural way of working may be rather unfamiliar to some therapists, but it can have a great deal to offer when clients need guidance in managing aspects of their experience which could endanger their future mental and physical health if poorly handled. Outlined below are some major problematic features of crises and the kinds of coping strategies which can prove helpful.

Physical self-care is important during crisis periods. During a time when psychological stress is high, vital aspects of self-care may be neglected because they seem to require extra effort and it can be useful to advise clients to create a simple regime of attention to their physical needs, including diet, exercise and rest. There is a significantly increased *risk of accidents* occurring during periods of heightened stress and clients should be alerted to this: they should be advised not to undertake risky activities and to take special care in routine ones. A judgement must be made about whether people are safe to drive.

Anxiety and tension are such common features in crises that a working knowledge of *anxiety management* principles is essential (Clark, 1989). Relaxation procedures (progressive muscular relaxation techniques; pre-recorded tapes; breathing procedures; and simple meditation exercises) are useful in reducing tension and providing clients with a sense of control. Cognitive control of worries, ruminations and self-critical or catastrophic thoughts is another major element of managing anxiety – identifying thoughts and behaviours which undermine a sense of control or maintain the experience of anxiety. Coping strategies include: distraction, scheduling times for worrying, self-challenging and substitution of coping statements. When anxiety takes the form of *panic attacks*, a vicious circle of mounting anxiety, hyperventilation and 'anxiety about anxiety' is set in motion. Explaining the nature of anxiety and providing a model of how this escalates during panic, while reassuring that this is not in itself dangerous, can be quite powerful, together with learning the further coping strategies above. The aim should not be to talk the client out of her anxiety or to help her 'fight' it, but to enable her to gain a measure of control and so create the space for emotional processing.

Sleep problems are a common and debilitating feature of crisis states which can result in exhaustion of the kind that makes finding rest yet more difficult and leaves people vulnerable to disorganization and ineffective coping. *Medication* can be useful but has its dangers and is often over-prescribed. Its value is in breaking the cycle of sleeplessness in the short term and so preventing total exhaustion; in fact, its use for this purpose may need to be encouraged for clients resistant to the idea of 'taking drugs'. However, use prolonged beyond one week maximum is likely to interfere with re-establishing normal sleep cycles. Even in the short term, over-medication can interfere with necessary emotional processing and reduce motivation for problem-solving. *Insomnia* over the longer term can be a source of considerable distress and it may be helpful to guide clients in responding to it (see Table 4.4). Some clients may be troubled by intense dreams and *nightmares*. The therapist should help clients see this as a normal process in which their mind is attempting to make sense of the events they are going through. Nightmares, in which there is an element of intense fear or helplessness, can generate a fear of sleeping which contributes to exhaustion. By encouraging clients to talk through nightmares in detail several times, exposing themselves to the frightening experience, they can start to assimilate them and the nightmare becomes 'only a dream'.

TABLE 4.4 *Responding to insomnia*

- Do not worry *about* sleeping:
  - you can't force sleep
  - you can manage on relatively little sleep
  - you are probably getting more sleep than you imagine

- Cut out caffeine and alcohol:
  - alcohol makes insomnia/waking worse over time

- In bed:
  - lie quiet and relax physically
  - don't *try* to sleep
  - keep clearing mind of thoughts e.g. by repeating one word at irregular intervals
  - persist (for about an hour)

- Re-establish association of sleep with bed:
  - only go to bed when tired
  - if awake after one hour, get up
  - go *elsewhere* and do something calm (read, listen to music)
  - when sleepy, return to bed
  - get up at usual time (even if tired and sleepy)

- Control anxiety:
  - remember worries seem larger when in bed
  - persistently put troublesome thoughts aside
  - use a calming visual image
  - focus on relaxing the body

- Re-establish routine pattern:
  - do not nap during the day
  - go to bed when tired in mid to late evening

Feelings of exhaustion, despondency and *depression* may be part of a process of grieving or they may be a secondary consequence of prolonged high levels of anxiety. During such states of temporary depression, it is important that the therapist help the client not to expect too much of herself: lowered activity and perhaps heightened emotionality can assist recovery and provide space for assimilation. Allowances should be made for this by reducing the level of life demands and enabling some 'free wheeling': the therapist may have to challenge the client's self-criticism and drive to push herself onwards. Sometimes it is appropriate for the person to create a temporary retreat situation; but it is often useful to create a routine with a manageable level of activity, perhaps through working at a reduced level. Activity scheduling – proactively drawing up such a routine – can restore the client's sense of control and ensure that some satisfying and effective areas of action are included in each day.

Involve family and social networks

Crises almost inevitably involve the disruption of a person's network of attachments and social supports. Indeed, it is often the network as a whole that is in crisis and the individual's difficulties reflect as well as affect those around them. Crisis resolution involves re-establishing the functioning of the social network and interventions should take particular care not to further damage the integrity of the social group by removing the person from their normal situation and so individualizing the problem. If this is essential, it should be part of a carefully considered strategy which acknowledges the competing risks. The therapist must view the crisis in its context and help natural support networks in their efforts to achieve a constructive resolution and restore disrupted ties. This may involve enabling the individual presenting in crisis to seek help from her normal supportive resources when she may feel inclined to withdraw from contact. It requires the therapist to have a degree of faith in the social network and to assume that, as a rule, it has the capacity to help: this attitude more readily engages other people's participation.

Different views can be taken, both theoretically and pragmatically, of the role of the family in a crisis situation (Sugarman and Macheter, 1985). Too often, perhaps, the family is seen simply as background to an individual problem: family members may be drawn on solely as a source of information and to understand the impact of the client's disturbance on others. However, the family is more usefully seen as a context for the problem, either a resource or a stressor for the client: family members need to be involved in modifying the ways they mediate stress. Indeed, the crisis situation may be redefined by the therapist as a 'family crisis': it results from reciprocal patterns of influence, with the individual in crisis only the 'identified patient' and the therapeutic approach being to treat the family system as a whole. In practice, different approaches might usefully be taken depending on the assessment of the family situation. If pre-crisis relationships were good, a conjoint treatment approach which taps the family's resources makes sense; if they were poor, the family may be viewed as a stressor which may in the short term be difficult to modify and an individual approach could be adopted. The approach may vary over the course of a therapy, with families who label the member in crisis as 'sick' being more responsive initially to being treated as 'background', while it may be possible to change the degree of their involvement with time. Where children or adolescents are presenting in crisis, family and network approaches are to be recommended in nearly all instances.

Where the need for a family intervention approach is established, they must be helped to see themselves as integral to the individual's difficulties.

The therapist should open up communication, help the members recognize and change patterns of interaction, reach compromise solutions to difficulties, discover new ways to relate to each other and reframe the issues with which they were struggling (Puryear, 1979). It may be helpful to convene a conference with the wider network beyond the immediate family at the second or third sessions, ensuring linkage of the family to a broader social context and exploring the problem as it pertains to everyone involved, airing the complaints of all parties and facilitating the consideration of possible solutions. People's connectedness with each other and the sense of unity of the group as a whole can be re-established. In some busy clinics dealing with a lot of people presenting in crisis, group work methods have been developed both for intake assessments and for intervention (Hoff, 1978). Such groups rapidly develop cohesion and the sharing involved normalizes problems and gives participants a sense of increased mastery over the situation. Again, the value of social participation in the crisis situation is emphasized by this approach.

Adapt the environment and mobilize resources

The therapist must be willing and prepared to mobilize external resources on the client's behalf. In taking this active role and in extending normal therapeutic boundaries to include the involvement of others, the therapist is acting decisively to contain a highly charged situation where there is the possibility of personal collapse or the threat to life. There should be an attempt to mobilize the client's energy to reach out to others and seek help for herself in effective ways. However, the therapist may need to be willing to take responsibility for making some of these initial decisions.

In involving others and making effective referrals to other agencies, the therapist has to go about this in a thoughtful and responsible manner. She should explore the readiness of the client to be referred to some other specialist and what this might mean to the client. She should be direct and honest about the suggestion to involve others, the reasons for it and her own limitations in what she can offer as an individual therapist. The nature of the agency referred to, its potential and its limitations should be explained and it should not be set up as the place for a 'miracle cure'. The therapist may wish to confer with the other people whom she plans to involve, but she should take care to do so in a calm professional manner and to release information about the client only with the client's clear consent (preferably in writing). Where it is possible, the client should be enabled to make her own appointments rather than have the therapist take over and do it for her.

It takes good preparation to be properly equipped to involve outside resources in effective ways. It means knowing what useful resources there might be in your local community: what available telephone helplines can offer as a support between therapeutic sessions; suitable places (religious retreats, nursing homes or health farms) which might be appropriate for use as a place of retreat or 'asylum' in some relatively informal, non-medical setting; the location of the nearest Accident and Emergency hospital; a contact in the local community mental health team and an understanding of their admission procedures. A record of a client's GP in case an emergency situation arises can be very important.

Agree a definite plan of action

The therapist should work to agree a definite plan of action with the client. The plan should be realistic, concrete and time-limited, specifying what will be done by whom and when. The plan defines the problem and a goal, reassures the client that something will happen and specifies a clear time-frame: as with many of the other elements in crisis intervention, this creates structure which contains the distress. The push for action provides a greater sense of control, increases hope and motivation and surfaces any possible resistance. The plan should be flexible and capable of dealing with changes in the situation: it should not be set up in such a way that if some elements of it do not work, this is viewed as a failure – something else can be tried.

It is essential to share responsibility with the client in drawing up the plan and for there to be active collaboration with any other people who have been brought in to help. The therapist should not take over and assume inappropriate control, although as discussed above, it can be legitimate to give specific direction where the client is chaotic and limited in her own capacity to make appropriate decisions. It is vital to obtain the client's commitment to the plan of action: she needs to agree what she will do next and recognize that she is expected to take these agreed-on steps.

Returning to the case of Elaine, the student in crisis in the earlier example, her counsellor Roger had asked her what she thought she should do next. She thought that she would be able to return to her friend with whom she was staying and 'patch things up' but wasn't sure beyond that. Roger helped her to prioritize the main issues facing her and they agreed on a way forward for each. The first issue Roger wanted to feel reassured about was Elaine's safety: it was clear that the immediate impulse towards suicide had passed but he was aware that she was not yet emotionally stable. They agreed that she would phone Roger briefly the next day to discuss progress and if there was a setback before then, Elaine felt sure that she could 'talk herself down' but might need help to do so and they decided that contacting 'Nite-line' would achieve that. Secondly, Elaine's lack of secure accom-modation was very unsettling and needed to be sorted out urgently. She felt able to go to the College accommodation office on the following day but asked for Roger's support; he agreed he would ring them and ensure that she was seen as a priority. Her friend's flat would be OK for the next few days and she could get emotional support there once she had explained more clearly how difficult things were and that she was doing something

TABLE 4.5 *Crisis intervention planning*

Actions targeted at goals
    specify concretely how will
    – manage specific risks/maintain safety
    – restore prior level of functioning
    – address concrete problems
    – work on personal issues

Maintaining contact
    – by whom
    – frequency
    – place: home/office
    – in person/by phone

Involvement of others
    – obtain consent
    – who: friends/family
            other involved professionals
    – how: seek/provide information
            involve as helpers/caretakers/collaborators
            involve in family/network therapy

Involve additional resources
    – telephone help-lines
    – specialist referral:
            medical/psychiatric/therapeutic
    – assessment for medication
    – arrange respite care/refuge
    – seek psychiatric admission

Obtain additional services
    direct to: social services/social security
                housing/legal/trades union
    advocacy with these services

Identify blocks to implementation
    – what might hinder the plan
    – what might escalate the crisis
    – fall-back plan

Identify time-frame
    – date for review of plan
    – end of planned intervention
    – follow-up

about them for herself. They agreed that it was best not to be in touch with either of her parents in the next week. Thirdly, the danger of failing courses and possibly dropping out of College had to be addressed rather than avoided. Elaine thought she could speak to her tutor about her late work as she became calmer and agreed to do this within two days; Roger said he was willing to be contacted by the tutor if this was necessary. They agreed to have a further session in two days time to review progress and contract for a 'few more sessions'. Roger had in mind that – if the situation had been contained – he would move to weekly contact for three further sessions during which he would raise the more fundamental issues of Elaine's family problems, low self-esteem, isolation and poor coping abilities, with a view to setting up a referral for longer-term work, probably with a trainee within the student counselling service.

Factors which might interfere with intended actions should be identified and ways of addressing them considered in order to minimize the possibility of failure. The likelihood of recurrences of overwhelming distress and difficulty should be discussed in advance and the plan designed to incorporate ways of coping with these. As the immediate crisis draws to a close, consideration should be given to how to deal with future trigger events and the reactions of other people to the crisis. The therapist thus gives a 'roadmap' for the future which supports the new learning that has been achieved. In any plan, the option of future contact with the therapist should be built in and it is generally helpful to schedule a specific follow-up as part of the process of termination.

At the end of each therapeutic contact during a crisis, the therapist should briefly reassess the level of risk and whether the plan that has been agreed reduces risk to an acceptable level. If it does not, of course, additional strategies and resources must be introduced and the plan of action changed.

Implications for therapeutic practice

These guidelines for crisis intervention are not hard and fast rules. They are general principles, focusing mainly on what might be different for many therapists from their normal style of working. As a crisis situation requires a flexible, eclectic and pragmatic response, it is helpful to be skilled in a wide range of techniques and to be able to adapt to the demands of a particular situation. However, it is also necessary to adapt the framework of crisis intervention to fit your own style and therapeutic orientation. Like any therapy, crisis intervention is best performed with a combination of discipline and creativity. Different facets of crisis intervention technique will be appropriate with different clients and at different points in the work. It can be helpful to organize our conceptualization of intervention during a crisis into stages (Baldwin, 1979), ordering various interventions into a sequence, with different therapeutic tasks to be undertaken in each phase. This is not a rigid pattern, however, and any crisis therapy might move back and forth between different stages of the process. This approach is detailed in Table 4.6.

As a normal part of human experience, all cultures have traditionally found ways to respond to the person in crisis which help them weather the storm and re-establish their life, possibly transforming their identity and shifting their role in the process. Seen in this light, problematic crises occur when these natural helping processes are insufficient: a crisis presentation in a professional context is as much a symptom of a breakdown in the social

TABLE 4.6 *Phases and tasks of crisis intervention*

Phase 1: Contact and Assessment
- Establish relationship of trust and containment
- Identify and explore meaning of precipitating event
- Assess level of risk and disorganization
- Encourage acknowledgement of crisis and expression of feelings
- Obtain limited relevant personal background information
- Assess dimensions of crisis situation
- Restore realistic perspective
- Identify viable options and courses of action
- Mobilize appropriate support

Phase 2: Focusing and Contracting
- Help conceptualize personal meaning of situation and link to biography
- Develop awareness of feelings and meanings that impair adaptive coping
- Support acceptance of reality
- Normalize responses to crisis situation
- Establish therapeutic alliance emphasizing appropriate levels of client responsibility
- Negotiate a shared definition of the core problem(s)
- Define goals and time frames for intervention
- Agree initial plan for resolving crisis

Phase 3: Coping and resolution
- Define and support client's coping strengths
- Explore past styles of coping
- Enable evaluation of alternative strategies
- Work through feelings and meanings which prevent adaptive resolution
- Support direct, appropriate responses to situation and communication with others
- Teach or help develop coping responses and problem-solving skills
- Define progress towards goals and reformulate plan
- Prevent diffusion of therapy away from crisis focus

Phase 4: Integration and termination
- Evaluate goal attainment
- Elicit and respond to feelings about ending without prolonging intervention
- Reinforce changes in coping and link to resolution of problem
- Anticipate and prepare for future situations and help integrate change
- Identify future support
- Provide information about additional resources or refer for continuing help

system which is failing to manage the person in distress as it is a breakdown in the individual. Caplan (1964) takes a preventative, 'public health' approach to crisis, attempting to strengthen natural helping systems in the community. There is a danger of a psychotherapeutic approach pathologizing crises by taking people out of their natural systems and weakening the ability of these to help. Therapists need to be alert to this danger in order to make a judgement about what an appropriate intervention might be, avoiding unnecessary or harmful responses. Psychotherapists and counsellors do have a significant role of a more public health nature in supporting, advising and consulting to other less specialist professionals such as health visitors or police, as well as to the client and her natural support systems. Such consultations sustain and guide the efforts of others to ensure that appropriate help is provided in the least stigmatizing context. It is also possible to take a 'health promotion' stance towards prevention by preparing vulnerable groups of people for possible future crises through 'psychoeducational' interventions, in such a way as to reduce the risk of damaging breakdown in the future.

Individual practitioners and services need to review their capability to deal with crisis situations. Individual therapists particularly should have a clear understanding of their limitations and what kind of clients and presenting circumstances they are equipped to deal with. We should not presume to offer more than we can realistically deliver. Crises may test our capacities to their limit. Where emergency situations are relatively common, training, high morale and supportive team working are essential to sustain staff under constant pressure. In the more common situation where crises are out-of-the-ordinary events, practitioners should ensure they find time and support to think through situations with colleagues as soon as possible afterwards and if necessary to 'debrief' themselves from excessively demanding or frightening encounters.

Conclusion

In the pressure to act which crises create, it is possible to forget that there are dangers to taking assertive action as well as good reasons for doing so. The balance of costs and benefits in taking any specific action needs to be weighed up in each instance. This balance is likely to be different when a crisis occurs while someone is in ongoing therapy rather than presenting for help in an acutely distressed state. The risks of intervening assertively or not are different in the two situations. The issues for crises during therapy are addressed in the following chapter.

5   Crises in Therapy

Therapists seek change in their clients – but not too much too quickly! For therapy to promote change, there generally needs to be a basic framework of stability in circumstances and social functioning in the client's life: psychological change feels more manageable against a background of continuity. Frequently, however, we are not so fortunate – there are disruptions in the client's life or her underlying difficulties re-surface in dramatic fashion. Crises often beset the course of the therapeutic work.

Therapy and crisis intervention

Dealing with a crisis occurring during the course of psychotherapy or counselling is different in a number of important ways from providing help when someone presents at the point of crisis. In an ongoing therapy, the client is known with greater depth and clarity than if she were presenting for the first time in a desperate state. Her history, her capabilities, her life circumstances and the meaning of the current situation, are likely to be much clearer to the therapist and so an assessment of risk can be made with greater assurance (rather than erring on the conservative side as will often be the case for a first presentation in crisis). Moreover, the context of an established therapeutic alliance is in itself a significant safety factor; this is linked to a pattern of mutually agreed ways of working and therapeutic issues which guide any intervention. All of this enables a more informed strategy for positive risk-taking in a therapeutic context than is possible for a crisis presentation in which both an assessment and plan of intervention must be created from scratch.

The strategy and goals for intervention are also different in the two situations. Crisis intervention prioritizes a short-term aim – restoring the client's normal level of functioning. As a strategy, crisis intervention allows plenty of latitude in appropriate interventions and extended boundaries. The strategy of psychotherapy is different; it has longer-term aims, a clearer contract and, typically, a specific therapeutic 'posture' with a more tightly defined range of techniques. These vary for different approaches of course, but all aim to maximize the client's responsibility for her own actions and to empower her to make her own choices about her life. It is this which can come under serious pressure in crisis situations. The client's message can be: 'Help – you've go to do something . . . now . . . or else!' The pressure – and the temptation – in a crisis is to short-circuit the work of empowerment and to do things for and give things to the client.

It is in the nature of a crisis to create pressures on the normal framework of therapy, raising questions about whether the overall strategy is adequate to the client's needs. Can the therapist meet the challenge of the crisis within her normal therapeutic framework, or does it have to be temporarily altered or even abandoned? It is this pressure to alter the usual ground rules of the therapeutic contract during a crisis which creates dilemmas for the therapist. Intervening actively in ways which change the framework of the relationship may have significant costs in being able to pursue the long-term aims of therapy effectively. In being pulled out of her usual therapeutic role by the demands of the crisis, a therapist risks being drawn into participating unhelpfully in some enactment of the client's customary life script – perhaps the very problem which led her to seek therapy in the first place. The therapist's crisis response may feed a maladaptive cycle so that old patterns are repeated rather than understood or changed. Mishandling crises can easily create an impasse.

The wrong crisis response may implicitly give a number of unhelpful messages to the client: that she is fragile and unable to cope by herself; that she is not up to dealing with the demands of her life; that other people's caring and concern are expressed only by 'doing'; that help is obtainable most readily by getting into a mess; that threats, urgency and emotional pressure are the best way to communicate needs. This may leave the client with reduced self-respect, increased passivity and less sense of responsibility for herself. At worst, it may result in a pattern of escalating crises as the client's resources are reduced and the threshold for obtaining help increases. Thus, the long-term goals of therapy – of increasing respon-sibility and choice and the capacity to relate skilfully to others – can be subverted by the urgent need to manage short-term risk. Therapists faced with a client in crisis have to resist being pushed to act without thinking through the implications of the choices available. Crisis intervention techniques for those presenting in the midst of a life crisis attempt to avoid these dangers by being strictly time-limited, circumscribed in their goals and are based on the assumption that the client was functioning at a reasonably adaptive level to which she can return. For clients with chronic difficulties in coping, crisis intervention can lead to precisely these problems of dependency and repetitive escalating dramas as a means of dealing with life.

When Gerry split up with his girlfriend and then a week later lost his job, he felt 'almost suicidal'. Cheryl, his therapist, felt deeply concerned and increased the frequency of his sessions to twice a week, making it clear that he should also phone her if he felt really low. She also said he mustn't worry about the fees until he'd got over this bad patch – it would be soon enough to think about those when he was able to get another job. Gerry did phone several times, sometimes late in the evening, complaining at length about how unfair the world was and that he'd had enough of it. Cheryl seemed to find little opportunity to explore these events – how they had occurred so close together, or even why they had hit him so hard. When she started to press Gerry to 'move on' and consider his future, he complained bitterly that there was just 'no way'. Cheryl was left feeling confused, angry and frightened about what he might yet do. She began to think of how she could just 'get rid' of this client who had become a burden and a pest.

Responding during a therapeutic crisis

As the emotional pressure on the therapist to act in a different way increases, the more she needs to be clear about the aims and the ground-rules of the work. Theorists who have specialized in developing work with so-called 'borderline' clients (who are prone to dramatic presentations) have been the most careful to develop clear protocols to deal with crisis situations (Kernberg et al., 1989; Linehan, 1993). The therapist needs the support of these frameworks to respond consistently: the middle of a crisis is not the ideal time to work out from scratch what is the best way to handle it. This does not mean being inflexible, but clarity is needed: in particular, the therapist has to know her role boundaries and the nature and limits of her responsibilities. There is a damaging myth which some therapeutic pairs get entangled in – that the therapist has both the power and the responsibility to ensure the client's survival. Ultimately, only the client can guarantee her own safety. While there are circumstances in which the therapist must act to protect the client, this is beyond the normal boundaries of the therapeutic contract. A therapist's primary responsibility is to ensure the appropriate conditions for the therapy itself (on the premise that this is in the long-term interests of the client).

It is essential to work within the limits of what you are prepared to offer:

- what you are sufficiently competent and confident to manage (not of course that you will always *feel* confident!);
- what you are prepared to tolerate in terms of anxiety and intense emotional involvement;
- what you can and will provide in terms of time availability, flexibility, rapid response and access to other resources.

If you cannot realistically provide what is likely to be required, ethically you probably ought to decline to start or to continue. You ought also to be alert to your own motivations for involvement in crisis-ridden situations. It is easy to be drawn in by the excitement of an urgent situation and the need to be needed; it can be gratifying to be the rescuer of a 'hapless victim'. These intense counter-transference reactions can endanger the therapy: either leading it into an impasse (as discussed in Chapter 9); or through encouraging the therapist to be a hero or martyr, compromising her own personal or professional safety (as discussed in Chapter 13).

Deciding on the best response to a therapeutic crisis is aided by having a way of categorizing the type and seriousness of the risk which it poses. Linehan (1993) suggests that risks can be:

- a threat to the life or safety of the client or others
- a threat to the effective continuation of the therapy
- a threat to the quality of life of the client.

Threats in the last category – to quality of life – such as self-harm or making self-detrimental choices, should normally be 'grist to the mill' and incorporated in the therapeutic work itself, however dramatic they may seem. Where acting-out compromises the conditions needed to undertake therapy – the client attends erratically, makes herself unable to pay fees, insists on receiving practical help or will only talk about the current drama – work on this 'resistance' is a priority: trying to understand the behaviour, finding ways of getting in touch with the underlying distress or revisiting the therapeutic contract and the client's commitment to it. Failing to re-establish the therapeutic framework is likely to result in an impasse (see Chapter 6); responding by inappropriately implementing crisis intervention procedures is almost certain to do so.

The majority of crises during therapy can be contained without the therapist being drawn into taking over-active measures. It is normally sufficient to acknowledge and validate feelings of distress, to provide an opportunity for understanding and catharsis, to redefine and de-dramatize the situation, and, on occasion, to draw anger away from the external situation and onto the therapist who can withstand it without retaliation. The containment provided by the established therapeutic relationship enables fear and emotional pain to be faced without the need for reassurance or active problem-solving which might actually be experienced as a rejection of the client's feelings. However, the more serious the crisis and the greater the risk of significant harm, the greater is the need for modification to the therapist's usual role in implementing a crisis intervention plan. Such interventions can be arranged as a kind of hierarchy of increasing activity and modification to the therapeutic boundaries as suggested in Table 5.1. Normally, the therapist's stance should be modified as little as possible consonant with safety: increased availability can be a powerfully supportive action, building on an established sense of security and hope. The implications of any change for the longer-term work still have to be weighed up and their meaning must be addressed with the client after the crisis is over. Some therapists with some clients may conclude that if there has been a major alteration of boundaries, the therapy can no longer proceed effectively.

Crises occurring during therapy differ enormously – in their source, their seriousness, their meaning and their implications for the future of the therapeutic work. It may be helpful to distinguish three broad types of crisis during therapy:

TABLE 5.1 *Responses to a crisis during therapy*

Increased availability
- added scheduled sessions
- scheduled telephone contact between sessions
- crisis telephone availability
- emergency sessions

It is essential to have a clear, practicable and tolerable policy about such contacts. Do not get into extended therapeutic work by telephone: brief assurance of concern, assessment of safety and problem-solving only.

Increased therapist activity
- focus on reality testing
- provide information/education
- teach coping techniques
- focus on specific problem-solving

Remain clear about the limits of therapeutic responsibility.

Involve family/network
- family/couple sessions
- family/friends act as advocates
- family/friends provide respite/'minding'

Client consent and active participation is essential.

Involve other services
- liaise with/co-ordinate others already involved
- link to others with specialist resources:
  GP
  telephone helpline
  community mental health team/psychiatry
  accident and emergency/hospital
- advise about provision of other interventions
  medication
  case management
  hospital admission: voluntary or 'formal'

Client should be helped to **secure her own safety** *as far as possible.*

- External – crises which are a response to external life events (such as bereavement or divorce) which impact on the course of the therapeutic work.
- Intrinsic – crisis events which arise as a consequence of the therapeutic work itself (such as an emotional 'breakdown') but which disrupt its smooth course.
- Repetitive – crises which are a repetitive pattern of coping with difficulties (such as drinking or self-harm) and which are from the outset, or which become, the focus of the therapeutic work.

These are not clear-cut divisions, of course: we are seldom quite sure to what extent a client has provoked an external event or dramatized her emotional response. However, these distinctions are a starting point from which to organize our thinking about the impact of crises on therapeutic work and to consider the most helpful ways to respond to them.

The impact of life events

Some therapists see psychotherapy as a time-out, a protected space for the client to reappraise her direction in life. Reality is not always so obliging. Especially in longer-term therapies, there is a significant chance of major life events occurring. These can have a substantial impact on the therapeutic work; they can be experienced as an intrusion. There may have to be a change in the therapeutic goal with the focus moving to helping the client cope with the psychological aspects of the event. However, external events often also become a part of the therapeutic work: the client's response may be problematic, possibly in ways related to the difficulties that originally brought her to therapy. Thus, depending on the goal of the therapy and the nature of the event, there may be a significant change in the work with a shift in goals and an altered therapeutic style, or alternatively, the life crisis may be incorporated seamlessly into the ongoing therapeutic process.

The therapist's stance should initially be one of respecting and facilitating the client's normal processes of making sense of and coming to terms with the life changes which the event has produced. Only when there is some difficulty or blockage within these natural processes of adaptation should the therapist actively intervene with the intention of restoring the integrity of the process of growth. For example, a major *bereavement* is a powerful experience but one that is not uncommon in the course of extended therapies. It may slow down general progress in therapy or it may greatly speed it up. Much has been written in recent years about the process of mourning and about therapeutic interventions when grief becomes frozen or distorted (Worden 1991), but we should *never assume* that we know what a bereavement means to someone, or how they are (or ought to be) feeling. Principally in this situation, the therapist needs to 'be with' her client – it is a situation of shared humanity. As with any stress, bereavement may bring into sharp relief both the strengths of the client and her characteristic difficulties. The therapist should enter into the dynamics of the mourning process with the client only after the most acute emotions have receded and where the client seems to need assistance to face the pain or to work it through. This should take place only at a measured pace and the therapist should guard against a wish to hurry the process. Much of this is also relevant to situations when a client is facing the impending death of another. It may be important, tactfully, to explore ambivalent feelings held towards the person: negativity to someone who is also important and loved is what most often makes the process of bereavement unusually problematic. The therapist can help with the gradual acknowledgement of these conflicts and yet also to encourage the client to act conscientiously.

If the client herself falls *seriously ill*, such a major change is likely to substantially take over the therapeutic agenda. It is essential to explore the meaning of the illness to the client, in both realistic and personal/symbolic terms. On the one hand, it might mean major changes in social role, future plans or financial status; on the other, it may be experienced as a punishment or a loss of personal power. Illness can be a 'narcissistic blow' – an attack on the sense of self-worth and inviolability and the particular characteristics of the disease or disability may have personal resonances which need to be explored. Fears of enforced passivity – both real and imagined – are amongst the commonest reactions that have to be worked through. For these reasons, the client may be inclined to deny the full seriousness and implications of her medical condition. In general terms, the major task may be said to be 'reality testing': helping the client distinguish her own assumptions, fears and imaginings from what is actually happening to her. Exaggerated fears of harm and magical expectations of cure may need to be gently challenged, working to help the client accept the realities of her situation and express her fears so that she can start to re-establish some sense of control and escape the experience of isolation and shame which illness can produce. The therapist may need to make a decision about how it is appropriate to maintain contact if her client is hospitalized or cannot attend sessions in the normal way. The value of continuing support may outweigh any dangers in extending the normal boundaries of therapy.

The meaning of therapy is dramatically redefined if the client's illness is diagnosed as *terminal*. The temptation can be to end the therapy early, but the therapist may be needed more than ever. All of the issues touched on above are applicable. The client should seek out the kind of information about her condition which she feels she needs and can handle. The therapist should try to help her to accept the realities of the situation to the extent and in the way that she is able to and to avoid sinking into passivity. How people might be helped to deal with the experience of approaching death in growthful ways has been much better understood in recent years (Orbach, 1999) but again it is not a question of technique but of human presence. The greatest problem in these circumstances is almost certainly the therapist's own feelings: her sense of helplessness; her guilt at being unable to do anything and at surviving; her fear of death itself.

Another intruding life event is the experience of some potentially *traumatic incident* such as being involved in a serious accident or being subjected to violent attack. Much attention has been focused in recent years on the psychological consequences of trauma and how to intervene with them (Bisbey and Bisbey, 1998; Scott and Stradling, 1992) but other painful and crisis-inducing aspects of these events must not be overlooked: their association with multiple losses and significant life changes which take place as a consequence. Traumatic events, like any life event, also have particular personal resonances and meanings. Trauma, like crisis, is not a general but an individual experience, profoundly dependent on who the person is. In particular, issues around the experience and meaning of passivity and loss of a sense of control are crucial (Yule, 1999). The aim of therapeutic work is to enable the assimilation of the experience which has so dramatically intruded on the person's sense of safety and continuity, to provide some conceptual framework to help make sense of strange or frightening post-traumatic reactions and to communicate that the pain of the experience can be borne. The therapist in this situation can work to counter denial and avoidance and so facilitate emotional processing but is in a position to do so in the context of an ongoing therapeutic alliance and at a pace which the client finds manageable, thus avoiding secondary re-traumatization. Fundamentally, the aim is to tackle potential blocks to the assimilation process: the therapist's in-depth knowledge of her client enables these to be identified and linked to the continuing work of therapy. The traumatic element is not the exclusive focus but is integrated with its wider meanings for the individual client.

Patricia had been seeing a private counsellor for about ten sessions, making slow but gradual progress with her agoraphobia, when she discovered that she urgently needed to have a hysterectomy. The therapist suggested that Patricia re-contact her after the operation when she felt well enough to resume. She did not feel she had much to offer Patricia until that time. Although told that the operation had been a complete success, after it Patricia felt very much worse psychologically – constantly afraid, frequently tearful and almost unable to leave her house. She felt strongly that she didn't want to see her counsellor again. Her GP urged her to see a psychologist from the practice who visited her at home and quickly understood that she had felt the operation to be like a violent invasion which had evoked memories of the sexual abuse which she had suffered for a period in her childhood. He had first to overcome Patricia's suspicion that other people abandoned you in times of need, like the counsellor and as she had felt her parents had done at that time. As he established some trust, he was able to help Patricia review and work through the experience of the hospital and then to consider how she might best deal with her childhood memories as well as her anxiety.

Dealing with the meaning of any event in ongoing therapy is complex. It may be important in appraising the situation to consider the client's part in creating or contributing to it. This is, of course, a delicate matter. What has just happened – the break up of a relationship, the loss of a job, a car accident – may be very painful, perhaps shocking. The last thing the client may feel she needs is to have her therapist make things worse by appearing to lay blame. As the event starts to be adjusted to and its meaning disentangled, however, the possibility that there was some contribution from the client may need to be explored. In traumatic situations, the sense of loss of control often paradoxically creates an exaggerated sense of responsibility with reactions of intense guilt and self-blame. It is difficult therefore to approach issues of realistic responsibility in a helpful way. Usually, it is necessary to allow sufficient time for the event to be substantially assimilated before this can be productively raised. It requires sensitivity to explore – for example – the client's poor judgement or excessive risk-taking which amounted to a kind of 'invitation' for something bad to happen. On the other hand, the therapist's own wish to keep the world predictable and meaningful can tempt her to blame the victim. A particular area of complexity is in relating the 'accident' to the ongoing work of the therapy. Accidents can undoubtedly be unconscious forms of 'acting out' – a way of dealing with and expressing distress and rage. Car accidents in particular can be a form of suicide attempt which may be conscious, or substantially out-of-awareness. In particular, it is vital for a therapist to consider any way in which such events may be a response to unexpressed elements in the therapeutic relationship: anger; a plea to be taken care of, or protected; self-punishment; or fear of progress.

These therapeutic meanings are also essential to consider in other major life events which impact on the work. Issues such as *pregnancy*, *marriage* or *divorce* may appear either as positive choices, impulsive or careless behaviours or accidents and misfortunes! Whatever the appearance, the therapist should give consideration to alternative implications – at this moment in the person's life and at this point in therapy. The emotional turmoil – including anger, frustration and intense longing – which therapy can arouse, can all too easily prompt ill-considered and irreversible actions which amount to a life crisis. The therapist should be active in supporting and pressing for a considered and reality based judgement, where possible playing for time, urging that thought be given to the decision; she should not too readily accept such sudden changes at face value. This is more difficult to the extent that the issues are presented in a crisis-like fashion. There is also a danger of being 'drawn in' too much to the decision and the conflicts around it. These very 'intimate' issues have a great potential for causing the therapist to over-identify with the client's predicament such that the therapist's own values and conflicts get involved. Hard work is needed in supporting the client to make her own considered choice when the stakes are so high.

Among other implications, some life events may pose a threat to the continuation of therapy. This may be most obviously the case for *employment* related changes, either due to a geographical move or to their impact on finances. Once again, the relationship of these apparently incidental life changes to the therapeutic process itself must be considered; that is, has this sudden crisis-like situation been 'engineered', functioning as a form of resistance to the challenges of the therapeutic work. With unpredictable financial reverses, it may be necessary (where a fee is being paid) either to arrange a temporary interruption or some way of accommodating the changed circumstances in order to continue (Bellak, 1981). Therapy should not suddenly be interrupted in the urgency of the first impact of, say, a redundancy: the task is to consider all realistic aspects of the situation and the options to deal with them. If necessary, the therapist may then consider how far she is willing to extend herself to deal with the problem with a reduced fee or a deferred payment. The meaning and the realities of these must be carefully considered: they can cause real problems in the therapeutic relationship, most readily avoided through the client taking responsibility for a loan. It will often be appropriate to give only the time necessary to consider the realistic problems and work through the psychological consequences of the event and then to interrupt the therapy. As with all life events during therapy, the pressures of an apparent crisis, though needing immediate attention, should not distract from the need to explore the wider personal meanings and implications of the experience for the client. Where this can be held in mind, external crises during therapy almost always represent an opportunity for growth.

Crises intrinsic to therapy

Some psychological crises arise directly out of the process of therapy: for better or worse, they are an intrinsic part of the work, a response to its emotional demands. In general, crises are a consequence of the kind of change which produces a discontinuity in our sense of self – and sometimes therapy provokes the possibility of just such dramatic change. Rather than being gradual and continuous, change may be experienced as a sudden or fundamental threat to our identity. The response ranges from increased anxiety and deeper unhappiness, through instances of prolonged agitation, acting out or depressive/regressive withdrawal and passivity, to more alarming and sinister symptomatology – major depression, severe dissociation and psychotic episodes.

A crisis in this sense may feel to the client like imminent 'breakdown' but the therapist may see its potential as a 'breakthrough'. This is a complex and fraught area in the psychotherapies. Most exploratory and expressive styles of therapy assume there will a degree of emotional turmoil and personal disorganization on the road to change, an element of 'adaptive regression' (Balint, 1968). The question is how much disorganization is safe and developmental. Some authors in the existential and humanistic traditions (Barnes and Berke, 1971; Schiff, 1975) see extensive regression and breakdown as the path to transformation. This is not now a widely shared view. Some people may indeed gain access to new parts of themselves and reorganize psychologically at a better level of functioning after severe breakdowns with psychotic features (Little, 1981; McCormick, 1988). However, there is too much risk of harm involved: some people never seem to resolve severe breakdowns entirely satisfactorily; others experience the breakdown as a kind of trauma in itself, feeling flooded by unmanageable experiences and humiliated by the loss of control. They can become phobic of any future emotional contact or personal risk-taking, resulting in a future impasse in the therapy. Of course, therapists should not themselves become phobic of creating disorganization in their client's unsatisfactory patterns in the interests of change – but a judgement must be made about manageable degrees of turmoil and appropriate levels of risk. The focus here is on therapeutic crises which might become setbacks.

Although these events are a common part of therapeutic 'lore' there is surprisingly little discussion in the literature about psychological breakdown in therapy and little good research evidence about how common it is. Bellak (1981) suggests that it is doubtful that major breakdowns occur solely as a result of psychotherapy and that careful assessment will pick up previous occurrences. Malan (1979) proposes that an assessment should always establish what is 'the worst things have ever been' since this may recur during therapy (see Chapter 8). The question is whether the client, the therapist and the circumstances of therapy can cope with the potential degree of disorganization that may arise. Internal and external resources are needed to manage the turmoil and sustain collaboration with the therapist without a serious risk of major breakdown. The therapist must be able to respond to and contain the likely degree of regression (Boyer, 1983). Thus, the risk of such therapeutic crises is to a degree predictable: nonetheless, they still occur in unexpected ways.

A *major depressive episode* – involving significant 'retardation' (slowing down of thinking and action) and profoundly negative experiences and beliefs which are hard to relate to the person's normal views of life and may be delusional – can be a very problematic occurrence in therapy. Psychiatric intervention is generally called for and some therapists believe they have little to offer, beyond perhaps continuity of support. Some would bring a temporary halt to the work (Kernberg et al., 1989) and if continued, it may have to be on the basis that it will be largely supportive – though more directive approaches of a cognitive-behavioural type do appear to contribute to recovery even in severe depressive episodes (Roth and Fonagy, 1996). Suicide is, of course, a danger in any depressive breakdown and must be monitored closely.

Some experience of *dissociation* is not uncommon in therapy. Signs are: experiences of feeling not quite present, being cut off from others, on the outside looking in, enclosed in a bubble and so on. Clearly, this is a way of cutting off from aspects of experience which are felt to be too much to bear. People prone to using this type of 'defence mechanism' may show such signs as frequent episodes of *déjà vu* or 'derealization' (the sense that the world is not quite real). This becomes problematic in therapy when such experiences become extreme or pervasive, with the person doing things in states of mind which they can barely recollect (Mollon, 1996). The appearance of such experiences may signal the possibility of an impending psychotic breakdown. Signs of dissociation, therefore, should be taken seriously. It suggests that therapy is touching on deeply problematic emotional material such as traumatic separation, deprivation, violence or abuse (often, though not always, from an early period in the client's life). The therapist must slow down and proceed with great care.

The emergence of *psychotic symptoms* during therapy can be the most alarming form of crisis for the therapist to deal with. Signs of the beginning of a disintegration in the client's contact with reality may be: dissociative symptoms as outlined above; paranoid features such as extreme suspiciousness and touchiness, or 'ideas of reference', that is – a sense that ordinary events in the everyday world have special significance in relation to the person; bizarre somatic sensations; intense excitement and agitation with compulsive talking and uncontrollable impulses; and fleeting hallucinations and delusions. The individual may substantially maintain her grasp on reality for a while but gradually develop fixed delusions, hallucinations and uncontrollable excitement or panic. Any therapist should urgently seek consultation if faced with this situation. It may be helpful for an experienced therapist to continue endeavouring to work through distress therapeutically – but it may not. While these may be regarded as the symptoms of an episode of schizophrenic or manic 'illness' in the context of therapy, it is also vital *not* to see them as psychologically *meaningless*, but as an idiosyncratic expression of an intolerable state of mind. It may be possible to help make sense of the experience and the therapist should ask herself whether the client is sufficiently accessible to be helped by this process. There is growing evidence that early manifestations of a psychotic process should be regarded as a 'critical period', during which psychological intervention to enhance self-esteem and social relationships can have a substantial impact on long-term adjustment (Jackson and Birchwood, 1996).

In this sense, therapeutic technique with emerging psychotic symptoms is not dissimilar to other instances of crisis intervention. It is vital for the therapist to remain warm and calm and not to be overtly alarmed by or critical of the client's symptoms. It is useful to try to trace and understand them as a response to a precipitating event. It may be necessary to modify the therapeutic approach to some degree, backing off from areas that are too difficult to explore. The aim is to help the client understand her seemingly incomprehensible experiences, to make sense of them and put them into context as being about herself and her emotional reactions. It may be useful to help her seek alternative explanations to her interpretation of events. The therapist may need to stop probing and focus instead on current realities. The client's fear may be countered with reality: things are seen as they are because she is upset. The therapist is helped in this task by the existence of an established therapeutic alliance. However, the therapeutic relationship may itself be the source of the trouble: alliance ruptures and therapist errors should be explicitly considered in an open-minded way as the possible root of the client's distress. The therapist is trying to provide as clear and uncritical an account as possible of the process that is taking place for the client. This kind of therapeutic effort may be able to 'head off' the deepening of transient psychotic manifestations. Nonetheless, the therapist should also be undertaking a risk assessment both of threats to safety (such as ruinous spending or criminal behaviour) and of the likelihood of an intractable episode of psychosis which requires more active crisis management including psychiatric assessment, social support and relief from stressors, respite care, hospital admission and medication together with a review of the continuing psychotherapeutic strategy.

Any crisis takes its meaning within the context of the ongoing relationship of the therapy and is likely to reflect its underlying themes. Therapeutic breakdowns can arise from the therapist herself becoming caught in some damaging relationship dynamic which escalates rather than contains her client's fear and rage. (This process is very similar to some forms of impasse and is addressed in detail in Chapter 8.) Sometimes a crisis is a kind of 'test' of the therapist's willingness or ability to respond and to 'care enough': this needs to be worked through and understood – but often it may need to be acted on too. The therapist may have to take enough concrete action to 'pass' but not so much as to prevent the meaning of the crisis being clarified. All such emotionally turbulent times require courage, honesty and a steady nerve from the therapist to maintain the structure of the overall therapy which provides the safety which the client needs. She must deal in the shorter term with the client's sense of being emotionally overwhelmed and look for wider meanings later. The process is the same as crisis intervention but with great care not to be panicked into over-reaction.

Clients prone to crises

While some clients 'achieve' crisis during the course of therapy and others have crises 'thrust upon them', some people seem 'born to' the state of crisis. The presence of recurrent crises in their lives is a major feature of their experience and may be the main presenting problem causing them to seek help. Such clients are on a continuum – from those who live in socially unstable life situations, through those who constantly involve themselves in interpersonal dramas, to people with enduring personal disturbances which present as recurrent crisis situations, possibly with significant risk of harm. The latter pattern has been termed 'furore' – a repetitive pattern of crisis behaviours which may have become the main vehicle for seeking help (Ratna, 1978). At the more severe, high-risk end, these include patterns of self-harm and self-destructiveness, recurrent suicidal wishes, serious eating disorders, some types of alcohol and drug misuse and other forms of severe anti-social acting out. As this list makes clear, these patterns can often be regarded as chronic relapsing conditions. They may be best approached from the perspective of relapse prevention and maintenance of stability as outlined in Chapters 11 and 12. Such relapses can constitute a serious crisis both in the person's life and for therapeutic intervention and require skilled handling.

With some clients, hearing about their lives in session after session can be like listening to a 'soap opera'. The client and those she is involved with participate in constant dramas which tend to overwhelm the sessions with incident and emotion. These 'crises' pose little real risk and hold no potential for change; they get in the way of any real work being done. Two lines of action are possible. If the person's life situation is so unstable and problematic, more practical forms of help may be needed – change of housing, benefits advice, debt counselling, child care help and so on – in order for further psychological help to become relevant. If this is not the case, then the dramatizing style of relating should become a main focus of the therapy. It should be confronted as both a way of avoiding working seriously on the problems which brought the client to therapy and as a way of avoiding painful feelings and emotional contact in life more generally. Such ways of relating frequently cover up severe experiences of deprivation or abuse. It takes patience and the capacity to maintain focus on the underlying difficulties to prevent this kind of presentation through dramas turning into a therapeutic impasse.

In the case of more severe damaging behaviours where the risk is higher, there are important strategic decisions to be made at the outset about what kind of intervention is most likely to be viable. Is it possible to provide psychotherapy or counselling? Is the kind of therapeutic work that you are equipped and willing to do the best available response? These are major assessment questions which must be addressed if a future breakdown or impasse in the therapy is to be avoided. If you decide to do therapy, the main task is setting up the conditions for your way of working to be effective. This means clarifying the responsibilities of both therapist and client in a therapeutic contract and within that being explicit about how different kinds of crisis will be handled (see Chapter 7). The main function of such contracts is to provide a structure which enables the therapist to take risks in the face of pressure without being blown off course. All of the issues concerning the therapist's counter-transference which arise in the context of suicide are relevant here (see Chapter 3). In long-term work with clients who are demanding, hostile, negative and consequently 'hard to like', a process of 'malignant alienation' may set in (Watts and Morgan, 1994). Carers or therapists withdraw sympathy, avoid contact with the client and express their aversion and frustration, often in hidden ways, colluding with a client's hopelessness and precipitating a breakdown in therapy. Such clients are typically unable to express directly their unmet needs to depend on others, due to past experiences of neglect and exploitation. This means they are likely to be negating of any help they receive. The therapist needs to acknowledge the extremes of dependency and hopelessness which are at the heart of her client's experience and to tolerate the negativity which covers it.

Any intervention with clients prone to crisis is likely to be a long-term proposition. The aim is the gradual amelioration of a self-destructive life-style. Crises are dealt with as disruptions to this change process and there is less emphasis on active intervention to ensure safety or on viewing the crisis as an opportunity: the crucial element is a continuing, stable and dependable therapeutic relationship (Clarkson, 1995). The degree to which the client can sustain elements of challenge and development in the therapy rather than merely be supported (with minimal expectations of improvement) is a crucial judgement made as part of an ongoing process of assessment of what is therapeutically viable. In either case, however, crises should be dealt with by working with the client to devise ways in which they can be defused and by identifying 'lifelines' which she can use independent of the therapist to help her get through each occasion of transient but intense pain. Ways must be found to prevent serious harm while reducing the probability of subsequent crises. The therapist's response greatly influences this, the more so where crisis-like behaviours are not simply a way of discharging painful emotions but are substantially a means of attracting help from others. The current crisis and the client's response should be related to the overall focus of the therapy: if this is not possible during the crisis situation, it should be undertaken afterwards. When long-term therapy becomes merely a process of repeated crisis intervention, it is failing to move towards its objectives and has become stuck in an impasse.

In structuring a pattern of long-term help, the therapist may wish to consider liaising with a wider network of helpers or making non-therapeutic help the principal intervention. This can take a number of forms. Practical and social welfare assistance has already been mentioned. A range of non-therapeutic 'case management' tasks include: organizing direct practical help, in addition to providing information about it; identifying resources and services and ensuring the client's engagement with them; co-ordinating the efforts of other professionals; advocacy on behalf of the client and actively interfacing with other professionals to ensure she gets treated appropriately. A case manager working together with a therapist can also undertake some of the more intrusive or controlling interventions which may be needed (including activities such as weight checks or dietary programmes for anorexics, body checks with self-harmers, breathalysing for drinkers and so on). Contracting for these case-management activities to occur separately can help maintain an appropriate framework for therapeutic intervention itself. Of course, any of these active measures can promote passivity or rebellion. As Linehan (1993) makes clear, the preferred therapeutic strategy is always to enable the client to be her own 'case manager' and for the therapist to support her efforts to organize appropriate resources and relate to other professionals and services as an 'informed consumer'. However, with a proportion of clients, this is simply not sufficient and for therapy to take place, someone may need to fulfil this role. Some counselling work can be undertaken by a single therapist acting in both a case management role and a therapeutic one – but there are many traps inherent in managing these complex shifting boundary conditions and it is better to separate the roles where possible. Clear communication is then needed between both parties, in the context of agreement about their respective roles – otherwise a disruptive splitting of attitudes to the client is very likely. Similarly, arranging to have back-up or adjunctive therapists involved in the care of some clients may be helpful to cover breaks in availability (when there is a much increased risk of damaging acting out) or to defuse the pressures of the therapeutic relationship when they become too much for one therapist to bear. An atmosphere of mutual support counters isolation and enables therapists not to feel swamped by the demands and negativity of these clients.

For clients who have serious difficulty in sustaining a continuing psychotherapeutic intervention, other long-term inputs which are less demanding can be of real benefit. Various forms of 'befriending' – in person or by telephone – can be a stabilizing influence, buffering the client's sense of isolation and despair. Similar to this but more impersonal, is the idea of a 'Crisis Card' by which a client prone to self-harm at times of crisis is offered the opportunity to get immediate help when she feels unable to cope, provided she has not already harmed herself. This help is typically from a duty psychiatrist on call at an emergency department who will talk to the client (either over the phone or in person) and possibly arrange an overnight admission. The client must contact the service instead of self-harming, otherwise she should go to medical casualty and receive routine treatment. These are forms of help which engage clients who are unable to comply with the ground rules of therapy: they experience them as more immediate and concrete and so more relevant. Help is provided at crisis points and under the client's control but in ways that are contracted for and so containable.

Conclusion

Managing the tension between competing demands has been identified throughout this chapter as crucial in dealing with therapeutic crises. On the one hand, therapists need to be able to intervene confidently and effectively when a crisis occurs in the course of a therapy – responding flexibly, changing their usual ways of working and altering the therapeutic focus. On the other, they must not be blown off track, react inconsistently or break the necessary boundaries of the therapeutic enterprise. This tension does not set up unmanageable contradictions but it does place considerable demands on the therapist: to retain clarity of role amidst pain and confusion; to stand firm on the conditions required for therapy in the face of pressure to be 'more helpful'; and to remain calm and emotionally available when venturing into uncharted territory. Skill, experience and good support is required and care should be taken not to work beyond your competence. Failing to negotiate the demands of this therapeutic storm will set the therapy off on the wrong course. Unless this can be corrected speedily, the likely outcome is either for the work to be terminated in an unsatisfactory way by one party or the other, or for it to reach a cul-de-sac. Crises are often followed by the development of an impasse, both in the course of normal development and in the course of a therapy.

6   Recognizing Impasse

Therapy is by its very nature an attempt to get out of an impasse. Impasses develop in people's lives when normal processes of development come to a halt and efforts to derive satisfaction and fulfilment are frustrated. In a sense, the various psychological therapies have been developed as the means of breaking through life impasses: therapists are in the 'impasse business'. Since therapy starts in impasse it should not come as a surprise that it often arrives at a further impasse. In fact, it is probably typical for this to happen to some degree and relatively few therapies run their course without getting bogged down at some point, albeit temporarily. The view that we take in this book is that an impasse, like a crisis, is a nodal point in development and has in it the potential for change and transformation. No one looks forward to an impasse but it is a situation which can be expected and may be viewed as a crucial part of the work rather than cause for dismay.

Defining impasse

Dictionary definitions suggest that an impasse is a deadlock or predicament affording no obvious escape. A deadlock implies a state of immobility resulting from opposing forces or aims. A word with a similar connotation is 'stalemate' – an unsatisfactory draw from which any move results in finding oneself in an even more intolerable situation. 'Stale' also suggests stagnation, the loss of free flow and movement towards a goal. The word 'impasse' itself is a metaphor of travel: a cul-de-sac or place from which there is no apparent way out in the direction of one's destination. Each of these images captures something of the experience of impasse.

Not every interruption to the flow of the therapeutic process is an impasse, however. Minor fluctuations within and between sessions are entirely normal. We should not expect a steady rate of development since change of any significance is likely to take time and effort (Mahoney, 1991). It is difficult to draw a clear distinction between what is and is not an impasse – but we could say that it is a situation in which more energy seems to be invested in sustaining opposition to change than in resolving it and that this state of affairs is sustained over a period of time that is significant in relation to the anticipated length of the therapy. There is a failure to improve in circumstances where improvement would reasonably have been expected (Weiner, 1982). It includes the client who never stops criticizing the therapist but keeps coming; and one who seems to explore her issues but changes nothing; the client who always has a reasonable excuse for not doing an agreed task; and the one in whom a deep mistrust develops, leading to a stand-off.

The notion of impasse may also be linked to other quite common situations in the process of therapy, including any ending in which there is no agreement between therapist and client. Thus, a client announcing 'out of the blue' that this is to be the last session is an instance of the sudden emergence of a serious impasse. Early dropout and the failure to engage with a process which the therapist believes should go beyond a few sessions is another instance of an unresolved difference on how to proceed. Taking a broad view of impasse in therapy suggests that all forms of therapeutic failure can come within its scope. They are not all the same of course and there is a danger of blurring useful distinctions, but this wide definition draws attention to their continuities and overlapping causes. Research indicates that on average about a quarter to a third of clients across all modalities of psychotherapy will fail to improve (Lambert and Bergin, 1994). Although this is worrying, it does seem to imply a lower boundary for the number of unresolved impasses within our work. It points to a high proportion of wasted effort and misdirection of resources. Managing impasse better is therefore about improving the efficiency and effectiveness of professional practice and service delivery.

Elkind (1992) reports a survey of psychodynamic psychotherapists in California of whom 53 per cent had themselves been clients in a therapy that had ended in a breakdown in the therapeutic alliance; of these, 72 per cent were left feeling harmed by the experience. Lambert and Bergin (1994) in their review of the psychotherapy outcome literature cite evidence for a worsening in the presenting problems or general condition of between 5 and 10 per cent of all clients. Deterioration effects are the manifestation of the most worrying forms of impasse. They demand our urgent attention to understand and prevent them. Although many clients may have been on a downward track which the therapeutic intervention failed to reverse, it is essentially the therapist's reponsibility to prevent deterioration (Mays and Franks, 1985). The first rule must be to 'do no harm'. Negative effects seem to stem from two sources: the choice of an inappropriate form of intervention which either creates or fails to arrest deterioration in the client; and the therapist interacting in such a way as to create a vicious cycle of harm, generally involving a spiral of covert hostility or exploitation within the relationship. In the worst cases, this results in direct abuse.

All this suggests that impasse is both common and important. However, unlike the dramatic character of a crisis in which there is likely to be a sense of panic and a pressure to act, an impasse is often hidden or unrecognized (Nathanson, 1992). It can be almost as if a spell has been cast – the therapist is trapped and immobilized. It is vital that the therapist wake up from this state of mind, that she recognizes and takes responsibility for the situation that she and her client find themselves in. Only then does it become possible *to identify what has become stuck* within the therapeutic process. This chapter provides the outline of a framework for understanding and responding to impasses which will be expanded upon subsequently. We will start with the concept of resistance.

The paradox of resistance

Resistance is an old idea but one that continues to be much misunderstood. Every model of psychological intervention is defined by its way of understanding what is necessary to promote change and what stands in its way. Therapeutic change is not easy, otherwise there would be no need to resort to the special measures of therapy. What stands in the way of change is resistance. Originating the idea, Freud (1926/1961) directed attention towards the pervasiveness of ambivalence about change in every person. The status quo, in the psychodynamic view, is an elaborately worked out compromise between conflicting unconscious internal forces. Other theoretical systems have, of course, objected to this formulation, some rejecting the idea of unconscious conflict, some the notion that resistance is to be considered as internal to the client and so on – they would conceptualize the obstacles in the path of change quite differently. Some would wish to jettison the term resistance because of its dynamic connotations. However, alternatives such as non-collaboration or non-compliance seem more limiting and it is probably better to use the established terminology to mean all those forces opposing change, however conceptualized. It is vital that every therapist knows how she understands this aspect of the process within her own model of practice: to ignore it is to invite difficulties. Subsequent chapters will consider different elements of resistance and so focus attention on different sources of impasse, drawing on a variety of theoretical perspectives.

Resistance can be thought of – using a relatively simple model – as comprising an array of forces opposing change. In the same way, those elements in a client's personality, her life circumstances and the therapeutic situation which tend to promote and support change can also be conceptualized as forces. These change-promoting forces can be termed the 'alliance for change' (broadening the common usage of the term 'alliance'). The two sets of forces oppose each other and the situation in therapy, at any one time, can be thought of as the sum of these opposing elements. Representing this graphically as a 'Force Field Diagram' provides a simple tool for analyzing the process of change (Lewin, 1951). Figure 6.1 provides a brief example. Typically where therapy is appropriate, the force field will be finely balanced but with the alliance for change predominating. Where an impasse has developed the resistances have increased to the point that change can no longer take place. Resolving this impasse might involve either increasing the predominance of the change-promoting alliance or reducing aspects of the resistance. This mechanistic approach to the therapeutic situation is obviously over-simplified, ignoring complex interconnections and feedback loops but it is a useful starting point that provides help in taking stock and guidance in finding a way forward.

James is a 28-year-old man, unmarried and living with his divorced mother. He presents as depressed, lonely and concerned for his future; he experiences social anxiety and has had limited relationships with women. He is successful at his work as a telecommunications technician and has hobbies in model making and as a member of a cricket team.

After eight sessions with an experienced woman counsellor, paid at full-fee in a local counselling centre – he voices doubts that things are 'going anywhere' after missing the previous session.

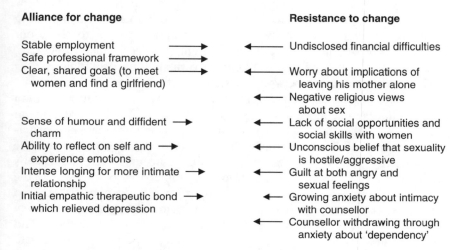

Speculative analysis

Alliance for change   **Resistance to change**

Stable employment ———▶   ◀——— Undisclosed financial difficulties
Safe professional framework ———▶
Clear, shared goals (to meet ———▶   ◀——— Worry about implications of
  women and find a girlfriend)   leaving his mother alone
                                        ◀——— Negative religious views
                                                about sex
Sense of humour and diffident ———▶   ◀——— Lack of social opportunities and
  charm   social skills with women
Ability to reflect on self and ———▶ ◀——— Unconscious belief that sexuality
  experience emotions   is hostile/aggressive
Intense longing for more intimate ———▶ ◀——— Guilt at both angry and
  relationship   sexual feelings
Initial empathic therapeutic bond ———▶ ◀— Growing anxiety about intimacy
  which relieved depression   with counsellor
                                        ◀——— Counsellor withdrawing through
                                                anxiety about 'dependency'

At this point, there is an impasse and potential drop-out. Forces against change look stronger. But the balance can be restored and movement resumed through the counsellor's awareness and understanding of James' and her own anxieties.

FIGURE 6.1   *Force field analysis*

The word 'resistance' does have some unfortunate connotations, however, which can lead to misinterpretations and mishandling by therapists. It suggests a combative approach, a battle, certainly something to be overcome. Resistance therefore seems to be something 'bad'; it is then a small step to blame the client for 'resisting'. However, resistance is inevitable – indeed necessary. Beck (1995) for example, says of cognitive therapy that blocks are an inescapable part of the process and are not to be avoided but uncovered, specified and conceptualized. All approaches regard working with resistance as the essence of therapy and necessary for real change: if this is not happening then it's not therapy.

Everyone appears to need their resistances: they provide stability in relation to both our internal and external worlds (Mahoney, 1991). All of the mechanisms which maintain consistency and control in our lives are ones which, in the context of therapy, might function as resistances to change. What identifies positive and adaptive coping structures is the degree to which they can be brought into awareness, placed under some conscious control and utilized in a flexible way rather than rigidly and compulsively. This conceptualization of resistance means that blockages in the path of change are being worked with continuously as part of the normal course of therapy: knowing about the resistance is part of understanding the client and helping her. The agoraphobic client who is making less and less progress on homework assignments may be indicating something of her worries about improvement – perhaps her concerns that increased independence will disrupt other relationships. The client who is becoming increasingly disparaging of her therapist may be providing a clue about how past relationships left her feeling ashamed and hopeless. Encountering resistances in therapy is ideally viewed as an opportunity – to refine our understanding of the client and gain insight into her wider difficulties, perhaps also for the therapist to refine her own skills and creativity.

There is a continuum between resistance and impasse, not an absolute divide. Impasse suggests some overall arrest in movement – but more than that it implies that something has been lost sight of or ignored. In an impasse, resistance becomes an unacknowledged or misunderstood enactment within the therapeutic process. It is corrected when it becomes possible to return to *working with resistance*. Impasse occurs when the client's resistance is too much for the therapeutic frame or too intense for the client's own resources or too great for the therapist's capabilities and so cannot be managed as part of the work. Resuming the work of therapy happens when it is possible to see that within this situation, difficult and uncomfortable as it is, there is something which is being communicated: something which is being missed or cannot yet be understood; something which is expressed as a failure. It is essential for the therapist to ask herself 'What is this impasse trying to tell me?' and 'Why has this distress or difficulty not been expressed directly?' This reframes the impasse as potentially positive and creates space in which learning is possible (including learning from mistakes).

Jim, a man in his mid 40s, consulted a young person-centred therapist, Raymond, about a mild sense of depression and general dissatisfaction which had persisted for two years. For the first few sessions things seemed to be going well. Jim discussed his fear of physical ageing, his financial insecurity and his sense of having lost direction. His mood lightened as he felt more optimistic. However, the work soon got bogged down; sessions seemed repetitive and circled back over the same old ground. Raymond began to feel that this was really not a very interesting case and that his client was not working particularly hard. He took other cases to supervision, neglecting the work with Jim. His supervisor pulled him up on this after some weeks. Looking at the work together, they found that Raymond's feeling of time slipping by and his vague sense of not knowing quite what to do appeared to parallel what the client felt. In talking about this, Raymond uncovered some doubts in himself that he wasn't experienced enough to help this older man. When he raised this experience of 'lostness' in the next session, Jim became more animated, feeling rather agitated and talking about his anger with young men at work overtaking him. At the next session, he disclosed the sexual problems that he had been having for some time. The therapeutic relationship deepened as Raymond facilitated Jim to explore his competitiveness and the pressure to perform which he felt in many aspects of his life.

The response to impasse

While the therapist commonly feels resistance to be an obstacle, a frustration, impasse tends to be experienced as a failure. This can lead to a complex set of interlocking feelings and responses which may feed back in a destructive loop, maintaining and intensifying the stalemate. While such sequences may take many individual forms for different clients and therapists, the origin of this vicious cycle may be viewed as a form of shame (Nathanson, 1992). The therapist experiences the developing impasse as a failure which challenges her sense of competence and efficacy. As the situation persists, it taps into her potential to feel shame and guilt in the face of her inability to help, undermining her sense of self-esteem as a therapist. Faced – even briefly – with an inability to help, we can all feel incompetent. Where an impasse extends over time this can deepen into a sense of fraudulence: we pretend to be able to help by continuing to offer sessions but the therapy can seem like a charade.

The danger is that this experience of shame and impotence will produce an atmosphere of helplessness, hopelessness and despair within the therapy. This can easily result in a focus on what is negative within the client's situation and the therapeutic process and positive resources are overlooked. This negative set generates incompetence and further failure. The therapist loses a sense of her own authority and avoids offering clarity or leadership within the sessions. Part of her response is likely to be frustration and mounting irritation – but anger towards a client may be felt to be unacceptable. Turning against herself, the therapist experiences both her failure and her anger as guilt; this guilty restraint will make it doubly hard to feel secure and respond with directness and freedom.

All these responses are very painful: various defensive reactions may arise within the therapist as a result. Passivity itself can be a comforting response and the inertia of the situation exerts a kind of 'spell', so that both therapist and client become enthralled by the pull of what is familiar and neglect the necessary discomfort of change. The therapist may simply deny that there is any real problem, neglecting to notice that there is little movement taking place. Frustration and anger with the situation may be directed at the client who is blamed for the lack of change. However, this is generally rationalized and cloaked in some technical vocabulary: clients are privately accused of 'being resistant' or 'lacking motivation'. These things may be true in part but labelling them in this way is not a thoughtful response; it is part of the therapist's defensive reaction to her own sense of failure and frustration. Blaming clients for their resistance is one of the most seductive and dangerous elements in an impasse. It can lead to the client being harmed. It encourages exhortation and intrusiveness by the therapist and promotes the tendency to make an assault on the client's defences and to demand high levels of experimentation or emotional expressiveness without proper agreement or a framework of safety. Through denial of the experience of failure and shame, the therapist may insist defensively on her competence and indulge in an excess of certainty. This results in a therapeutic stance which is closed off from feedback from the client and from the results of her interventions. Denying that anything is wrong, the therapist persists in doing more of the same. This is the worst possible response to a developing impasse. It is dangerous to need always to feel competent. It is not at all useful for the therapist to slip into helplessly doing nothing or, in a panic, trying anything – a tactic which may be used either aggressively or ineffectually. However, these reactions do at least acknowledge that things are not going well.

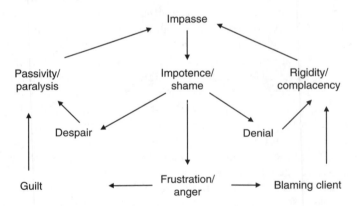

FIGURE 6.2 *Therapist responses to a developing impasse*

Our proneness to shame as therapists is not sufficiently widely recognized. It originates partly in the contagion of the clients' sense of shame at their failure to cope without help, and partly in the limitations of what anyone can do to help when dealing with extremes of confusion and distress. However, it is probably also connected with the way many therapists are trained and the contexts in which they work which create the pressure of needing to 'know' and to 'get it right' in situations where it is very difficult to be clear what is going on and what is to be done. More appropriate support and a better education in 'not knowing' would help us deal with the experience of impasse more constructively.

In order to break the vicious cycle of impasse two things are necessary:

- to recognize explicitly that an impasse is developing;
- to contain discomfort sufficiently to be able to evaluate its causes.

Each of these issues will be addressed in turn.

Recognizing impasse

According to Socrates, the recognition of ignorance is the beginning of wisdom. We learn most from our mistakes. In order to do that, it is essential to stay alert, open and alive to the discomfort of error and ignorance. This makes it possible to start to rectify things by seeing sooner rather than later that they are going wrong. In seeking to recognize an impasse we are often trying to peer into a mystery because impasse is, by its nature, often deceptive in its appearance. Indeed, since it can be painful to face, we may want it to stay hidden. We need some pointers which alert us to the existence of a problem and the need to search for its source. This is no straightforward matter in therapy: what might be a vital indicator in one model of practice may be misleading or irrelevant in another. For example, a person-centred therapist who challenges a client's sense that people despise her by asking for evidence, might wonder how she is being drawn into invalidating her client; whereas this would be a legitimate tactic from a cognitive-behavioural standpoint. More than this, each therapy, each client–therapist pair, is unique so that the ways in which they might get stuck are individual to them. It is the capacity to take a 'second look' at the process which makes supervision so vital in detecting, as well as resolving, impasses.

As a rule of thumb, a therapist should monitor any particular therapy against her idea of what the process 'should' be like. If one has a sense, developed through theory and experience, of what to expect of a 'normal' therapy process, then it is possible to ask what some significant deviation from it might mean. More specifically, it is possible to identify a number of possible signs which occur quite frequently in the context of a developing impasse. (These are outlined in Table 6.1.) The therapist needs to be alert for information coming both directly from the client's words and actions and also from her own reactions. It is useful to consider all aspects of the process including frame and boundary issues, progress towards aims and goals, how the tasks and techniques of therapy are being implemented, and how the depth and momentum of the therapeutic process is progressing.

Perhaps most crucial of all is the therapist's ability to locate in herself signs that she might be giving up, stopping working as hard as she might expect on the client's behalf, and allowing things to drift by working repetitively, complacently or cynically. Indeed, many of the indicators in

TABLE 6.1   *Signs of developing impasse*

Client	*Therapist*
framework:	**framework:**
missing appointments	missing an appointment
repeated lateness	starting late
failure to pay fees	extending sessions
	failure to take normal notes
	failure to invoice normally
goals:	**goals:**
symptoms getting worse	confusion about appropriate goals
new problems being presented	loss of direction
prolonged lack of progress on goals	loss of momentum
(in spite of apparently 'good' sessions)	
acting out (which is not responsive to	
challenge)	
techniques:	**techniques:**
request to change mode of therapy	deviations from usual practice in session
requests for consultation/referral to	loss of normal session structure
another therapist	loss of confidence in efficacy of techniques
failure to bring relevant material	
repeated failure to undertake assigned tasks	
process:	**process:**
decreased overall depth of rapport/	dreading client's arrival
engagement	boredom/inattention
unacknowledged negative affect shifts	working harder and harder
within sessions	irritability/arguing
omissions/disconnectedness in	loss of empathic relatedness
material presented	loss of sense of meaningfulness
failure to report significant information	of material
reservations expressed (directly or indirectly)	aimless chat
about therapeutic process/goals	judgementalism
continued failure to reflect on self and to	dreaming about client
'own' problems	

our list are similar to those used by therapists and supervisors to detect the interference of counter-transference issues in the process of therapy (Robertiello and Schoenwolf, 1987). As should be clear from the previous section, the therapist's counter-reactions to the client's resistances almost always get involved in the development of an impasse and prevent her from being able to think clearly about what is going on.

The analysis of impasse

When one has identified signs that an impasse may be developing, the next step is to pause for thought and give time to evaluate the situation. As the saying has it, 'When you find yourself in a hole, stop digging'. However, it is always hard to rethink a case. In therapeutic work, we generally get so close to the client as a person and so immersed in our relationship with them, that our view, both of the person and of the relationship, becomes a highly developed gestalt which may not be easy to change. In an impasse, the deadlock includes the therapist's view of what the therapy is about, resulting in a preoccupation with one way of understanding the situation and so making it more than usually difficult to disengage and seek an alternative perspective. An impasse involves a certain kind of blindness: if it persists after we have become aware of it, some element is probably still not being seen and addressed. Pressing issues are being neglected as a result of blind spots or tunnel vision on the part of the therapist and lack of awareness or concealment on the part of the client. To analyse an impasse is to try to bring into focus an aspect of the situation which is being neglected and to make it explicit within the therapeutic dialogue.

Therapeutic models inevitably have a narrowing effect on our view of the client's situation. Impasses sometimes happen because what is hard to articulate within the therapy is just what is ignored or poorly addressed within a particular model. To be part of a particular therapeutic school is to have an identity and a reference group which increases the therapist's sense of personal security – this can enable anxieties to be borne and risks to be taken. But a single paradigm also limits the range of one's vision (Kluft, 1992). It excludes certain ways of thinking. With a woman presenting with an episode of obsessive-compulsive checking, the psychodynamic therapist might be tempted to focus on this as a defence against rage towards her critical mother who died recently, ignoring what a more problem-orientated worker might see – how the recent stresses created by bereavement and redundancy could be tackled directly. However, it might require a cognitive-behavioural orientation to think through the self-perpetuating cycles of anxiety-reducing actions and how these could be reversed. This might still overlook what a family therapist would attend to – the way that the client's symptoms provide a focus for worry in the family which protects her husband's self-esteem. Any one approach could get bogged down by neglecting vital issues. In relation to impasse, perhaps more than any other topic within psychotherapy, it seems appropriate to take a broadly integrative approach. The best therapeutic stance for resolving impasses is one characterized by imaginative but disciplined flexibility. This should be reflected in the way in which theory is used to guide practice.

In taking the difficult step of reanalysing a situation in therapy and identifying areas of the process which have been overlooked, it is helpful to have a framework for identifying, locating and analysing blocks within therapy. Such a framework is offered in Table 6.2, which also serves as an outline for the subsequent chapters on this topic. There are four main areas within which blocks can occur:

- the way in which the basic contract and aims of the therapy have been set up and the degree to which it has been possible to engage the client in an appropriately collaborative way within this frame;

- the degree to which the client's social ecosystem and the therapist's professional context supports rather than undermines the therapeutic work;
- the accuracy with which the individual characteristics of the client have been assessed in making an appropriate strategic choice of format and technique to address her problems;
- the manner in which the therapeutic process is being handled and the therapeutic relationship kept free from unacknowledged repetitive cycles of interaction.

The purpose of having such a framework in mind is to draw attention to neglected elements, ask difficult questions and become more objective. It helps to remove the 'blinkers' which involvement with the client has created and to transform a personally painful situation into a more manageable one. This particular framework attempts to be relatively inclusive of the many complex, multifaceted ways in which impasses develop; each of the issues raised is addressed in detail in subsequent chapters. It is, of course, only one format for considering the issues and other protocols have been proposed by different writers including: Green (1988) from a systemic viewpoint; Beck and Freeman (1990) from a cognitive viewpoint; and Kluft (1992) and Weiner (1982) from an eclectic psychodynamic viewpoint.

A comprehensive scheme for analysing therapeutic impasse of this kind underlines what a complex process the work of therapy is. The protocol which we have provided might suggest that it is possible to examine each element in turn, identify which are problematic and take action to rectify the situation. If only it were that simple! It is one possible starting point – but only a starting point. Therapy is a process of mutual influence between the interacting 'systems' of client and therapist, each embedded in their own social networks and practical constraints. An impasse does not exist in any of the interacting elements alone. Each element affects and is affected by others and an impasse exists as the complex product of their interaction. Indeed, a factor in creating an impasse may be for the therapist to have an overly linear and individualistic view of causation. Bateson (1972) proposed that wisdom is the appreciation of the interconnectedness of things. Tackling and resolving impasse requires exactly this capacity.

Three elements interact within the therapeutic situation: the relevant aspects of external reality; the internal world of the client; and the therapist's responses to each of these. The external world exerts real pressure on both client and therapist but they are always 'interpreted' pressures, the world as seen by the participants. The therapist never sees the client 'in themselves' but only as they present in the context of this particular therapy. Equally, therapists change their responses in more and less subtle ways in relation to the individuality of each client and the demands of any particular encounter. It might be said that resistance is not characteristic of a person but of a relationship. In understanding how an impasse has developed, the therapist must reckon on how any of the potentially

TABLE 6.2 *Factors contributing to impasse*

Contract and engagement

Frame:	Practicalities – not manageable
	Logistics – arrangements unclear, misunderstood or unacceptable
Alliance:	Tasks – roles misunderstood; style or rationale not acceptable
	Bond – therapist/client mismatch; lack of engagement
	Goals – unclear; not agreed; inappropriate

Social ecosystem

Culture:	Differences – not understood or appreciated
	Explanatory System – incompatible
Social network:	Significant Others – obstructive
	Systemic Function – not appreciated
	Key People – not involved
Service system:	Referrer – not informed or on-board
	Co-professionals – ill co-ordinated, with weak boundaries
Therapeutic organisation:	Therapeutic role – not validated/legitimate
	Culture – professionally unsupportive

Client factors

Bio-medical:	Organic illness – causes or contributes to symptoms
	Psycho-pharmacology – interferes with experience or misattributes change
	Substance misuse – ignored when interferes with experience
Psychological:	Ego strength – lacking for style of therapy
	Motivation for change – insufficient (at out-of-awareness level)
	External supports – inadequate during crisis
Therapeutic:	Focus of work – wrong for client
	Degree of structure – inappropriately high or low
	Therapist skill/support – inadequate for level of client disturbance

Therapeutic process

Alliance:	Ruptures – not repaired
	Negative spirals – develop unchecked
	Misalliance – not recognized/addressed
Transference:	Reality testing – not preserved
	Regression – left unbounded
	Intensity – beyond therapist capabilities
Counter-transference:	Therapist character – unconstructive or immature
	Therapist vulnerabilities – result in hostility or rescuing
	Therapist responsiveness/availability – not sustained

problematic issues has interacted with other elements to produce the current deadlock. The complexity of this situation could, of course, promote paralysis by analysis. In seeking to understand, a therapist might feel overwhelmed by the difficulties and disengage so that the pernicious cycle of impasse begins again. The process of re-evaluation has to be undertaken in such a way as to facilitate movement. Various measures can be used to ensure that this is the case, beyond simply analysing causes; these are elaborated in Chapter 10. Ultimately the therapist only really has control

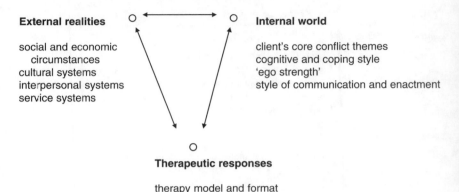

External realities

social and economic
   circumstances
cultural systems
interpersonal systems
service systems

Internal world

client's core conflict themes
cognitive and coping style
'ego strength'
style of communication and enactment

Therapeutic responses

therapy model and format
skill and accuracy of response
therapist's internal reactions

FIGURE 6.3   *Interacting elements within impasses*

over herself. In this sense, it is the therapist's responses or her contribution to the therapeutic interaction which is at the crux of attempts to resolve an impasse. Counter-transference (or personal congruence), therefore, is always central.

Conclusion

These various conceptual perspectives on analysing impasses can be used as tools to help structure an understanding of the situation by:

- highlighting significant issues;
- linking these to each other to create a complex picture of their inter-relationships;
- directing attention to points of leverage to effect change.

However, it may not be necessary to follow the whole route to articulating an integrative 'formulation'. Sometimes it can be more useful simply to have generated various alternative perspectives. This enables movement within the therapist's sense of her place in the interaction. A feeling of fluidity and psychological space is introduced in place of the deadlock.

Inevitably our attention is drawn to the more serious instances where therapy runs into trouble. However, probably only a minority of therapies run their course without getting stuck or going off track to some extent, at some point. What is crucial is that these instances give rise not to recrimination, but to learning. What is needed is a respectful, optimistic attitude towards the client and the therapeutic work. Through all the many perspectives which can be offered and are considered in the following chapters, it is this stance of humility and perseverance which is at the heart of dealing with the difficulties of an impasse.

7 Impasse and the Alliance

The conclusion of a therapy is often inherent in its beginnings. Getting things off to a good start – which does not necessarily mean an easy one – can be the best guarantee of ensuring a positive outcome. By the same token, an impasse often stems from how things are set up at the very beginning. Either therapy never really gets off the ground, perhaps resulting in early dropout, or else trouble is stored up, waiting like a time-bomb to explode at some critical point in the future. Foundations have not been laid which are capable of withstanding the pressures that the therapeutic work places upon them. Two closely related issues – the collaborative element of the therapeutic relationship which provides the basis for working together on the resistance to change and the defining framework of the therapeutic enterprise, embodied in a contractual agreement specifying their mutual responsibilities – constitute the main components of the therapeutic alliance. Impasse occurs where this alliance breaks down or proves unequal to the challenge posed to it by the client's – and the therapist's – resistance.

Collaboration and the therapeutic alliance

In the previous chapter, we defined the alliance of forces for change as all those elements in the situation supportive of positive development. A more conventional notion of the therapeutic alliance emphasizes the background elements within the therapeutic relationship itself which support the process of change in the client. An extensive literature has expanded this concept from its psychoanalytic roots to provide a key integrative concept with a large empirical research base: the strength of the alliance overall is the best predictor of success across all forms of therapy (Horvath and Symonds, 1991). Table 7.1 outlines major elements of the alliance drawing principally on Bordin's (1979) conceptualization. These provide an outline for major elements of the therapeutic contract (Sills, 1997): the contract can be thought of as the framework of the alliance. An impasse always calls the therapeutic contract into question: the issues of 'Where are we going?' and 'How are we getting there?' are thrown into relief by the sense of things not moving. Collaboration has broken down and resistant elements in the therapeutic situation dominate.

The therapeutic relationship – the bond element of the alliance – mediates collaboration on tasks and goals: it lies at the heart of the development of an impasse and of its resolution. The framework of the alliance and

TABLE 7.1 *Elements of the therapeutic alliance and their contract implications*

1 Therapeutic bond	2 Therapeutic goals	3 Therapeutic tasks
– Client's positive expectations of help from therapy	– Clarity and agreement on overall goals	– Clarity and agreement on the tasks of therapy
– Client's positive response to therapist as expert helper	– Appropriateness and achievability of goals	– Clarity and agreement on appropriate ground rules
– Client's friendly sense of collaborating with therapist	– Agreement on and success in achieving intermediate goals	– Understanding of each party's responsibilities
– Therapist's empathic understanding and involvement	*leading to*	– Client's understanding of therapeutic task rationale
leading to	– Explicit contract of what work is aiming to achieve	– Client's working capacity to undertake therapeutic tasks
– Client's overall positive affectional bond to therapist with implicit interpersonal contract of trust and collaboration.	– Agreement on opportunities to review progress.	*leading to*
		– Clear explicit contract on ground rules: attendance, scheduling, fees and payment, notice of changes, policy on missed sessions, confidentiality and communications
		– Possible agreement on consequences of ground rules not adhered to
		– Informed consent on ways of working
		– Informed consent on mutual roles and responsibilities

perhaps particularly the interpersonal bond, supports the tougher and more painful aspects of the work, which may not be possible without it. Without a reference point in the alliance, the therapist's more challenging interventions may come to be seen as hostile, critical or demeaning. It is easy for both parties to find themselves locked into a pattern of misunderstanding which is hard to break. However, sometimes renegotiating the contract or repairing the alliance can be a 'new start' leading to a breakthrough. It can then seem as though the initial mistakes 'had to be made' to achieve this new level of understanding. Safran and Muran (2000) place the detection and resolution of 'alliance ruptures' at the heart of the change process. The earlier such a pattern of re-establishing a damaged alliance is set, the less intractable any future impasse situation will be.

Clients arrive with a mixture of expectations about getting help for their problems. They have both hopes and fears and the balance of these must quickly be tipped towards the positive in order to hold them through the early stages. It may be appropriate to support them with interventions which emphasize the provision of help by a capable professional whose robustness, acceptingness and competence can be relied on, thus creating the necessary atmosphere of safety and trust. It is a valid strategy to reinforce the client's hope of improvement and wish for emotional support enabling the client to mobilize her personal resources which have been undermined through feeling overwhelmed by difficulties. However, the intention in most psychotherapy is to ground the relationship in a connection with the client's maturing self which can be engaged in seeking solutions to her own problems. While in early stages of work, and with acute distress, the 'expert' element of the therapeutic bond is likely to predominate, in longer-term work the therapist's role must shift towards mutual collaboration (Luborsky, 1984). Crucially, it is seldom appropriate to place too much reliance in the early stages simply on the 'expert' type of bond. The lack of a developing collaborative working relationship from the earliest sessions is bound to result in impasse or dropout.

Ensuring client/therapist 'fit' and consciously matching therapeutic dyads in order to enhance the bond is a way of overcoming difficulties of engagement. Excessive dissimilarity of social background and circumstances and of cultural beliefs and values may put an excessive strain on each person's capacity to form a bond. Subtler dissimilarities in terms of personal style, key areas of vulnerability and interpersonal orientation are harder to specify but go to make up the 'chemistry' which can make or break therapeutic encounters (Feltham, 1999). The fit between client and therapist enables a positive partial identification to be made between them as a foundation for their collaboration. If you are unable to find something to like about a client it is best to find someone else to work with her (and the same advice might be given to clients).

Working towards collaboration

The failure to negotiate the basis of a therapeutic contract represented by early dropout constitutes a victory of resistance over the potential alliance for change. This is not necessarily a disaster and real problems arise if the therapist regards not 'losing' the client as the main criterion of success in the early stages. The need to keep the client at any cost can push therapists into taking on clients whom they should not, setting up relationships which are insufficiently challenging or subtly seductive, and making unhelpful compromises with the ground rules: all of these will lead to an impasse at a later stage. The client may herself have many reasons for not pursuing therapy and it is important to respect the choice that she makes, even if this is to dropout. However, awareness of this need for respect can sometimes predispose a therapist to an excessive degree of passivity, rather than inspiring her to identify and address problems in terms of what the client can appropriately manage. It is generally best if a choice not to pursue therapy can be discussed as an explicitly negotiated decision rather than risk leaving both people feeling as though they have failed at something.

Adopting this attitude is most likely to clarify difficulties as they arise and minimize the proportion of people dropping out needlessly.

While a collaborative relationship is essential for any ethical attempt to promote psychological change, therapeutic styles and stances differ markedly and this collaborative element is expressed in various ways. In more actively structured styles, such as the cognitive-behavioural, the client is invited explicitly to participate in setting session agendas, determining the focus of work and developing homework assignments. The directive component of this model makes explicit attention to collaboration essential since an impasse is frequently the result of a power struggle in which the therapist is cast in an authoritarian role. This danger makes it vital to actively solicit and genuinely value the client's input and feedback, particularly with those who tend to be unassertive (Beck and Freeman, 1990). In exploratory approaches, collaboration is often more implicit. To the extent that the therapist is deliberately less active, it is vital that they be more alert to signs that the client is just 'going along' with a process in which they may be feeling uncommitted or imposed upon. It is especially important to notice emotional shifts at specific points in a session when a client may be responding to how the therapist has just behaved (Safran and Muran, 2000). In a more active exploratory stance the therapist inquires repeatedly about what the client is thinking and feeling in relation to the process and to the therapist; encourages her to raise concerns, objections and doubts; and takes those seriously, working to develop a genuinely shared understanding. Therapeutic decisions should be jointly arrived at and any differences of view fully acknowledged and explored. Ideally, therapist and client are functioning as a team – both are working and both are feeling responsible for their role in the process.

Such fully shared responsibility is, however, likely to remain an ideal – if anything it is an outcome of the work rather than its precondition. One of the commonest sources of impasse is to have failed to establish appropriately shared responsibility for crucial elements of the therapy and for the client at some level to be waiting passively to be helped. This can be bound up with unrealistic, even magical, expectations of the ability of a parental figure to meet the client's needs and smooth her path through life. This is accompanied by a corresponding sense of incapacity on the client's part – that there is just no way that she is able to manage her life by herself and should not be expected to do so. There may also be an underlying sense of entitlement – that she deserves the help of others, perhaps in compensation for the hurts and deprivation that she has suffered earlier in her life or in some more recent trauma or injustice (Stark, 1994; Strean, 1985). These irrational and normally unstated assumptions can lead to a kind of false alliance which blocks the work until they are identified and confronted. Under the guise of collaboration the client is supported in perpetuating unrealistic and self-defeating attitudes. Both client and therapist are protected from their fear of taking full responsibility for their feelings and actions and an impasse results.

It is therefore important not to overvalue rational collaboration as though it were something which can be willed into existence by the therapist. The therapeutic alliance involves an element of both conscious and unconscious collaboration, based on positive early experience and the client's impetus towards growth and maturity. However, all relationships also involve resistance and a reluctance to give up the safety of attitudes which enable us to avoid taking full responsibility for ourselves. This kind of resistance expresses itself in interpersonal forms in the therapeutic relationship, often out of the awareness of either party (see Chapter 9). People are complex and contradictory with many different 'parts' to them. In negotiating in a collaborative style, it is important to stay aware that you are speaking, as it were, to only one part of the client.

Nor does collaboration mean simply going along with what the client wants. It has to be a genuine negotiation or the therapist will simply undermine her own contribution to the client's development. Sometimes there is a case for allowing a certain diplomatic ambiguity or vagueness about some issues such as goals at the start of therapy to enable an alliance to be formed so that further work can be done – but there is always the danger of sowing the seeds of a later impasse. In working to create a collaborative atmosphere, there is a risk of making inappropriate compromises in either the framework or the process of therapy. The therapist may be reluctant to provoke conflict through expressing a difference of view with the client; she may simply wish not to offend. Early in a therapeutic relationship there may be an urgency to offer some form of help, even when the client is not willing to accept what the therapist believes to be the minimum conditions for effective work. The therapist may make inappropriate compromises and collude with the client's unreasonable wishes to be totally in control. In doing so, she avoids letting the client experience the consequences of her own decisions about engaging with the therapeutic process. In general, there is a balance to be struck between the support and emotional safety implicit in a collaborative relationship and the strategic challenge to resistance that characterizes effective therapy: collaboration must not become a disguise for collusive avoidance which will also lead to an impasse.

Establishing the therapeutic framework

Therapists' discussion of the therapeutic contract with their clients is too often limited to a brief mention of some basic ground rules. A more complex vision of what is involved is essential: a focus on negotiating an agreement about the framework contributes greatly to preventing impasses later; an understanding of the ways in which contracts may be flawed and the ability to renegotiate them can rescue a therapy from deadlock. A secure frame is needed for any work that intends to deal with difficult or fundamental issues of change. The process of contracting can assist pragmatically by focusing the therapy, and ethically by informing the client's choice and protecting her from power inequalities, but it also safeguards the therapeutic work, defining what is supposed to happen and spelling out the conditions which are needed (Sills, 1997; Yeomans et al., 1992). A contract which defines a secure frame creates a safe place for both client and therapist in which difficult work can be done. It protects the therapist's role and so secures her ability to work and think. Pressures on the therapist's stance and on the therapeutic framework are the norm in working with more difficult, fragile clients who are particularly prone to intractable impasses. They attempt to involve the therapist beyond appropriate limits in ways that confuse and compromise the dynamics of the therapeutic process and can draw her into responding in such a way as to reinforce and reward the client's unhelpful behaviours, while at the same time devaluing the therapeutic sessions and over-taxing the therapist. The contract acts as a reference point when there is pressure to deviate from initial agreements. It encourages the client to reflect on her current, emotionally charged expectations, in contrast to the original rational agreements which she made. For the therapist too, it heightens her awareness of an inclination to deviate, under the pressure of the situation, from what she had originally set up as the ground rules which she needed to work within. Difficulties experienced in holding to the contract – or in setting it properly in the first place – are likely to point to counter-transference issues arising from the intense involvement with the client.

Deirdre went for therapy some time after she had been left by her husband. She had sorted out the practicalities of her life but was experiencing anxiety and some agoraphobia. She had been brought up by an over-burdened single mother. She attended a centre where a low fee was agreed on the basis of her income but other contractual issues were not discussed. In the first six sessions she felt warmly supported by the therapist concerned. Then, on several occasions, she cancelled sessions at short notice and asked for time changes which the therapist altered schedules in order to meet. The therapist felt it important to be as helpful as possible and not to overburden her client further. However, on one occasion she refused to change the session time, though feeling quite guilty about this. Deirdre was hurt and distant in the next session, leaving the therapist feeling terrible. Two sessions later, when she asked for a further reduction in the fee, the therapist quickly agreed. A series of increasing demands followed, for changed times and phone contact. When the therapist finally confronted Deirdre about the meaning of this, under pressure from her supervisor, Deirdre became furious, shouting that the therapist 'did not really care'. She did not return to another session. By making 'real' the client's neediness through responding with actions, rather than maintaining clear ground rules and helping her make sense of her feelings about them, the therapist precipitated a destructive, regressive spiral, which could only end badly.

The basic elements of a contract follow directly from the framework of the therapeutic alliance (the goals, methods and rationale of the work), together with the 'business' of therapy (the length and frequency of sessions; how appointment times will be set and the policy on missed sessions; any fees and how and when they are to be paid). Perhaps most crucially, the roles and responsibilities of client and therapist should be defined: the responsibility of the client to attend, to come on time, to stay and to participate actively in the work; the therapist's responsibilities for scheduling sessions, attending and working in the session time, for confidentiality and for asking no more of the client than is in the contract. Saying something about the therapist's responsibilities makes it clear that the process is a 'two-way street' and also provides an opportunity to clarify the limits of her involvement – not only what the client may expect but also what the therapist will *not* do. The meaning of all this to the client can be explored later but it needs to be given in a 'matter of fact' way early on, as part of the contract.

The process of negotiating a therapeutic contract is the first collaborative task of therapist and client. It should be a dialogue with each taking an active and responsible role. It sets the tone for the subsequent relationship. The process of creating the contract is likely to be a microcosm of the dynamics that will unfold between therapist and client and the complexities of these should be noted, without treating the process as primarily a therapeutic one. Particularly with clients bringing difficult issues, it is not a good sign if they express no doubts or do not ask questions. Superficial compliance is not useful and must be explored. The therapist should check out the client's understanding and agreement and not ignore any objections, pursuing these with patience and persistence to arrive at a genuine contract rather than a pseudo-agreement (Yeomans et al., 1992). A common error is being reluctant to pursue these issues due to anxiety about setting limits and so eliciting objections and hostility. The opposite mistake is to bear down on the client in a controlling and aggressive way, rather than negotiating from a 'matter of fact' sense that the therapist's conditions are those she regards as the minimum to create a secure frame and a successful therapeutic process.

It is possible to identify clients who are likely to create threats to the therapeutic frame by being alert to problematic interpersonal patterns in their life story, to difficulties in the nature of the interaction with the therapist at this early stage of setting up the work (such as missing appointments or making special demands) and perhaps most clearly, by considering the course of any previous therapy and particularly the ways it was disrupted or unsatisfactorily terminated. In this respect, it is useful to contact a previous therapist, with the client's permission, to get an alternative view of the problems to that of the client. By considering all of this evidence, the therapist can identify specific potential threats to the therapeutic framework which could create an impasse or breakdown later in the therapeutic work (Kernberg et al., 1989). It is possible to make specific contractual provisions in relation to such identified potential threats. The main issues of this kind fall into a few broad categories: self-destructive and homicidal impulses (dealt with in Chapter 3); problems created outside therapy by involving others in a way damaging to the work (dealt with below); and poor attendance or participation in therapy sessions, which includes missing sessions, arriving under the influence of alcohol or other drugs and not maintaining sufficient income to pay the fees. It is vital that the client should understand concerns of this kind and participate in considering what steps can be taken to ensure that she does not destroy the therapy. If she is unable to acknowledge the threat and respond to reduce its impact, it is unwise to commence therapy: there is no secure contract. Without this process of defining the limits to therapy and to the responsibilities of the therapist, a belief in the omnipotence of the therapeutic process is ratified rather than challenged, a belief which is likely to be tested and found wanting at a later stage.

Marsha had had two previous therapy experiences for her problems of intense fluctuating, emotional states of both anger and anxiety, during which she had done damage to other people's property and herself. John, the therapist in the NHS department, had access to previous notes which indicated rather erratic attendance and then dropout. He planned a five session extended consultation for assessment and contracting for possible long-term therapy. Marsha cancelled and rearranged the first session, came 10 minutes late to the second and cancelled the third – she had various plausible excuses: her childcare arrangements, transportation problems and feeling unwell. Indeed, John had felt as though he was being quite harsh when he queried the meaning of her lateness. Discussing this with colleagues, he saw that this was probably linked to Marsha's own expectations about relationships and that in view of how the previous therapies had gone, whatever the reality behind the practical difficulties, they also served his client's resistance to getting help with her own destructiveness. In the fourth session, he linked together a number of features of her history and problems and said that he thought she did need the therapy and could use it but only if she was able to attend: therapy could not happen if she was not there. John commented on the missed sessions, lateness and how her previous therapy had gone, saying that they had to consider seriously the possibility that she would not attend regularly. He wondered how she felt: did she agree that she should come to all sessions and that she could commit herself to this? Marsha responded that she really wasn't sure and John said that it was best that they know now rather than proceed with therapy under circumstances that just wouldn't work. Marsha looked a little surprised but said yes she could see that. In the next session, Marsha said she thought she did want therapy but what if she did miss a few sessions? John commented that that was an important point and that she ought to know that if that happened, they would have to review the situation to see whether the therapy could go on – that 'therapy really can't take place without you here and it would make more sense to end than go on pretending that you were in therapy when you really weren't'. Marsha seemed relieved if anything that this was all being taken seriously but then asked, 'Well how many sessions could I miss before you'd stop things?' John said, 'I'm not talking about a threat or a punishment – it's about understanding whether you're making it impossible for any helpful therapy to take place – we would talk about that if it ever happened'. They agreed to take three more sessions together to decide whether to go forward with open-ended therapy and finally did so. Marsha felt more secure than with previous therapists and worked more productively with her angry feelings.

Such threats to the therapeutic frame may often present themselves in the guise of 'real' difficulties, stemming from the circumstances of the client's life. It can be difficult to distinguish the ways in which clients distort their perceptions, or are responsible for creating interfering situations, or fail to find ways around difficulties, from genuine practical limitations inherent in the client's life and social situation. There can be pressure from the client to make alterations to the normal therapeutic framework which are essentially a resistance to committing to therapy; or represent a demand for the therapist to become an 'all-giving parent' rather than a realistic collaborator; or seek to make the client an exceptional case who is a 'special' person and warrants extra-special treatment. However, the therapist needs to exercise good judgement about this and to negotiate around what is actually practicable; she should not overlook or misinterpret real limitations and practical problems. If the client is required to make an excessively burdensome journey, or attend at very inconvenient times, or pay more than she can afford, an unhealthy lack of realism has been built in to the very structure of the therapeutic contract which will be its downfall. A secure frame is needed in relation to both the client's psychological and her social realities.

Therapeutic goals and motivations

Therapeutic impasse and failure is frequently attributed to the client's 'lack of motivation'. This cliché blames the client and excuses the therapist – at the very least it fails to think the situation through. No client lacks motivation: the therapist has to try to discover at the start and on an ongoing basis, what the client does appear to be motivated to do and what she does not. This may be better thought of as identifying the client's various goals (together with those of the therapist) and her degree of commitment to them. Obviously, the idea of 'goals' fits well with a structured and problem-oriented approach to therapeutic work while defining them in an exploratory model is more challenging. However, an over-simplistic understanding of goals – unquestioningly accepting what the client says are her goals, for example – can be equally misleading: there are usually many goals at different levels and in diverse areas of a person's life, many of them contradictory. Ambivalence about what we want is part of the human condition. A series of common goal conflicts in therapy are outlined in Table 7.2. Where such conflict and ambiguity is not adequately explored it is a frequent source of impasse.

One important form of protection against impasse from this source is that therapist and client should discuss and mutually agree the goals of their work together. It is the therapist's job to translate the client's stated ambitions and aspirations into a form which is an appropriate goal for the kind of work she is offering to do. Part of her skill is negotiating a definition of the problem that is likely to lead to change, so that working on the issues viewed in this way will create some improvement in the client's life. A client may see herself as 'weak' and needing to 'become stronger' or, perhaps more subtly, as needing to 'get more confidence'. The therapist would probably do better to work on developing a more concrete, shared understanding of these problems so as to redefine goals, say in terms of behaving more assertively in certain situations, or being less self-critical and more affirmative more of the time. In this process of negotiating the understanding of the problem, there is a real danger that the client's and the therapist's goals will in fact differ in ways that are not acknowledged. For example, a therapist may believe she has agreed to work with a client on her perfectionism and self-critical tendencies when the client is still coming simply to reduce her anxiety and so improve her performance and achievement at work. An appropriate initial goal here might be to work on understanding what interferes with the client's work and makes her anxious. It makes sense to construct intermediate goals on the road towards the eventual aim. However, it is vital to keep the goals related to the client's stated concerns.

TABLE 7.2   *Goal conflicts in therapy*

Commitment to change can be *undermined* by:
Fears about how change will damage other people.
Fears about solving current problems because of having to tackle other larger ones.
Having to give up some of the gains that 'problems' provide.
Having to give up the gains of being in therapy.
Fears of the unknown, giving up the security of the familiar.
Sense of threat to the survival of one's current 'self'.
Anxiety about trying and failing to change
  – seeing change as all or nothing
  – anticipating criticism from therapist or others.
Changed behaviour would bring negative reactions from others.
Coping with immediate problems and environmental stresses leaves no time or energy to make larger changes.
Problems are viewed in terms of other people needing to change.
Other people want the client to change but she may not want to.

Goals can change and develop over the course of therapeutic work and it is easier to keep track of this process and to avoid working at cross-purposes if goals are stated as clearly as possible. This is a familiar process in a problem-oriented style of working but still requires careful consideration by more exploratory therapists. Failing to be explicit about goals for the work may come about because of the therapist's unwillingness to tell the client that she cannot get what she wants from therapy, paralleled by the client's wish to avoid facing its limitations. It is not uncommon for a client's real hopes to be that other people in her life, perhaps her partner or parent, will change. Many dream of having a different life, or of having had a different early experience and though they claim to know this is unrealistic, may retain an underlying expectation that the therapist can magically change things.

The client's expectations of what an outcome to the therapy could or should be, can thus be a crucial area at the heart of the work. The frustration of not making progress may be necessary to prompt a review of how realistic is the view of the change expected by both parties and to reconsider the client's ability to achieve her goals, in the light of the time, personal resources and life situation that she has. The therapist can never know ultimately what is and is not possible for her client: what needs to be explored is what might stand in the way of change and what disappointments might have to be faced. There is a very real difference between the 'motivation' that someone has to seek relief from distress and unhappiness and her willingness to work actively and bear the discomfort involved in making difficult changes in awareness, in behaviour and in life choices and to give up the 'gains' which the problem might bring. A woman suffering from agoraphobia might be unhappy about her restricted life and wish to be free of the anxiety which besets her; but this might involve tolerating anxiety during exposure work, learning new skills in managing her feelings and social encounters, revising significant aspects of her self-concept and sacrificing the relative safety and the control of her husband which her symptoms provide for her.

Aspects of this conflict have classically been discussed in terms of 'secondary gain' – the original source of a problem comes to be overshadowed by other benefits which accrue as a result of having the problem. These maintain the difficulty and alter the balance of the wish to change. Such 'pay-offs' commonly include: avoiding responsibilities; getting others to do things for you; getting your own way; and attracting sympathy and attention. On occasion this can make the 'sick role' very attractive and the person does not need to admit or express her needs directly. At worst, the invalid may come to control her whole environment and tyrannize her family. A wider family intervention may be necessary (see below). The issue of secondary gain can be particularly intractable when pay-offs are concrete, such as financial awards through compensation, litigation or from welfare/disability benefits. Finding a way to discuss this frankly while not being drawn into a position where you influence these claims is the best stance; experience suggests that psychological intervention is frequently ineffectual while litigation is pending and is best delayed until after its conclusion. Less obvious gains may come from subtle interpersonal roles: being the victim provides an excuse for escaping pressures and the opportunity for self-pity; an identity as a suffering individual can provide psychological safety and a familiar though restrictive relationship with others. The therapist can easily be drawn into these interpersonal 'games' if she accepts at face value what every client *says* about their motivation and intentions rather than recognizing what they actually *do*. Being able to accord these covert goals a degree of respect and legitimacy – seeing them as understandable in terms of the client's experience of how she can have her needs met – is a helpful starting point. It removes the element of shame and assists the therapist to work steadily towards enabling the client to make conscious choices rather than be trapped in her automatic, self-defeating actions. This may be at its most difficult where the pattern is one of confounding all help, 'seducing' a series of therapists and defeating them – thus confirming a sense of grievance and bitter victimization while experiencing a kind of victory. Therapists should be alert to such patterns and avoid being drawn into engaging in a power struggle by accepting and perhaps amplifying the self-defeating patterns (see strategic approaches in Chapter 10, p. 168).

Motivation – and an apparent lack of it – often crops up in relation to helping people change socially undesirable behaviour. Understandably, therapists and a wider network of other interested parties can become invested in the importance of people stopping smoking, giving up heroin use, not gambling compulsively and so on. However, similar pressure for change is around in relation to many intractable life situations. The reality is that many people may not *yet* have reached a point where the benefits of change seem to them to out-weigh the costs, even though others in their life believe this to be obvious. They may also believe they are not able to change. When this situation exists, clients may be pushed into 'treatment' by well-meaning family or friends or by the legal system, only to be then told that if they are not motivated they can't be helped! Any small glimmer of self-awareness that changing their behaviour might be worth trying is obliterated by shame, guilt, disappointment and a retreat into the comfort of the familiar pattern.

Most people are not permanently stuck in this supposedly 'unmotivated' state. Sometimes they oscillate between a desire for change and avoiding it. Prochaska and DiClemente (1984) have proposed that there is a pre-dictable process of change with identifiable stages which such clients go through, sometimes repeatedly. (Their model is considered in detail in Chapter 11 in relation to relapse.) What has been described above is the pre-contemplation phase when someone perceives change as undesirable or unattainable; and the contemplation phase, characterized by overt ambivalence. Until clients have worked through some of their ambivalence and the balance has tipped in favour of change, they will appear 'unmotivated' and discussion and setting of change goals would be premature. Specific techniques have been developed in recent years to help clients break through the impasse that can occur when they are unable to resolve their ambivalence. Drawing on ideas from both person-centred and cognitive-behavioural ways of working, Miller's (1983) approach, termed 'motivational interviewing', regards the therapist's primary task as enabling the client to move through the 'contemplation stage' in the process of change. This means encouraging the client to talk about her ambivalence but to do so in a semi-structured way: see Table 7.3.

TABLE 7.3 *Motivational enhancement*

Direct the client *first* to talk about the '*good things*' about the status quo.

Then assist her to discuss the '*less good things*'.

Seek to identify: – patterns in her behaviour
– concern about its consequences
– what she believes might enable her to change.

Employ general active listening skills – but focus on eliciting *self-motivating statements*.
The client thus hears herself talk about:
– her ability to change
– the desirability of change.

Therapist reinforces the positives through attention and hopeful comment – but two *golden rules* are:
Don't put words in the client's mouth.
Don't assume ambivalence is resolved until the client is able to convince you that it is.

Sheila talked in detail in her first session about her conflicts over whether or not she should tackle her binge drinking. She didn't believe it was damaging her health or her social life but she did feel embarrassed about it and worried that she seemed to have no control once she had opened a bottle of wine. She had tried to stop before but didn't succeed. She came for counselling because the previous week her seven-year-old son had to wake her up, because she had slept through the alarm and she was deeply ashamed that her drinking was affecting him. The enthusiastic therapist said at this point 'So you recognize now that you really are going to have to get your drinking sorted out this time'. This resulted in Sheila falling silent; the therapist had elicited heightened resistance. Sheila remained uncertain that she would be able to change and was highly sensitive to being only partially understood. Even worse, the therapist's tone implied disapproval and coercion: as if she knew what was best for Sheila and Sheila ought to agree.

In working with people whose motivation to change is fragile, there is a real danger of eliciting psychological 'reactance' (Miller and Rollnick, 1991). If a person perceives themselves to have been controlled or accused of something undesirable, with the implication that they *must* do something, they will regard this as a threat to their personal autonomy. The natural reaction is to argue, deny or defend. This reactive battle may be fought more strongly when the person is herself struggling internally with that demand or accusation, that is, when she is feeling ambivalent. Even the most broad-minded therapist may experience puzzlement, discomfort or disapproval when a client indulges in behaviour which appears to her to be overtly destructive. It can be very difficult for the therapist to deal with her own feelings about this, to know how to achieve an empathic stance and to create a collaborative working relationship. The client in her turn, has perhaps progressed to a potentially painful phase of ambivalence and con-flicting motivations: the possibility of exposing herself to someone else who may judge her is now on the cards, together with giving up the very thing which provides psychological comfort and escape. The therapist must try to bear in mind how hard clients in this predicament find it to deal with their own feelings, to trust that they are going to be understood and to achieve the beginnings of collaboration.

Negotiating the tasks of therapy

For the therapist, it is all too easy to assume that a client knows 'what you are about'. The client's expectations regarding what being in psychotherapy or counselling involves come from many sources – some personal, some cultural. When she arrives at the first session, it may be a first-time experience or expectations may be derived from previous therapy, possibly conducted on a quite different model. Practising regularly in our own way of working can restrict our vision and lead us to believe that a client readily understands and agrees with what we expect of her. Misunderstandings of this kind are not uncommon and if not resolved are very likely to result in an impasse.

Each model of therapy has what can be described as a set of 'tasks' which the client and the therapist undertake and through which it is assumed that the process of change is facilitated (Bordin, 1979). There is a rationale for these tasks which gives meaning to them in the context of the model, linking them to the client's goals. This way of characterizing therapy is more obvious in structured therapies which are overtly task-based – self-monitoring, undertaking exercises, homework assignments and so on. However, non-directive ways of working are also based on assumptions about the format of the relationship and about which activities promote change – experiencing at depth, observing your own process, telling your dreams and so on. This way of proceeding in therapy – these 'tasks' – in a sense, define a 'role' for the client (and for the therapist). Whilst this way of speaking might seem alienating to some, it draws attention to the specialness – and the strangeness – of the therapeutic situation: people have to learn how best to use it. This is sometimes known as 'socialization' into the client role and evidence has long suggested that specific attention paid to this process improves therapeutic success and reduces dropout rates (Orne and Wender, 1968).

Of course, a great deal of 'socialization' takes place implicitly through the ongoing process of interaction. However, it is helpful if the client has some overall understanding of the therapeutic process, not only of its goals but what the work is to be and how it will be undertaken. Again, this is easier within a model with a significant didactic element where learning about it is explicitly part of the change process. For example, cognitive therapy must initially enable the client to understand how distorted thinking may be related to the problems she wants help with: that her feelings of depression say, can be the consequence of a sequence of thoughts in which she blames or disparages herself. In a more exploratory therapy, there is a difficulty and a danger: by trying to explain too much, the therapist takes herself out of the role that she will adopt in the rest of the work and may encourage the client to adopt a role which is unhelpful – expecting the therapist to be like a teacher, being encouraged to use intellectualization and argument in ways that are defensive and misleading. On balance, even in psychodynamic and person-centred work, providing a brief overall rationale for the work and an introduction to the way of working is very helpful (Luborsky, 1984). Such information provided at the beginning of therapy can act as a reference point for any later difficulty: Has the person understood what therapy involves? Perhaps there was something that the client didn't want to hear at the time it was first explained?

It is a complex and contentious issue how best to set up and manage induction to therapy and there are several different approaches, each with pros and cons:

- as part of the later phases of a consultation prior to therapy when an appropriate referral is being discussed, explanations can be provided and the client's questions answered;
- during an assessment by the therapist, perhaps as an element of a separate and explicit 'contracting phase';
- in an assessment or extended consultation blurring the distinction between therapy and assessment by using some therapeutic interventions in order to see how the client responds to them (allowing the client a more informed choice of what this form of therapy will actually be like for her);
- setting up a 'trial therapy' with a contract for a relatively brief period of work, between four and twelve sessions, with the decision to continue or to end being made at a review point.

Many feel that it is unhelpful and inappropriate to open up sensitive issues with no guarantee of continuing. On the other hand, it is important for clients to have some sense of what they are letting themselves in for if they choose to embark on an extended therapy in order to avoid misunderstanding, disappointment and stalemate.

Ensuring an understanding of the overall rationale of therapy at a general level can be supplemented by procedures which, as part of the early intervention, share with the client a specific formulation of her problems in terms of the model. Again, this is a cognitive-behavioural procedure (Beck, 1995) but one that has been expanded in cognitive analytic therapy (CAT) (Ryle, 1990) to include a more dynamic understanding. In CAT, at around the third session the therapist typically writes a 're-formulation letter' to the client, explaining how she understands the pattern of difficulties the client has presented. This ensures that specific elements in the therapy – individual interventions such as assignments or in-session challenges – are related not only to the rationale of therapy as a whole but are linked closely in the client's mind to her individual problems and goals. Understanding the relevance of particularly difficult and challenging aspects of the therapeutic work may minimize resistance arising from felt needs to maintain security and re-establish control and so serve to prevent an impasse developing. An example in exploratory work is the use of interventions directed at the therapeutic relationship itself – transference interpretations or process comments. These are not only emotionally intense but can be confusing to clients who fail to see why talking about the 'here and now' of therapy has anything to do with what brought them there in the first place. Briefly orienting the client to the point of such a comment – that what happens between her and her therapist may be an example of what she struggles with elsewhere – can ease resistance and resentment and prevent it from escalating unhelpfully. There is a continuing need to ensure that the client understands and assents to the rationale for what the therapist is doing and the way in which it is relevant to her goals.

This ongoing feedback process about the work and the state of the therapeutic alliance can be more or less explicit. Again, this is clear in structured approaches where the success or failure of particular interventions and assignments is designed to contribute to an ongoing mutual conceptualization of the difficulties. However, in exploratory work it is also vital for the therapist to note her client's response to the interventions which she makes, to receive implicit feedback about the state of their relationship and monitor the level of their rapport (Malan, 1979). Tracking fluctuations in the level of rapport acts as a continuous feedback channel providing information about the client's participation in the work and her authentic collaboration with the therapist (Safran and Muran, 2000). It is equally important to look continually for evidence that the client is capable of being collaborative with the particular work being done at this point in therapy. A woman used to a busy practical life looking after other people may have had little experience of talking about herself or reflecting on her own feelings and motivations and may need time, practice and modelling to enable her to do so. Preparation and explanation can only take the client so far; it is essential to go at her own pace rather than put pressure on her to engage in work that she is not yet ready for. Therapists need to be flexible and to manage their own frustration in this process. Bad timing and inappropriate expectations about the work to be done will lead to an impasse. Flexibility, creativity and responsiveness are needed on the therapist's part: she must be accurate in her judgement of what can be expected of the client. Indeed, for clients who are 'veterans' of previous failed attempts at therapy, Duncan et al. (1997) suggest that placing a premium on understanding and respecting the client's own 'theory of change' and framing interventions to work with it is the best way not to repeat earlier impasses. This 'solution-focused' strategy makes room for and utilizes the client's existing skills and resources in circumstances in which these might easily be neglected.

Resistances in the social network

When an individual client enters the consulting room we are not necessarily in touch with or informed about all the relevant 'players' who are involved in creating or maintaining the problem with which she presents for therapeutic help. Therapists accustomed to understanding problems solely in the light of what they mean for the person opposite them are vulnerable to encountering therapeutic impasses which arise from the role which the client and her difficulties play in a wider social network. This individual bias can obscure perception of the problem as part of an ongoing, circular interactional pattern, or system, involving many other people. We may need to shift our framework of understanding resistance in order to appreciate it as part of a broader relational 'ecology'.

At one level, there is simply the difficulty of dealing with the client's friends and family during an individual therapy. They can be important allies whose co-operation it is vital to secure. They may support the client to stay in therapy at difficult moments when she may be inclined to drop out. Alternatively, they may seek to disparage or invalidate the work, through fear or misunderstanding, in ways that diminish her commitment. The client may need to be helped to communicate effectively with her family about the therapy and be supported in making a decision for herself. Where parents or a partner are paying fees for therapy, such difficulties are increased; active preparatory work may be needed to avoid later problems, perhaps even negotiating some early joint sessions to consolidate their support. Friends and family may also seek some active involvement – asking for advice, wishing a progress report or expressing fears for the client's well-being. It is essential that such contacts be handled with sensitivity: giving someone concerned for the client's well-being the 'brush-off' can harm her and the therapy but responding while preserving the therapeutic framework is tricky. Concerned others can be given information about the therapist's credentials and about the type of therapy being offered in general terms, but, of course, not about the client or her therapeutic work. Such refusals of further information must be framed in terms of the nature of therapy rather than of the person inquiring. The focus should be on the therapist herself and on the caller's own concerns. You should not consult to the caller about how she should cope with the client.

However, a real shift of perspective towards a more systemic view of the potential for therapeutic impasse takes account of the complex inter-relational dynamics which go to make up a family system (Dallos and Draper, 2000). The family is a multi-generational, rule-governed social network which has strongly 'morphostatic' properties, that is, patterns of interaction linked together in ways which maintain continuity and sameness in the overall structure of relationships between its members. Any change in one member reverberates throughout the whole system. These processes of communication or 'feedback' crucially affect and constrain the choices of any individual; everyone's actions influence each other in a circular fashion. This has a powerful impact on the capacity of any family member to change on her own (Lerner and Lerner, 1983). The individual client with the presenting problem comes to be seen from this perspective as only the 'identified patient': someone who both expresses a difficulty on behalf of the wider family network and also serves an adaptational function within it, maintaining and protecting the integrity of the current family structure. Sometimes after one problem is resolved another one emerges to rebalance the situation. It becomes necessary for the therapist to consider what might be the disadvantages of change for *each* person in the family network. Frequently, it will be found that the family as a whole is stuck in a developmental impasse, its efforts to negotiate a transition point in the family lifecycle blocked. There is an attempt to 'hold the clock back'. The difficulties of the client, presenting perhaps as an impasse in individual therapy, represents a compromise between the pressures for and against change within the family: her symptoms help keep the need for change alive but, at the same time, monitor the options and protect the status quo in case someone in the family is imperilled by its destabilization.

An impasse frequently arises when the client feels caught in a loyalty trap between the therapist and her family. She is pulled two ways – by the therapeutic relationship which stands for change and by her family which stands for sameness. Change is thus associated with betrayal and loss and she experiences both intense guilt and separation anxiety. This situation can escalate into a power struggle, with the therapist asking her to relinquish her symptoms and the client feeling pressurized to choose. In this tug of war, family loyalty typically holds the upper hand. The therapist can become caught in seeing the client as the sacrificial victim of her family – someone who needs to be rescued from them (rather than someone who has an investment in the status quo): the therapist has lost her neutrality and has become the person with the greatest investment in change.

To avoid this trap, the therapist needs to construct a *systemic hypothesis*, which enables thinking about the adaptive functions of the client's problems and her immersion in the system of family beliefs. She needs to identify what the problem behaviours are trying to accomplish and to appreciate both the real and imagined risks to the client and to other members of the family. As with understanding ambivalence in individual work, this allows the client's 'rejection' of help to seem less hostile and devaluing. To arrive at this hypothesis she needs to gather information about the family, the pattern of transactions between its members and how the identified client's symptoms are embedded within these. A *genogram* supplies crucial information about multi-generational patterns of relationship and ways of expressing difficulty. Drawing this up with the client enables her to become aware of these links and encourages curiosity and, potentially, communication with other family members, including those who are estranged. The systemic technique of *circular questioning* within a family meeting seeks to explore hypotheses about how beliefs and feelings are maintained by complex transactions such as coalitions between members which have formed and changed around nodal events in the family's history. Having arrived at a systemic hypothesis, it is possible to offer it to the client or to the family as a whole in terms of how the problems being faced contribute to the cohesion and ongoing well-being of everyone in the system. This re-framing of the problem by providing a positive rationale for how it protects others, often permits the therapist to gain greater access to the dilemmas faced by everyone in the system and frees her from the position of urging the client to change and engaging in a power struggle with the family (Fish et al., 1982). This can lead to the client gaining a clearer sense of personal responsibility for her part in maintaining family patterns and a capacity to observe these as they unfold, but does so in a validating, non-shaming way. It helps her to evaluate the pros and cons of changing or maintaining the present situation. It permits her to achieve clearer, more straightforward, person-to-person relationships within her family and to face her own anxiety about separating from it.

Of course, systemic approaches to therapy also encompass many opportunities to get stuck in an impasse – and often for similar reasons to individual work: disagreements about goals; being drawn into replicating a repetitive family pattern; choosing a therapeutic style which alienates the client family; becoming convinced of the rightness of your own ideas (see Carr, 1990; Green, 1988). However, the systemic perspective alerts us to how any psychotherapy – whether individual, couple or family – can be rendered ineffective if it fails to take into account the wider system of relationships which surround whoever is being seen in the therapy room. The correct frame must be found in which to address the real problem successfully. Widening the network can deepen understanding, bring hidden agendas to the surface and provide new leverage for change.

Successful therapy requires implicit agreement about the goals of change. From a systemic point of view, the question is, of course, whose goals? Therapists need to establish to whom the problem is a problem: this person might be called the 'customer' and they must always be included in the frame. The customer is not always the client or her family. It can turn out to be the professional who referred the client who has become hopelessly entangled with the problem, leaving the referrer feeling trapped and exasperated – the referral is an attempt to escape the entanglement. The danger is that the therapist will be pulled in as a substitute, either playing the same role as the referrer or else politely defeated by the client who simply wants to return to the old relationship with the referrer. This often happens with medical practitioners and social workers who play a long-term supportive role in someone's life. It is generally best to take a systemic approach by inviting the referrer to an early session or otherwise adopting a consultative stance. It is unwise to try to prise the parties apart or to imagine that you can do much better than the previous therapist. Re-framing the prior relationship in terms of its positive systemic value is a better tactical starting point.

In many complex therapeutic situations, the therapist finds herself to be just one member of an extensive network of involved professionals. The situation may involve several agencies and individuals with overlapping roles and competing agendas. Psychotherapists are always in danger of seeing themselves as the people doing the 'real' work: but even here, there can sometimes be several people with therapeutic roles involved. It is important to try to understand how the referral to you has occurred as a function of these complex systemic dynamics and what elements of the client's agenda are actualized by her alliances and conflicts with different elements in this network. Her internal conflicts will often be replicated within the professional network: it is the responsibility of the professionals to build trust and create the relationships which allow these conflicts to be resolved so that they can focus on helping the client (see Chapter 13). Impasses commonly arise through lack of clarity about boundaries and responsibilities and the power struggles which result as different agencies and practitioners try to work out their positions. Such situations require collaboration but are often beset by a lack of communication. It is helpful to clarify who else is involved with the client and to get permission to consult with them. A meeting or case conference may facilitate a process of clarifying why each individual, professional and agency is needed, what are their appropriate domains and what boundary problems might exist between these functions. It is usually essential to agree who is the key person who will co-ordinate the various pieces of work, is responsible for communicating regularly with others and ensures that the client is properly informed.

Entering any system of family relationships is akin to entering a different culture with its own beliefs, values and rules. It is multi-generational with complex roots extending far beyond the individuals presenting with a problem. As such it should remind us of the complexities and risks of helping anyone from a class, ethnic or cultural background other than our own. It is essential to be as aware as possible of our own agendas and of the ways that we might be seeing issues in a different light or expecting changes of people which are unacceptable to them (Kareem and Littlewood, 1992). One way to deal with this is to ensure that our understanding of the therapist's role and our own value system is explicit and included in the contractual negotiations that frame the therapeutic work. However, such explicitness is not always possible through our own lack of awareness. There can be real difficulties in the way of establishing a common language and unacknowledged assumptions and circumstances may introduce perceived differences of power which significantly affect the relationship. Openness to learning from the client, consultation and above all a willingness to extend ourselves beyond our own assumptions are essential to ensure a deepening awareness of our own participation in those complex social processes which if unattended to lead to confusion and impasse.

Conclusion

The most fundamental issue regarding the mutual expectations held about all therapeutic work concerns the responsibilities of each party. It is vital that the therapist be clear about how she views her own roles and responsibilities and their limits, and be capable of communicating these to the client equally clearly. The client's expectations in relation to goals, motivations and the terms of the contract, are crucial. On the one hand, she needs to have some belief that it is all for some purpose and that change is possible. However, she must not assume that change will be easy or that the work will be done *for* her. Each of these opposing expectations might form a major focus of therapeutic work but if they are not identified as issues and dealt with at an appropriate stage they will undermine any possibilities of success in the longer term.

8   Impasse and the Therapeutic Strategy

Naturally, therapists like to believe that therapeutic knowledge and technique are the most important determining features of the progress of therapy. However, the research literature suggests that the greatest contribution to the success of therapy is provided by the characteristics of the client (Garfield, 1994). This means that it is essential to consider what the client brings to the development of an impasse, although it remains the therapist's responsibility to create the circumstances which are most likely to be helpful for any individual – not just facilitating the process of the therapeutic interaction but also selecting an appropriate format for the work overall. This chapter is concerned with this responsibility and the choices of therapeutic strategy that derive from it.

A medical model of diagnosis and treatment implies an assumption of power and unilateral control which is anathema to the ethos of psychotherapeutic work and is contradictory to its methods and goals as conceived by most theories. While these reservations are right and proper, they have too often resulted in a lack of attention to the skills and processes of assessment and formulation during the contracting phase. There is already enough helpful literature attempting to redress the balance: our aim here is to draw attention to certain common client issues which can predispose to creating an unproductive therapeutic contract and to consider appropriate strategic responses. Assessing these issues as they present themselves is an essential part of negotiating your way around or through a therapeutic impasse. Again, prevention would be better than cure, and many impasses might be avoided by undertaking accurate assessments early in the process of therapy. However, even with care, mistakes will continue to occur. These issues must often be considered in terms of a 're-assessment' of the client in the context of an ongoing therapy where there is a need to extricate the work from a developing impasse.

Undertaking a review of the therapeutic process when a failure to achieve goals is implied, with possibly a consciousness of error on the part of the therapist, may involve frustration, disappointment and guilt. The process requires alertness and frankness and a capacity to manage the feelings of both parties. Serious difficulties are most readily avoided and changes most easily made if an early review is scheduled, perhaps as part of a 'trial therapy' (see Chapter 7). Even when sensitively and courageously handled, the issues of choice and responsibility are complex. It is the therapist's responsibility to make an informed judgement about how to proceed on the basis of what she has learned, without presuming to know with certainty what is right for the client. Responsibility for choices is shared by the participants to a degree appropriate to their different roles and knowledge. Clients can only make choices where they are informed by experience of the options – or at least what is on offer in this relationship – and this is one of the strengths of a trial therapy. However, a therapist must also take responsibility for her part in the choice of whether and how to proceed and must feel empowered to decline to participate in what she judges is not going to be helpful.

Biomedical conditions

One possible source of impasse lies at the interface of the psychological and the biophysical. Feeling emotionally distressed and feeling physically unwell are closely associated with each other. Physical symptoms may be part of the picture of complaints which bring people to therapy or they may arise during its course. However, such symptoms may occur either as an expression of psychosocial distress, or from an underlying biophysical illness, or from both together. Psychotherapy may of course be appropriate for many people suffering from physical illness and disability but the focus and goals will be about coping and adapting to the condition. Obviously, an impasse is likely to result where psychotherapy is being used to treat what is substantially due to a biophysical process. The worst scenario is when misattribution of symptoms delays recognition of a dangerous medical condition requiring urgent treatment. Taylor (2000) provides comprehensive guidance on distinguishing psychological from organic disorders. How large a problem is this? Striano (1988) summarizes studies undertaken in a range of American clinics which claim to demonstrate that about 15 per cent of patients receiving treatment for mental health problems had an undiagnosed physical illness which caused or significantly worsened their psychological symptoms. Clearly some therapeutic failures might be attributable to the involvement of undetected biomedical problems.

This is a difficult issue, precisely because it lies outside the realm of competence of psychotherapists. Over-attention to the possibility of physical causes may undermine the therapist's confidence in pursuing difficult emotional issues and inappropriate medical referral can deflect attention from the crucial personal problems. It can promote in some clients an intractable defensive belief that their difficulties are solely physical in origin. However, a cautious approach by the therapist and good communications with a reliable medical practitioner should enable her to avoid creating an impasse by colluding with avoidance of the underlying emotional issues, while not ignoring instances where medical intervention is needed. During therapy, clients should never be dissuaded from consulting their doctor though the meaning of this can be explored. As for the therapist's recommending that the client seek medical assessment (or even requiring this as a condition of the treatment contract), this should always be considered where a new physical symptom presents itself or a long-standing one is reported to have become more severe or to have changed significantly. Daines et al.'s (1997) advice on this is summarized in Table 8.1. With some clients, admitting to physical illness may seem to be a blow to their self-esteem and sense of control – it is essential to challenge this in their best interests. Experience with 'somatizing' and 'hypochondriacal' clients suggests that the most effective approach is to give careful, patient attention to their physical symptoms and to enable them to feel accepted and to be assured that proper medical investigations have been undertaken.

TABLE 8.1 *Physical symptoms needing medical assessment*

Symptom	Medical referral should be considered if:
Headache	• Recent onset and unusually severe and disturbing; wakes person at night; follows recent head injury; accompanied by severe visual disturbance or other symptoms not typical of tension headache or migraine.
Anxiety/tremor	• Possible presence of goitre (swelling of thyroid gland at the neck) or bulging eyes – indicating hyperthyroidism. Slow tremor at rest, diminished during movement – indicating Parkinson's.
Shortness of breath	• Always refer (although often anxiety).
Chest pain	• Always refer and assume it is medical (particularly if of recent onset) until proven otherwise.
Palpitations	• New symptom or above age of 35 years.
Dizzy spells	• Results in loss of consciousness; or has rotational element (vertigo).
Dyspepsia/gastrointestinal problems	• Generally refer, especially above age of 40 years or associated with weight loss.
Fatigue	• Recent onset or no other psychological features.
Backpain	• Generally refer, especially if at all disabled by it e.g. limping; if associated with weight loss; or has additional physical symptoms.

Marjorie, a 45-year-old married woman, was referred by her GP to a behavioural therapist for treatment of agoraphobic symptoms, panic attacks and generally raised anxiety, which had started to occur in the past three months. Marjorie had suffered two bereavements and moved house over the past year. Some symptoms had been attributed to the start of her menopause. After seeing her for ten fortnightly sessions which combined bereavement counselling with anxiety management, the symptoms had not improved and the anxiety was if anything more pronounced. The therapist believed that he had noticed some slight change in Marjorie's appearance around her eyes and, on enquiring, she reported some stiffness and swelling in her neck. The therapist discussed the case by phone with the GP who agreed to undertake tests of thyroid function. An overactive thyroid was detected and corrected by medication. The therapist continued to see Marjorie supportively until the thyroid functioning was reported to be normal. Anxiety and panic attacks substantially disappeared and some remaining agoraphobic symptoms were addressed by the therapist with a graded exposure programme which was successful within three sessions.

Misuse of drugs and alcohol

All too often, therapists fail to assess adequately whether the misuse of alcohol or other drugs forms part of their client's presenting difficulties. It is an issue which should be asked about at an early stage and if there is any indication that over-use is an issue for the client, a detailed exploration of the history, current patterns, amount, meanings and consequences of this behaviour is needed. Alcohol is much the most commonly misused drug in our society and it is important not to ignore or make assumptions about the effect it has on any given individual's functioning. The client's use of other, particularly illegal, drugs may cause more comment on the part of the therapist but is even more likely to be glossed over by the client when it is not the main issue in a referral. In order to discover the full situation, it is vital to be factual and to avoid moralizing. However, the more common problem for therapists is the opposite one: although the issue is alluded to by the client, it is not directly addressed by the therapist. There are a number of cultural and personal factors which contribute to this avoidance: discomfort about their own drinking; regarding questions about drinking habits as too 'personal'; or fear of implying a moral judgement about private behaviours. It is often omitted because therapists are not confident they have the knowledge or skills to proceed if the client's drinking *was* acknowledged to be a cause of her problems.

A further reason for this neglect, is the common view that substance misuse is always a symptom of other psychosocial problems and is simply a way of coping with unpleasant emotional states. This is true to some extent: relying on alcohol or any other drug that alters mood is an indication that there was, or currently are, underlying difficulties from which clients are seeking to escape. However, when this reliance develops into regular or heavy use of the drug, it is the drug using behaviour itself and its social, emotional and physical consequences which begin to dominate the person's life. Instead of trying to interrupt the vicious cycle by focusing on underlying difficulties which started the drug use, it is more appropriate for client and therapist to negotiate a cessation or a major reduction in the drug use before other issues can usefully be tackled.

Another argument against assuming 'substance misuse' is a symptom only, is that, whether or not the client sees it as particularly central to their lifestyle, psychotropic drugs affect mood and behaviour, with short-term and long-term effects. Depression, anxiety, agoraphobia and anger are likely to be exacerbated or may gradually become features of a regular drinker's/drug user's life. Eating and sleeping patterns are affected. Additional disruptions of mood and behaviour may occur when someone is coming off a drug, leading to a roller-coaster emotional life for some people. Substance misuse may be at the root of social problems involving money and work and may be involved in interpersonal difficulties, particularly in marriage. These issues will not be successfully tackled unless substance use is brought within manageable limits. Moreover, the therapeutic process itself is likely to be seriously compromised. Allowing clients to be even mildly intoxicated when attending sessions signals that the therapist does not see this as particularly problematic and also means that little lasting impact is made by that session's interventions. Continuing to drink heavily or take non-prescribed drugs between sessions minimizes and dilutes the effectiveness and continuity of the therapeutic process: it functions as a very destructive form of resistance to involvement in change. It is virtually inevitable that an impasse will develop unless it is dealt with.

For most competent therapists, it should not be necessary to refer everyone who drinks heavily or indulges to some extent in illicit or pre-scribed mood-altering drugs to a specialist. In line with an exploratory treatment option, the plan may be to challenge constantly the persistence of the behaviour as a therapy-defeating resistance, encouraging the client to take responsibility for this, to understand what is taking place and to bring it under better control. However, it might be necessary to make the substance misuse the initial target and work to arrive at an agreement with the client that this is so. A structured intervention to reduce this pattern of behaviour would then follow.

If it becomes apparent – or the client clearly states – that her sense of reliance on a drug is sufficiently strong that she cannot contemplate being able to come to sessions drug-free, therapists should consider with the client:

- whether referral to medical services is needed for detoxification;
- the extent to which ambivalence about change is preventing them even 'experimenting' with being drug-free, even for one day at a time;
- whether they are ready and willing to be referred to a specialist facility.

In her initial interview, at 2.30pm on a weekday, Jean appeared quite confident and eager to engage in therapy. The therapist was vaguely aware of a light smell of alcohol in the room after she had left, but thought no more of it. In the second session, at 11.30 in the morning, Jean seemed rather different in manner: she appeared more anxious and restless. Although the therapist had in the first session referred to the need for clients to be drug-free in the sessions, as part of outlining the counselling contract to Jean, he had not asked in any detail about her current drinking or other drug use. He commented on her anxiety and the client replied by asking if she could smoke and at this point the therapist realized he needed to explore alcohol/drug-use issues. He did so by asking about how she normally coped with anxious situations and was then able to elicit from her that she expected to find it difficult to not smoke for the therapeutic hour, and to attend without having had a drink beforehand. She would normally have a lunchtime drink of two glasses of wine, and most evenings either a bottle of wine or several glasses of spirits. The therapist explored both these concerns with her in a non-moralistic way, focusing on the ambivalence she felt about trying to cut out drinking at lunchtime, and reducing her evening consumption. She decided to do both, in spite of initial difficulties. She recognized that late-morning and late-afternoon anxieties were mainly related to minor with-drawal symptoms which she had got into the habit of avoiding by 'topping up' her blood alcohol level.

Clients are very often ignorant of the connections between the behaviour and the psychological distress they experience, and may be relieved when the therapist is willing and competent to discuss possibilities. If the issue is left in abeyance, client and therapist can become mistrustful, increasingly evasive and judgemental, and impasse becomes inevitable. Therapists may need to extend their knowledge about dealing with alcohol and other drug problems to increase their security in responding to them (see Edwards and Dare, 1996; Miller and Rollnick, 1991).

Certain other behavioural patterns such as disordered eating, excessive use of cigarettes and coffee and disordered sleep patterns have an ana-logous biophysical impact on psychological states, acting in a circular way to disturb emotional equilibrium and exacerbate the difficulties which they were intended to deal with. Each of these can promote the development of an impasse within a therapeutic contract aimed at co-existing problems. Each may need to be explored in detail and brought into the work as an explicitly targeted issue.

Psychotropic medication

Many clients who attend for psychotherapy or counselling have in addition been prescribed medication to help with their psychological symptoms. Sometimes this is appropriate, even essential; sometimes it is less appro-priate or actually problematic. Psychopharmacology rests largely on a different model of the causes of psychological distress and disturbance to that of psychotherapy. The main issue is the degree to which this can be seen as a complementary approach or as a competing one. To avoid impasses arising from this situation, the therapist needs to have a basic understanding of the uses, effects and side effects of the main classes of psychotropic medication: Bond and Lader (1996) provide a brief outline. However, it is even more important that you explore what medication *means* to your client – what is hoped for from it, how it functions as part of a network of relationships with others. Broadly speaking, there are three types of situation in relation to psychotropic medication that have the potential to create an impasse.

In some conditions, medication may be very appropriate (indeed perhaps the main treatment of choice) and may be needed to make psychotherapy possible. However, either the therapist or the client may be reluctant to condone the use of 'drugs'. While this applies to major mental illness (dealt with below), it also commonly arises in relation to taking antidepressants in cases of moderate to severe clinical depression and obsessive-compulsive disorders. The therapist should be able to negotiate in an informed way with the client and perhaps, in some cases, to consider including continuation of medication as part of the conditions of their contract to enable the psychological intervention to be most helpful. The meaning of the use of pharmaceuticals to the client – often concerned with fears of dependency or control – should be explored.

There may be occasions when medication has been prescribed inappropriately or as a competing intervention to psychotherapy. In either case, it may interfere with essential therapeutic processes, particularly free access to emotional states and possibly clarity of thinking. This can be a serious problem and there are dangers of being drawn into a struggle for control with the client's medical practitioner. It is wise to be alert to the way in which this might be being 'set up' by the client as part of a long-term interpersonal pattern of disowning responsibility. It is important not to be drawn into exhorting the client to stop their medication but rather to explore the issue with her and to facilitate her discussing it with the other people trying to help. It may sometimes be appropriate, with permission, to contact others involved in the case. The therapist may need to choose between stopping or continuing the work within the acknowledged limitations of the situation.

Medication may be being prescribed appropriately, inappropriately or irrelevantly (in terms of its effectiveness) but is problematic because any changes during therapy are attributed to the drug treatment. This can be frustrating and dispiriting for the therapist. The issue needs to be raised in relation to firstly, the therapeutic contract and what the client wants; and, secondly, to the way in which this view of medication has come to act as a resistance to the client's feeling responsible and empowered.

Joseph, a 19-year-old student, was experiencing serious social and educational problems and was being treated simultaneously by an experienced therapist and in the psychiatric outpatients department. He was depressed and often inarticulate, had self-harmed and had suicidal ideas. A new junior psychiatrist was concerned about his odd way of expressing himself and put him on a low dose of anti-psychotic medication in addition to his anti-depressants. The therapist did not know this and was in turn alarmed by a deterioration in the clarity of his thinking processes. The therapist had to contain his anxiety about a possible imminent psychotic breakdown and to try to explore what might be influencing Joseph's state of mind. In this way he found out about the change of medication and, after discussing it further with the client, contacted the psychiatrist in charge of the case. They agreed to monitor stopping the new medication and found that this rapidly restored Joseph's previous mental state, still distressed but more accessible.

Psychiatric disorder

The diagnostic categories used in psychiatry typically do not offer much help when choosing the format or guiding the process of psychological therapies. It is necessary to be able to appreciate and access a subtler level of an individual's psychological vulnerabilities. However, it is important that a therapist recognize the main forms of 'major' mental illness which do have important implications for intervention. In particular this means the main psychotic conditions: the schizophrenias; mania and hypo-mania; bi-polar disorders; severe/major depression; and organic brain disorders. This is not the place to discuss these conditions in detail but therapists should possess a basic knowledge which enables them to identify their possible presence; they should have to hand a basic psychiatric textbook for refer-ence (for example, Goldberg et al., 1994); and have access to appropriate professional consultancy.

Not having an accurate history, or simply being inexperienced with major psychiatric problems, can mean that the therapist fails to recognize the presence of these severe continuing difficulties and vulnerabilities until the work is already under way. It is through not recognizing the limitations which these conditions impose on psychological interventions that the potential for a damaging treatment impasse exists. On the one hand, there can be a developing stalemate as the client rigidly defends against or seems to avoid or be unable to explore feelings. This is, in a sense, perfectly appropriate for the client and misguided attempts to challenge this way of preserving psychological safety can be a dangerous error. On the other hand, the therapist may become aware of signs of deterioration in the person's mental state as a consequence of her attempts to uncover unmanageable feelings. Alertness to this possibility may enable her to 'back off' in time to seek consultation from someone experienced with these problems.

The point here is not that psychotherapy is never appropriate with people suffering from major mental illness but that the limitations and the risks must be properly recognized. The risks are of unwittingly provoking or simply encountering some form of severe breakdown, either into an acute psychotic state or severe withdrawal or into suicidal or violent acting out. It is obviously crucial not to contribute to such 'de-compensation' but also to be in a position to deal with these circumstances should they arise (see Chapter 5). Therapists must be realistic about their own skills and experi-ence and, if appropriate, choose a therapeutic strategy with limited aims. It is also essential to negotiate a framework that enables adequate liaison with other involved professionals: poor communication can sabotage well-planned care and lead to an impasse or a crisis.

Psychological capabilities and therapy

While psychiatric diagnosis does not greatly help in most psychotherapeutic work, exploration of the psychological capabilities of clients is a crucial route to understanding impasse and therapeutic failure – either by predicting and avoiding it, or in appraising what is going wrong and what can be done to retrieve the situation. A therapeutic contract always involves a 'plan' of therapy, a strategy, whether it is spelled out in detail or not, whether it is consciously adopted or made by default. Ideally, this should be based on some formulation or initial understanding of the client's issues by the therapist, as well as on a process of negotiation with the client. Too often both of these elements are more implicit than explicit. There is a legitimate concern not to reduce the client's uniqueness to some 'formula' – but equally, every therapy is not entirely new territory: other therapists have made these journeys and there are 'travel guides' available in the form of models which can inform choices and point out potential dead-ends. Assessment and formulation enable the therapist to avoid some difficulties and identify potential resources.

It is important to make a judgement about the client's capacity to undertake demanding personal change and exploration in a safe, productive way. This is an element of the therapeutic alliance – the 'working alliance' founded on the client's ability to undertake the tasks of any specific therapy. While it is important not to exclude unnecessarily people who might benefit or to stick over-cautiously with relatively easy work, there are very real problems that can arise from the misjudged use of expressive therapies in the wrong circumstances: risks to the physical and psychological safety of the client, but also deterioration in the ability to cope with and enjoy life, and wasted effort and loss of hope. There are risks for the therapist too: in our experience, a high proportion of complaints to professional bodies, many of them justified, occur as a consequence of clients being taken on for work which is inappropriate or for which the therapist is insufficiently experienced. Mays and Frank (1985) in their classic work on 'negative effects' in therapy conclude that the major issue is the failure to identify 'high risk' clients and to ensure their assignment to adequately skilled therapists.

Experienced therapists often have good 'intuitive' abilities which enable them to pick up on the psychological strengths and limitations of their clients and to gear their work accordingly. It is helpful to structure and formalize these processes, in order to enable well-informed decisions to be made by therapists and appropriate guidance to be offered to clients about the form of help they need. Bauer and Kobos (1987) integrate and summarize work on treatment suitability and selection for short-term psychodynamic therapies in terms of five factors: psychological mindedness; ego-strength; ability to sustain co-operative relationships; motivation for change; and availability of a focal issue (see Table 8.2). However, especially for the first three of these factors, they are essentially the same as those commonly held to be related to the chances of success in long-term exploratory therapies as well. In fact, the work of Safran and Segal (1990) suggests very similar considerations are relevant to selection for more ambitious forms of cognitive therapy. If a potential client is relatively deficient in these areas, longer-term work (say more than six months) is probably necessary, for there to be a significant chance of change and even then it will be more difficult work. Even in the presence of these three psychological strengths, without substantial motivation and a relatively well-defined issue to focus the work on, short-term therapy is also unlikely to be sufficient.

TABLE 8.2 *Selection factors for short-term therapy*

1	Psychological mindedness	• able to attend to and communicate thoughts, feelings and fantasies • capacity for self-reflection and curiosity about responses
2	Ego strength	• Toleration of frustration and stress through adaptive coping mechanisms • impulse control • goal-directed activities resulting in life achievements • sustained interests and creative endeavours
3	Ability to form and sustain relationships	• have meaningful long-term relationship • sense of basic trust in the benevolence of others • capacity to develop therapeutic alliance
4	Motivation	• wish for change rather than relief of distress/symptoms • interest in understanding problems • ability to be actively involved in process of change
5	Therapeutic focus	• identification of central issue linking different problem areas • ability to collaborate in developing relevant focus • realistic acceptance of limited goals

These factors, although useful pointers to the likelihood of benefit and appropriate length of contract, do not take us far enough in terms of predicting impasse. The risk of therapeutic breakdown is highest for people who are assessed as having so-called 'borderline' personality structures (Kernberg et al., 1989) and they frequently experience a variety of intense and intractable difficulties in treatment. Brooke (1994) offers a helpful way to approach this area in terms of the cohesiveness or fragility of the self-structure – while drawing on psychodynamic theory, this approach is more phenomenological and closer to therapeutic experience. Problems which exist within the context of an established and coherent sense of self should be distinguished from those which are essentially concerned with the very issue of self-cohesion. To have a fragile or incoherent self is to feel split, fragmented or precariously unstable much of the time; there is little room for imagination and memory; feelings are labile or dead; conflict is experienced externally, between oneself and other people, and so there is a sense of persecution; longings for closeness and separateness are in continual conflict. These structural features of a person's internal world can be detected at assessment or as they emerge in the work and may be marked by a series of 'clinical indicators' which are presented and organized in Table 8.3.

TABLE 8.3 *Therapeutic indicators of fragile self-structures*

Self-fragmentation	Self-cohesion
1 Widespread personal problems (i) 'Diagnosis' of Personality Disorder: i.e. long-standing, wide-ranging, poor social functioning, causing distress to self or others. (ii) Vague, global presenting problems: laconic presentation (after initial reticence), especially boredom and emptiness. (iii) Diffuse, multiple symptom profile: lack of focus other than 'self' issues. (iv) History of severe maternal/paternal deprivation.	**1 Areas of success in life** (i) Has several long-standing interpersonal relationships: so able to withstand inevitable conflict and disappointment; especially where bond sustained despite separation. (ii) Educational or occupational achievement: able to work under stress for long-term goals; especially if maintained in unstructured, self-generating context.
2 Lack of articulated self story (i) Personal history lacks detail: presented in vague, global, stereotyped or ambiguous terms; seems ungrounded in relation with real people. (ii) Lack of childhood memory: dissociation from history and little content recalled.	**2 Articulated view of self and others** (i) Presents detailed, differentiated memory of history: represents interior continuity; integration of experiences and self boundaries. (ii) Significant others described in detail: good differentiation of self and other; capacity for concern. (iii) Insight into family functioning and its bearing on difficulties: sense of continuity with past; capacity to make connections.

3 Sense of responsibility and insight

(i) Feels responsibility for difficulties: requires sense of agency and boundedness; ability to tolerate conflict rather than project it.

(ii) Presenting symptoms 'ego-dystonic': especially for personality problems, where must own (rather than reject) both sides of self; especially some contact with pain and dependency.

(iii) Concern for impact on others: tolerate and own ambivalence (loving and hating) to others; others seen as separate with own needs and vulnerabilities.

(iv) Accounts of close relationships in which experiences ambivalence: experience conflict within oneself; face and forgive losses.

4 Continuity of self experience

(i) Therapeutic continuity between early sessions: especially if worked on issues between them; shows able to remain focused and contain distress without falling apart.

(ii) Presents need for privacy to be respected: differentiated degrees of disclosure emerge with deepening rapport; sense of flexible (not brittle) boundedness.

(iii) Therapeutic alliance established at professional level: maintained despite transference pressures; sufficient boundedness to tolerate professional/personal tension and negotiate contract.

3 Lack of responsibility and reflection

(i) Severe disavowal of responsibility for difficulties: other people/circumstances blamed; unable to own any experience that conflicts with this.

(ii) Problem behaviours are 'ego-syntonic': not feel troubled/confronted by own behaviour; defends actions as justifiable; lack of self-reflection.

(iii) Severe lack of insight into defensiveness: destructive defences without anxiety or conflict.

4 Discontinuity of experience and behaviour

(i) Poor impulse control: e.g. serious destructive or self-destructive behaviours; due to rigid splitting defences; aggression not integrated; unable to tolerate conflict and ambivalence.

(ii) Radical discontinuities in experience: very rapid shifts in feeling states; conflicting descriptions of history/ people; large differences between adjoining sessions.

(iii) Premature access to deep states: 'primitive' disorganized feelings/images/impulses readily available; indicating lack of processing and symbolization.

(iv) Unusually deep rapport in first session: result of primitive idealization and weak boundaries; unable to hold onto experiences and conflicts as internal.

Challenging defences, uncovering warded off thoughts and feelings and exploring the interpersonal process have very different effects for people with these differing structures: for someone with a cohesive self, such challenges tend to produce initial anxiety followed by relief; for clients with a precarious self, such challenges tend to result in regression and fragmentation. The therapeutic issue is whether this is tolerable, manageable and productive in any particular therapeutic context. Such reactions can have serious therapeutic consequences and may result in a variety of chronic impasses or breakdowns. Of course, it is important to bear in mind that there are not two different categories of clients – everyone has elements of both cohesiveness and fragmentation: an assessment at any stage should always explore the balance between the client's weaknesses and her strengths. Traps lie in wait during the assessment, however: clients who too easily and quickly show apparently positive signs for therapy – such as getting in touch with feelings and establishing deep rapport – might be demonstrating their relative vulnerability and fragility; they may lack a firmly established sense of appropriate privacy and adequate emotional control. It is possible to do productive work with quite fragile people (even, with appropriate goals, in the short term) if there is sufficient self-cohesion to maintain the alliance with the therapist. However, the therapist's expertise and her personal ability to 'hold' the client during states of regression and dependency are crucial.

Jean, a 23-year-old woman, had recently returned to her home town after travelling abroad for two years. She sought therapy from the counselling centre at the university where she had enrolled, citing a number of issues around depression and her relationship with her parents. At the initial interview, she reported a previous suicide attempt, experiences of cutting her arms, drug use and confusion about her sexual orientation. There was a sense in the session of barely suppressed rage. The clinical picture therefore was of a severely 'borderline' young woman. However, there was a clarity of intent and focus in her request for help, suggestions of insight in her ways of talking about her parents and some capacity to experience and tolerate depression. She had sustained a number of valued commitments (being an activist about environmental concerns) and spoke with affection of a number of friends around the world. On balance, the decision was for an experienced therapist (who felt he could make the necessary commitment) to take her on for the full period of her university course, provided she was able to sustain that. In spite of some self-destructive acting out and one suicide attempt, she persisted with and benefited considerably from the therapy.

It has to be understood that dealing with clients with fragile self-structures:

- is usually difficult;
- involves long-term work;
- requires a high degree of skill, determination and strength in the therapist;
- generally requires good containing structures from the professional system around the therapist.

Consultation is essential and the therapist must confront honestly whether she has the expertise, the motivation and the context needed to see the situation through to a constructive conclusion – indeed, whether that outcome is realistically possible at all.

Forms of impasse with fragile clients

In working with clients who have significantly compromised self-structures, there is a strong possibility of encountering a number of severe and intractable forms of impasse as a consequence of the joint struggles of therapist and client to manage the pressure of painfully disintegrated emotional states. Any chance of resolving these depends on recognizing the difficulties for what they are. The therapist is frequently drawn in to become part of the problem (see Chapter 9). It may well be possible to enable the therapeutic process to move on through skilled work if the therapist can see what is going on and free herself from contributing to the deadlock. She needs to be able to bear the frustration involved and tackle the difficulties thoughtfully.

Psychic retreats

Commonly such clients develop what has been termed a 'psychic retreat' (Steiner, 1993): a way of providing an area of peace and protection which insulates them from meaningful contact with other people. These retreats can take many forms: distance maintained by cold condescension or mocking dismissal; isolation wrapped in self-hatred and destructiveness; unsatisfiable, vengeful demandingness; a false, superficial appearance of interpersonal contact, and so on. Relief from pain and anxiety is 'purchased' at the cost of isolation and stagnation, but this way of functioning is clung to since it has come to seem that any alternative is worse. The client may seem immobilized and inaccessible, or else ventures forth to make contact but immediately withdraws. An impasse develops in which the therapy is stabilizing but not growthful.

Negative therapeutic reaction

Resistance is not intuitively difficult to understand. The negation of the helping process makes sense when the client is having to face distressing truths about herself, make difficult choices in life or try risky new ways of acting. A more puzzling phenomenon is when real therapeutic progress or the relief of distress is met with its reversal, when improvement seems automatically to lead to its negation. This paradoxical response is known as a negative therapeutic reaction. It is as if there is an almost immediate 'relapse' after improvement. The capacity of this reaction to result in an impasse is obvious. Simplifying an extensive literature somewhat, it is possible to distinguish two constellations of conflicts, which seem to contribute to causing clients to respond in this way: firstly, guilt and masochism; and secondly, envy and narcissism. The patterns are not entirely exclusive and individuals may well experience elements of both.

Guilt and masochism

Socialization processes can be distorted by adverse circumstances, resulting in a punitive, intensely guilt-inducing and critical self-concept and a set of values which glorifies suffering. Childhood experiences which result in an intolerable sense of guilt can include events such as the loss of siblings or parents, or a relationship with a mother who is chronically depressed or ill. The child experiences guilt at the imagined damaging effects of her assertive strivings, but may simultaneously feel inadequately cared for and supported, leaving her with an unfulfilled longing for a nurturing relationship so intense that it is experienced as a frightening merger in which she loses independence and identity.

Two general tendencies result from these 'superego' dynamics. One is a fear of success and a parallel pursuit of failure: guilt at worthwhile achievement produces a need for punishment, in which people behave so as to ensure further failure and possibly retribution. This can be seen as related to worries about the damage which can be done through strivings for separation and independent success: these fantasized 'crimes' leave the person feeling unworthy and are reawakened either when some success in life, such as promotion at work, comes along or when the therapist encourages the client to feel more worthwhile. A second version involves the idealization of unhappiness and suffering – a kind of martyr complex, in which the client sacrifices her own needs to those of others, avoids any pleasure and actively maintains and promotes a position of suffering as a means of winning the love and approval of an internalized parent. Obedience to these demands removes the potential for guilt while suffering itself is gratifying through maintaining an approving relationship with the demanding internal figure. Therapy may be experienced as a kind of penance and it becomes important to the client to counteract any indication that it is possible to improve her life since this would result in the loss of security and protection. This 'sado-masochism' functions as a defence against underlying feelings of depression and clients might break down in this way.

Envy and narcissism

Narcissistic difficulties are centrally connected to the fragility of a person's self-esteem. The self is experienced as fundamentally weak and empty and any sense of vulnerability or neediness is threatening and dangerous. There is a fragile balance maintained within the person between helplessness and a compensating grandiosity: some people appear 'touchy' and over-sensitive while others seem remote and difficult to contact. The client feels the process of therapy exposes her weaknesses and forces her to feel helpless, needy and at risk. She is likely to experience the therapist as humiliating her and may need to retaliate and to restore a sense of power and autonomy by triumphing over the therapist. Thus, an intense competitiveness develops in which the client discounts well-intended comments because she experiences them as an attempt by the therapist to show off. The therapist can easily be drawn into this and interpretations may intensify such reactions. This kind of overt competitiveness can be dealt with when it is spotted, by 'backing off' a little and by exploring it at the right time.

In more severe cases there may be hidden envy of the therapist which can lead to subtle destruction of any progress. Any attempt to help evokes this envy which causes the client to disparage and devalue the work being done and her own vulnerable feelings. This wipes out any developing experience of emotional contact. Indeed, any successes are complicated by a sense of sadistic triumph due to this rivalrous element. In this respect, the two strands in negative therapeutic reactions – guilt and envy, masochism and narcissism – can link to one another: the feeling of emptiness leads to envy which can pervade any activity or relationship with a sense of destructiveness and spite leaving the person feeling full of guilt and self-disgust while also provoking fear of retaliation and a sense of persecution which further reduces the possibility of safe contact with others. In these circumstances, the process of safely uncovering and healing a person's underlying experience of hurt, vulnerability and depression is likely to be slow and painstaking at best and always fraught with the risks of therapeutic reversal or breakdown.

Malignant regression

Regression takes place when a person's psychological functioning shifts to a lower level of complexity and differentiation and will often seem to represent the emergence of earlier, more childlike states. Such a process can be part of many forms of change or developmental transition and is regarded as a vital transformative experience by many therapies. An impasse can arise in relation to the client's (or therapist's) fear of letting go and losing control which blocks access both to earlier pain and the opportunity to grow beyond it. It is very possible that the client in therapy will touch on states of mind equivalent to the worst they have ever been (Malan, 1979) and they need the personal strengths and supports which will enable them to go through such a phase in a relatively controlled and productive manner. However, in some clients with fragile self-structures there is the possibility of creating a 'malignant regression' – one which is prolonged and destructive and in which the client loses those capacities for self-observation and therapeutic responsiveness which enable her to work through the experiences which have been revived and to benefit from the regression (Little, 1981). Therapeutic breakdowns of this kind constitute a particularly damaging type of impasse. They take a number of forms: destructive acting out in suicide attempts, violence, impulsive life damaging decisions, or psychotic breakdowns – these constitute a therapeutic crisis and are dealt with in Chapters 3 and 5. They can also become delusional transferences which are unresponsive to therapy; and intractable dependencies in either dramatic or more subtle forms.

Dependency

Psychotherapy and counselling are often accused of 'creating dependency'. Of course, there is no 'creating' about it – people's dependency needs are frequently strong but feared and hidden. Uncovering these feelings is potentially a progressive step but only where they can be worked with in such a way as to enable the client to manage the experience of interrelatedness better. Feelings of dependency are quite likely to develop in any therapeutic relationship however brief, but longer and more intense therapies will increase this and technique has a crucial influence.

Long-term therapeutic relationships may be helpfully supportive but too often constitute a subtle, unrecognized impasse in which little developmental work is done – both client and therapist feel gratified by the mutual attention which they offer each other. Much more obviously damaging, however, are malignant regressive dependencies in which the therapy is taken over by an intense demandingness in the client who insistently seeks love and esteem from the therapist in the form of some concrete action, doing or giving something to prove that love. These gratifications are never enough and the client's state of mind seems to be one of addictive craving. The therapist may be pressed to extend the boundaries in various ways – lengthening or rescheduling sessions; making concessions on fees; permitting out of session contact or social encounters; hugging and giving gifts. Many of these activities can have their rationale, particularly in humanistically oriented work. However, in such situations there is intense pressure: the client can display extreme suffering and vituperation if not gratified; if the therapist complies it feels like an intensely and mutually rewarding experience. This situation tends to occur in people who have experienced severe childhood deprivation and it evokes in the therapist a desire to make up for what the client never had, to 're-parent' her. Some theorists support this point of view (Schiff, 1975) but going down this road is courting disaster.

Rosemary, a nurse in her late 30s, sought therapy from a humanistically oriented counsellor. While very capable at work, she had experienced many somatic complaints and was subject to episodes of depression. She reported a very distressing personal history: a chronically sick mother who had died when she was 11 years old and a father who had physically abused them both before leaving the family when she was six years old; she had been in foster care and stayed with various relatives and had been sexually abused in her early teens. The therapist, a charismatic woman in her 40s, provided a great deal of warmth and displayed obvious concern for Rosemary, whilst also using emotionally intensifying cathartic techniques to help her get in touch with her rage and her neediness. Rosemary responded with intense gratitude to the sense of care and relative safety; she attempted to do the work her therapist wanted and after six months applied to train as a counsellor herself. Subsequently, she started to become more childlike in sessions and this was encouraged as getting in touch with her true feelings. She started becoming more demanding, asking questions which the therapist answered and making phone calls which the therapist thought it appropriate to respond to. However, these demands began to escalate with constant calls and intrusions into the therapist's personal and professional life. The therapist started to become both alarmed and irritated and pushed Rosemary to 'take more responsibility for herself'. She tried to draw boundaries, ordering her client to stop making phone calls and refusing recognition outside of sessions. Rosemary felt intense distress and confusion, trying to comply with her therapist's wishes but also feeling compelled to telephone and driven to meet her in various ways. The therapist finally ended the work with three weeks notice, saying that she had done all she could do. Two weeks after the termination, Rosemary took a serious overdose and was admitted to the local psychiatric hospital where she stayed for three months.

Need or neediness

Where there is a regression towards a benign and developmental dependent state, it is important that the therapist accept, understand and be capable of 'carrying' the client for some time, providing her with the experience of being safely watched over. This recognition of need can allow the necessary mourning of what was not available in childhood, rather than embarking on a hopeless mission to make up for it. The distinction between need and neediness (Ghent, 1993) may clarify these distinct therapeutic situations. When a child's needs are responded to with neglect or punishment, they become dissociated; it being impossible to express them directly, they then continue to go unmet; this is experienced in part as an injustice, filled with resentment and indignation; the individual comes to have a sense of entitlement to compensation for the deprivation which she suffered. While this looks like 'need', it is largely an expression of rage and its demand-ingness has a vengeful quality. In this situation, the client presses and manipulates to get immediate satisfaction or provokes alienation and so confirms her state of deprivation. Clients who are needy in this way are dominated by resentment and a sense of grievance and it is this hostile element which has to be faced and survived rather than 'bought off', while remaining sensitive to signs of emergence of the underlying state of vulnerability and need. All such situations require the working through of loss – the childhood that was not available – which means that both grief and anger must be encountered without short-circuiting either.

Fragile self-states where revenge is to the fore can result in an insistent demand for compensation and life being dominated by a sense of injustice.

It provides a life focus through an endless search for revenge while living 'in hope' of future redress. The sense of grievance is kept alive because it defends against the experience of loss and mourning. Such states are hard to work with and are almost certain to result in impasse where there is a real claim for compensation being pursued. Unfortunately, one way in which therapies break down when it has not been possible to face the rage hidden in the idealization of the gratifying therapist, is for the client to be finally rejected. Sometimes this results in the client pursuing a vengeful complaint against her therapist.

Psychotic reactions

Full psychotic breakdowns constitute a clear therapeutic crisis in which other resources must be called upon – probably involving the psychiatric services and possible hospitalization. Occasionally regressions of this kind, if well handled by an experienced psychotherapist, can be developmentally helpful (Boyer, 1983). However, even brief non-recurrent psychotic episodes can have a deeply traumatic effect on the individual, leaving them much less secure with their own inner worlds. Preventative measures – assessing the risk, spotting early signs and helping to reduce pressure – are preferable in most cases. This is equally true of those psychotic-like phenomena which take place within and in relation to the therapeutic situation – situations of 'delusional transference' in which grossly unrealistic and inappropriate perceptions of the therapist are formed. The client loses sight of the professional role of the therapist and can no longer maintain a self-observational capacity, the 'as if' quality of the therapeutic relationship: the sense of the therapist as therapist is lost. Perhaps the classic form of this is the erotic transference in which the client falls in love with the therapist and may seek signs that this love is returned. Delusional, paranoid or jealous convictions may also develop in parallel or as an alternative. In some cases, these damaging forms of impasse result – insofar as they can be understood – from the therapist's unwillingness or inability to effectively address the client's frustration and anger, both past and present, and bring it into the therapeutic relationship in a manageable form. From this point of view, psychotic phenomena of this kind are desperate self-destructive defences against unmanageable feelings, particularly rage. Bellak (1981) suggests bringing in an 'auxiliary therapist' as an emergency measure to address these impasses by focusing on the client's relationship to the therapist from a fresh perspective.

Selecting the therapeutic strategy

A common problem in psychotherapy is over-attachment to a single therapeutic theory and technique: this may be a significant cause of impasse. Typically, clients are then blamed for being resistant or unmotivated for (our particular form of) therapy. Therapists should rather consider how they may be being inflexible and not imagine that they are always the best people to work with every client. The focus in assessment should be on the responsibility of the therapist to negotiate and guide towards an appropriate contract of therapy for this individual person. We should be selecting appropriate interventions rather than 'suitable' clients. This does not mean that every practitioner should be able to do every kind of therapy. The value of an orienting theoretical framework which provides discipline and containment for the therapist is widely acknowledged – each practitioner should consider the flexibility and breadth of approach which they can accommodate within their theoretical base. However, there is also a need for a framework to guide judgements about selecting the therapeutic strategy so as to match therapeutic format and style to the needs of an individual client.

Much of the decision-making around therapeutic strategy, particularly in relation to clients with fragile self-structures, can be thought of in relation to choosing 'supportive' or 'expressive' therapeutic approaches. It is important to be clear that these are not two 'types' of therapy but a continuum. The distinction is probably best considered a shorthand for combining several overlapping dimensions of technique, each of which can be varied to meet the needs of individual clients. These are outlined in Table 8.4. This continuum is related to the goals of the therapeutic work – whether to aim for a more extensive and fundamental psychological change or for a more limited stabilization and adaptation within a current life structure. However, the degree of change possible from supportive work should not be underestimated: it may be a matter of pace and the time-frame over which elements of the self can be retrieved or developed. Nonetheless, a quicker pace and more ambitious goals carry greater risks of both impasse and breakdown.

TABLE 8.4   *Dimensions of support and exploration*

Supportive	Expressive
Structured	'Free form'
Active	Passive
Didactic	Exploratory
Reflect feelings	Interpret/deepen feelings
Clarify what is consciously known	Seek what is out-of-awareness
Modulate feelings	Deepen experience of feelings
Greater therapist transparency	'Opaque' therapist
Focus on current problems	Focus on past hurts
Focus on relationships 'out there'	Focus on transference
Focus on 'there and then' feelings	From on 'here and now' feelings
Less frequent sessions	More frequent sessions
Shorter sessions	Longer sessions
Slow pace	Fast pace

One way to approach these issues is to acknowledge that in expressive therapies (as opposed to more supportive or structured work) we are, in a sense, inviting the client to 'break down'. Past pain and anxiety may well be experienced in the here and now of the therapy. We must ask what this experience will mean for each particular client, and whether it can be contained within the frame of this therapy. This requires crucial judgements to be made about the safety of the therapy as outlined above in relation to regression. The risks must be appraised in the context of three factors:

● the client's ego-strength, resources, capacity to bear stress and sustain relationships;
● the degree of social support available from the environment naturally, or which can be provided in addition by the formal care system;
● the capacity of the therapist and the professional system surrounding her to bear and cope with this disturbance.

The technical judgement which must be made is whether it is possible to provide the minimum therapeutic setting needed to contain the potential disturbance safely and productively rather than for it to escalate into a breakdown or freeze as an impasse.

These choices can be considered in terms of the therapeutic alliance (see Chapter 7). Clients with more fragile self-structures tend to have more difficulty forming an alliance. The *weaker* the alliance, the *more supportive* the therapy has to be – in effect what is being 'supported' is the maintenance of the alliance. Often this means both reducing the demandingness of therapeutic tasks and goals and also increasing the security of the interpersonal bond with the therapist – but without colluding with the client's resistant wish not to change at all. With each individual, sustaining the alliance has to be managed in terms of the particular strengths and vulnerabilities of that person. Therapeutic format and style may need to be readjusted in order to find a way out of an impasse and to discover the most productive way of working with a particular client.

A number of other considerations should be taken into account in choosing the therapeutic format most likely to be safe and successful. Increasingly, there is a professional and institutional expectation, particularly in the public services, that therapeutic choices are based on evidence of what is likely to be the most effective approach for a specific problem. Roth and Fonagy (1996) review good quality psychotherapy trials in a comprehensive effort to identify demonstrably effective therapies for a range of psychological disorders, classified according to the DSM-IV diagnostic system (APA, 1994). They are able to find indicative evidence that certain disorders do respond specifically to certain structured approaches. In spite of the limitations of the research evidence, it does now appear appropriate to use such techniques, often cognitive-behavioural ones, as the strategy of choice for certain presenting problems – or at least to adopt them as the initial approach. If an impasse develops with these techniques, then other approaches could be considered, based on the more detailed understanding then available. On the basis of detailed work assessing both research evidence and the current professional consensus about good practice, clinical guidelines and referral protocols have been developed for initial therapeutic 'disposition' on the basis of problem type and complexity (Parry, 1998).

Generally, however, the broad personal characteristics of clients do not seem strongly to predict outcome within therapy types (Garfield, 1994) and, certainly, psychiatric diagnosis is a very coarse categorization for therapeutic purposes. The most hopeful approach to analysing what creates or prevents therapeutic failure is to consider the ways in which therapeutic style and technique interact with client characteristics in such a way as to strengthen and promote the working alliance or, on the contrary, to put a strain on it so as to eventually undermine it, leading to impasse. For example, Hutchins (1984) discusses the effects of the style and preferences of client and therapist in their modes of experiencing and communicating and the need for synchrony in their use of thinking, feeling and action orientations.

Chris, a businessman in his 30s, started to experience panic attacks with increasing frequency. His GP referred him to the local behaviour therapy service but he did not return after the first session. He told his GP that he really wanted to 'think things through' and 'get his ideas together' about where his life was going. He repeated these rather vague sentiments to the person-centred counsellor in the Health Centre who agreed to take him on. After five sessions of trying to help him get in touch with his feelings about various aspects of his career and a new love relationship, the counsellor felt she was getting nowhere – her client remained suspicious and the sessions seemed superficial. She discussed this frankly with the client, who told her he appreciated not being 'pushed around' the way he felt the behaviour therapist had done, but that he really couldn't take on board this 'touchy-feely stuff'. Respecting what he had to say, the counsellor discussed with him the way forward. They agreed to try some written exercises and then discuss these in sessions and to try to 'understand his ways of thinking' as a first step. She drew on a recent course on personal-construct therapy and techniques for exploring his conceptual world. Over the next six sessions, he disclosed how the emotional neglect and bullying he had suffered as a child had affected his attitudes and beliefs about intimacy and agreed a further six sessions to work on this.

Beutler and Harwood (2000) have proposed an integrative model of treatment selection which attempts to provide structured guidance on how to tailor therapeutic strategies to the needs of individual clients. The client characteristics which influence choice of therapeutic style are detailed in Table 8.5. They adapt the form and style of therapeutic response to match the needs of the client by 'going with the grain', rather than putting excessive strain on the alliance and creating unnecessary resistance by

TABLE 8.5 *Matching therapeutic strategies to clients*

I	Problem complexity	Therapeutic targets
	Complex, severe adjustment patterns	► Broad conflict or cognitive assumptions focus
	Simple, single symptoms/problem	► Narrow symptom or problem-solving focus
II	**Coping style**	**Experiential mode**
	Externalizing	► Behaviour or problem focus
	Internalizing	► Affective focus
		Cognitive focus may act as bridging technique
III	**Locus of control**	**Therapeutic style**
	High reactance/need to maintain control	► Exploratory, collaborative, low directiveness
	Low reactance/wishing to cede control	► Structuring, authoritative, high directiveness
IV	**Level of impairment**	
	High arousal/anxiety/disorganized	► Supportive, non-confrontive, holding
	Low arousal/well organized	► Confrontive, expressive, demanding

Source: Adapted from Beutler and Clarkin, 1990

expecting the client to adapt excessively to the therapeutic model. Mismatches are likely to lead to relationship ruptures and a struggle by the client to create the kind of response from the therapist which she expects. The client's expressed preferences are obviously also an important guide – but once again a judgement may need to be made about whether they are based on an implicit wisdom about her needs or a resistant desire to avoid a necessary challenge. Matching at the level of the individual client and therapist may also be important in terms of the developmental opportunities for relating which a therapist offers by virtue of her unique personality characteristics. Mismatches at this level may create damaging impasses (see Chapter 9) – but there are few guidelines for predicting the subtle interactional 'chemistry' involved.

Conclusion

Providing a trial of the therapeutic approach in the early sessions allows the therapist to test out the suitability of a given style of work and gives the client the opportunity to make an informed choice: this can be an effective means of discovering what is likely to suit a particular individual. Adopting a tentative and negotiative stance from the beginning may allow the therapist to adapt her approach in response to the client's explicit preferences and a judgement of her needs. Changing the therapeutic strategy, however, is still a complex undertaking and should be done only on the basis of a considered reassessment of the client's needs and capabilities, rather than simply out of frustration. It must be managed in a collaborative way and with openness to the implicit feedback provided by how the client responds to the changes. The therapist must be continuously alert to what such proposed or actual alterations in strategy might mean to the client's perception of the therapeutic relationship.

9   Impasse in the Interaction

An impasse is always mediated by the therapeutic relationship: whatever the main source of the block it will be expressed and experienced through the interaction between therapist and client. The client hopes for, but in some measure dreads, change; the therapist works for change by maintaining the alliance while trying to stay productively focused on her awareness of the forces of resistance. An impasse threatens when the flexible equilibrium within the interaction between alliance and resistance is lost more than momentarily. Not only is the client unwilling or unable to move forward in the face of an experience which is too intense or alien to be accommodated, the therapist too has lost her balance. The therapist in a productive interaction has an 'equilibrating' function, facilitating the client's contact with experiences which are painful, frightening or new, but keeping these within manageable limits. This depends on the therapist's own ability to negotiate emotionally charged experiences and challenging or confusing personal interactions. An impasse is manifested in her loss of balance in this area. An experience of 'counter-resistance' is virtually always hidden at the core of an impasse.

Resistance and the therapeutic relationship

In thinking about impasse, we have placed an emphasis on the qualities of collaboration and negotiation. It is essential not to overvalue rationality in resolving breakdowns in this process or to place too much reliance on direct discussion. Collaboration is not solely – perhaps not even mainly – a conscious process undertaken explicitly and in words. Much of the meaning of an interaction is implicit, latent within the quality and feeling tone of the therapeutic conversation. At one level, the implicit balance of resistance and resolution gives a sense of the therapist and client working jointly, perhaps in a way that is personally demanding but still collaborating on problems the client brings. At another, the meaning given to the joint experience – the meaning of the relationship itself – is being worked out.

Ruptures and deadlocks in this process of collaboration have many sources. Some can be addressed through strengthening conscious collaboration around tasks and goals (see Chapter 7). However, many of the ways that the balance of collaboration breaks down are bound up with emotionally charged concerns, often partly out of awareness, which are triggered within the relationship between client and therapist. Indeed, there is an intimate interdependence of these technical and relationship factors. The quality of the bond mediates the process of negotiating tasks and goals and vice versa (Safran and Muran, 2000). The meaning of any technical intervention depends on the interpersonal context in which it is applied. The quality of this process of working together *is* the therapeutic relationship. This conversation embodies the forces of both alliance and resistance. It is dynamic and reciprocal at both conscious and unconscious levels and it establishes the conditions for change.

Margaret, a young woman who had been sexually abused in her early adolescence, had already received 12 sessions of counselling about these experiences and felt that this was sufficient at this time. However, she wished to receive further help with some remaining agoraphobic symptoms. The therapist responded by changing to a more directive technique in which she asked the client to keep diaries of her experience as she undertook agreed homework assignments. After two sessions the client did not return, worrying the therapist that she had put on too much pressure. She was able to persuade the client to attend to discuss the issue and found her frightened and suspicious. Sharing this perception, they were able to talk about how intruded on, exposed and out of control Margaret had felt. The therapist seemed to transform in her mind from a helpful and protective figure to an abusive one. Two further sessions were spent relating this frightening 'transference' experience to her past experience and expectations of abuse. Shared consideration was then given to how the client could feel more in control of the programme of homework tasks.

Many traditions of psychotherapy place the therapeutic relationship centre stage. The emotionally charged personal interactions between therapist and client are either the main vehicle or a crucial component of the change process. However, there are problems in discussing this area due to the extensive differences in vocabulary between the different traditions, some marking a significant divergence of stance, others more of appearance than reality. The psychodynamic tradition has the most extensive and well-articulated literature on this area and current 'relational' models (Mitchell, 1988) integrate thinking from a wide variety of analtyic and other sources in ways which remain close to clinical experience. Ideas about impasse framed in these terms should be accessible to practitioners from a range of therapeutic traditions.

There is an intimate relationship, in this view, between the interpersonal and the intra-psychic. Our experience of ourselves and of the world is developed primarily through our relationships with other people. Our sense of self is created as a cognitive-affective schema – a template of interpretation and action – which defines the 'self-other' relationship (Safran and Segal, 1990). Research on infant and child development helps us understand better the crucial role of the child's attachment to caretakers and of their emotional attunement to its needs (Bowlby, 1988; Stern, 1985). Persistent misattunement whether through subtle distortions of communication or gross neglect, deprivation and abuse results in areas of experience being cut-off – dissociated – distorting the experience of self in order to maintain a viable, acceptable relationship with significant others. These patterns of self-experience and relationship shape subsequent behaviour in other social contexts. To the extent that they are charged with anxiety, they are rigid and do not flexibly adapt to the range of relational possibilities. These distortions form the foundation of many of the interpersonal and symptomatic problems which are the 'life impasses' for which people seek therapeutic help.

Anne, a 29-year-old nurse, sought therapy for the depression and emptiness she felt after a series of unsatisfactory relationships with men. She had grown up with a mother who was often depressed and in need of care and comfort. Anne became a helpful daughter but turned to her father for a sense of being loved and valued. When he left the marriage for another woman when Anne was 12, she felt alternately desolate and furious and kept only distant contact with him. For the first ten sessions of weekly therapy Anne was compliant, considerate and eager to please the therapist but he felt irritated, stifled in his efforts to be helpful and shut out from the distress for which Anne had sought help. After the first holiday break she seemed to become a different person, being by turns dismissively rude or silent in sessions. The therapist felt even more distant and distracted. Anne missed several appointments and when the therapist insisted on payment for them, pointing out with some annoyance that this was agreed in their contract, she did not return. Both therapist and client were left feeling hurt and confused.

This example of a therapeutic failure may seem obvious as it is recounted – a clear example of 'transference' – but it would be much more confusing to be part of. It draws attention to three further, crucial components of a relational perspective; the ways in which:

- past relationship patterns form the basis of current ones and how these are frequently re-enacted in the therapeutic context;
- 'vicious cycles' are provoked within relationships which confirm our worst fears and perpetuate a distorted conception;
- therapists are almost inevitably drawn into participating, to some degree, in those patterns.

In considering the development of an impasse, close attention to the emotionally charged and anxiety-laden elements of the client's relationship with the therapist will cast a clearer light on how the process has become stuck (Strean, 1985). These issues will be explored below. We shall deal initially with the anxieties and resistances presented in the interpersonal context of therapy, first by the client and then reciprocally by the therapist.

We then move on to deal with the ways these interactively form the creative context of the therapeutic relationship: within this, the 'same old' impasses arise for the client but with the possibility of discovering a new resolution.

Responding to interpersonal resistances

Resistance, the sum of the forces opposing change, inexorably finds its expression within the interpersonal field of the therapeutic relationship. Resistance is both defensive and adaptive, simultaneously a means of avoiding painful experiences and of sustaining a viable form of relationship. The therapist needs to respect the client's struggles and to search for understanding. Within the resistance are the seeds of therapeutic knowledge and of transformation. However, resistance is an effort *not to know*. The status quo is maintained by disowning painful elements of the person's experience and denying frightening interpersonal realities. People cling to these distortions, repeating and maintaining the familiar painful impasses within their lives. In a sense, there is a failure to grieve – to let go of these illusory protective convictions and face the real losses, failures, frustrations and dissatisfactions which they have suffered. In confronting resistance, the therapist is often faced with a kind of pseudo-grief – feeling sorry for oneself, feeling victimized, blaming others, feeling depressed – in which there is an insistence that things should be different than they are (or were). It is difficult for all of us to move into the realm of interpersonal risk and to lose our familiar refuges.

Cataloguing the major anxieties which clients bring on entering therapy, however, can amount to a round-up of the 'usual suspects'. People fear:

- shame and exposure of fantasies, impulses and vulnerabilities;
- intimacy which may be experienced as submission, dependence or sexual excitement;
- dependency, passivity, or helplessness;
- merger and loss of identity;
- aggression – anger, destructiveness, and the damage one might do;
- criticism, blame and guilt;
- humiliation – being demeaned, shamed or despised;
- rejection – being invalidated or not accepted;
- abandonment – being left alone or left out;
- competition, jealousy and envy.

Such a list is inevitably simplistic and stereotypes what needs to be understood within the richness of each individual's lived experience but it serves to remind us what is at stake for clients when they enter the therapy room. Overall, these anxieties are about a vulnerable 'regressive' state of mind being actualized in the therapeutic relationship.

Typically, clients 'manoeuvre' to get the therapist to do something which interrupts the fuller emergence of these fears. Fine (1982) divides the pressures that the resistance creates into two types: pressures to change the frame or tasks of therapy; and subtle interpersonal pressures in the interaction. Common forms of these are outlined in Tables 9.1 and 9.2. The tendency is for the therapist to collude subtly with the avoidance and so have an impasse-promoting effect, either deadening the process or simply escalating the anxiety. What is needed is for the therapist to communicate her understanding and acceptance of the resistance. This requires confidence in the therapy being offered and not being frightened by the client's fears: the anxiety probably needs to be made explicit. It means overcoming the magical idea that if you talk about these things then it's just like carrying them out. Therapist errors are of course common in these circumstances (see Tables 9.1 and 9.2). These pressures cause us to make errors in technique which the most basic counselling training teaches us to avoid. We can be drawn in to advising, reassuring, praising, approving or criticizing. There are many ways to get it wrong. Fundamentally, perhaps, the common problem is ignoring the probability that the client is avoiding something – the therapist may fear the potential hostility or distress created by bringing it into the open. The difficult issue is to be able to stay focused on and keep working with these interpersonal expressions of resistance – to be aware of them and explore them within the context of each client's ability to keep anxiety within tolerable limits.

To find a way through the impasse, what is needed is for the therapist to regain her balance, staying empathically close to the client while holding the resistance in view as the focus of her work. The balance sought is one between the need to challenge the resistance and the need to accept it. This parallels the fragile equilibrium within the client: the conflict between the pain and anxiety that is warded off and the fuller sense of self and relationship that is sought; between the pain and limitation created by the distortions and the safety achieved in the only way that is known. A helpful shorthand is to divide this work with resistance into two alternative tactics (Stark, 1994) – confrontating or joining:

1 *Confronting* – here attention is drawn to the implications of what the client is doing as resistant; these are explored and clarified and an understanding arrived at which illuminates what is latent in the client's experience, her anxieties and longings; the opportunity is thus provided to elaborate these further, make links to other areas and work through the issues.
2 *Joining* – the therapist silently identifies to herself that the client's actions are resistant; rather than challenging this, she gives an empathic characterization of resistance, noting that it is something the client needs to do and has value for her at this time; this indicates an acceptance of the validity of the resistance but with a paradoxical quality that implies the situation will change.

TABLE 9.1 *Resistance through pressure on frame and tasks*

Behaviour	Possible implicit meanings	Therapist response errors
1 Persistent lateness	Mistrust/anger; Submission/ rebellion; Maintain distance Diminish therapy importance	Admonish Indulge
2 Persistent cancellation	Avoid anxiety of encounter as above but more pressing	Fail to challenge/charge full fee – and so: Appear to condone Seem to have no personal/ professional needs. Afraid of client's hostility
3 Phone contact: 'arranged' issues	Unable to bear separation Craving love/attention Romantic attachment Reassure that therapist is alive (= possible rage)	Avoid issues not being dealt with in sessions Reject rigidly – fail to deal with real issues (should listen briefly and 'refer' to next session)
4 Require additional sessions	As above	Give in readily versus refuse rigidly
5 Arrange extra-therapeutic contacts	Voyeurism/curiosity Exhibitionistic display Desire special/unique relationship	Participate in those wishes Stimulating or defensively avoiding contact
6 Reluctance to pay fees	Wish to feel cared for (unconditionally) Wish to feel special; Rebel against arbitrary parental demands; Humiliation at having to pay/'prostitution'	Accept and so reinforce the infantilization Fail to set date to end (after exploration)
7 Keeping secrets	Shame of exposure (Sense of power/triumph) Fear of intrusion	Focus on finding out Ignore feeling of relationship created
8 Prolonged silences	Defiance Passivity Fear of fantasy/feeling Fear of lack of interest	Impatience Succumb to boredom (should find out what 'talking' means)
9 Persistent demands: ask questions, prolong sessions etc.	Powerlessness/turning tables Unable to bear frustration/insist on gratification	Be forced to gratify Ignore implicit threats
10 Ask for new therapeutic modality/medic-ation	Test confidence/competence and strength of holding Disparage therapist/work	Comply Ignore aggression Fail to review (internally) and restore own confidence
11 Ask for consultation with other therapist	Humiliate or intimidate therapist Provoke criticism	Prohibit Act defensive or scared

TABLE 9.2   *Subtle interpersonal resistances*

Behaviour	Possible implicit meaning	Therapist response errors
1 Compliance: pleasure to treat but no change	Defiant Masochistic	Ignore lack of progress Irritation
2 Exploring reality issues only	Fear of revealing inner world and of closeness Victim position gratifies Relieved of responsibility	Pushing to reveal self Insist that client 'accept responsibility' Attempting to problem solve for the client
3 Exploring dreams and fantasies	Avoids daily reality Relieved of responsibility	Become fascinated Confront with 'hard facts'
4 Intellectualizing	Fear of loss, out of control of emotion Fear of being overwhelmed/ engulfed	Argue Philosophise together Irritation Fail to notice fragility
5 Over-emoting	Being rescued/infantilism Masochism Exhibitionism	Persist in seeking catharsis Paralysis and voyeurism Comfort Fail to promote thinking
6 Somatizing	Avoid inner world/feelings Secondary gains and masochism	Insist it is psychological Fail to accept how they experience distress
7 Confusion/not understanding	Resentment/competition Fearing being controlled/taken over Feels chronically misunderstood	Paralysis Fail to enquire about feelings in here and now
8 Negative therapeutic reaction (see Chapter 7)	Revenge/defiance Masochism, envy, hopelessness	Demoralization Fail to see pattern
9 Refers other clients	Express care/gratitude Placate/engratiate Become colleague Refer to hidden part of selves	Accept gratefully! Reject without exploration

Thus, in the case of a young man in his fifth session with an older woman therapist who has observed that he has looked around the room rather suspiciously, spoken reticently and kept asking questions about her, it might be possible to say: 'It seems that you are feeling quite suspicious, perhaps of me and my motives. You may even be worried that I will betray you in some way'. And perhaps go on to elaborate: 'You may feel that I am going to exploit you'. And even add 'The way you felt your mother did'. However, it may be better in the circumstances to attempt to empathically join his anxiety saying: 'I wonder if you are feeling quite mistrustful of me; in a way I have not really earned your trust yet and it is probably wise from your point of view to hold back a bit'. It may be clear from this example that provided the therapist is aiming to be empathic, the distinction between confronting and joining the client is not clear-cut but it is tactically useful to be aware of the different emphases available. A less 'interpretative' style of exploration would phrase interventions differently and invite more work by the client, but the distinction is still applicable. The underlying issue is that is that focusing too directly on resistance can sometimes heighten it and so compromise collaboration and the sense of emotional safety. Joining the client is frequently a crucial move in resolving an impasse in which the interaction has become fearful and combative.

The therapist's counter-reactions

The roots of therapeutic impasse are often embedded deep in the ground of the therapist's personal responses. She is frequently drawn to participate in relationships in ways that perpetuate the stuckness. This means that ways of identifying and articulating her reactions are a powerful tool for facilitating movement in stuck situations. Clarity of awareness about emotionally charged responses is at least as useful to the therapist as it can be to the client. The person-centred 'core condition' of therapist 'congruence' addresses precisely this issue. However, two significant obstacles lie in the way: terminology in this area is particularly muddled; and the culture surrounding professional discussion of the issues is often lacking in real frankness. The common term – counter-transference – is derived from psychoanalytic theory but used much more widely so that its theoretical underpinnings have all but disappeared. The way it is used and its technical application is multiple and confused. The term 'counter-reaction' might be proposed as being less encumbered by theory and more clearly applied to the full range of the therapist's responses to her client, but it is likely that counter-transference will continue to be the word most commonly employed for this vital dimension of the therapeutic relationship.

It is helpful to distinguish between 'objective' and 'subjective' counter-transferences: that is, whether the major contribution to the therapist's response stems from some way in which the client is acting or feeling, or from the therapist's own issues in the relationship (Racker, 1968). The *objective* counter-transference can be viewed as a vital source of information to be used in the work: this perspective will be dealt with in a subsequent section. *Subjective* counter-reactions are what was originally meant by the term counter-transference – the therapist's own personal history, emotional vulnerabilities, automatic assumptions and customary defensive distortions are mobilized in response to a particular client's material – her 'buttons are pressed', in the common usage. To the extent that the therapist's reactions are mostly defensive and tend to involve ignoring or invalidating or deadening what the client is bringing, this counter-reaction has come to be known as 'counter-resistance' (Schoenewolf, 1993; Strean, 1993). Signs of this could be excessive silence, changing the subject, intellectualizing, reassuring, being over solicitous, being bored, over-supporting, failing to confront and so on. An impasse is created because the therapist can't bear her client's pain (presumably because it is too close to her own) and so deflects the client from focusing on what needs to be brought into awareness. Such counter-resistances are, of course, usually out of the awareness of the therapist and are often justified and covered over by the use of some technical rationale. More obtrusive counter-resistances result in therapists breaking basic ground rules – being late, forgetting sessions, prolonging sessions – but the significance and relevance of these lapses may simply be overlooked.

When a subjective counter-reaction seems to involve more of an active distortion of how the client is perceived, the 'counter-transferential' (rather than the counter-resistant) elements of the situation are more to the fore. The therapist seems to relate to her client in ways driven by pre-existing assumptions and patterns in which some fantasy-laden internal drama is set in motion; it may perhaps be possible to relate this quite directly to significant figures and relationships in the therapist's own personal history. The intensity of the therapeutic situation has potentiated an emotionally charged reaction from the therapist which seems to have more to do with her own needs and fears than with those of the client. Such counter-transferential responses can either result in intense emotional reactions in the therapist or be transformed into some enactment within the therapeutic relationship. Where this goes unchecked over a number of sessions, it can result not only in stalemate but in the most damaging kinds of therapeutic breakdown. The client may experience not merely frustration and disappointment but be subject to a traumatic reliving of feared situations, coloured by the present day emotional charge supplied by the therapist's own over-involvement.

Andrew had been rather depressed for a couple of years and was experiencing marital conflicts, sexual impotence and heavy drinking. He had felt greatly helped by his therapist Brian whose interest had strengthened him and helped him be more in control of his behaviour. Indeed, he came to express admiration in the sessions and to extol Brian's qualities to friends. He started to run down other people at work, saying that his bosses were smug know-alls and when Brian refused to side with him in this dispute, Andrew lost his temper and did not come to the next session. Andrew was superficially apologetic on his return but continued to make criticisms of various people in his life while Brian felt rather aloof and remote, wondering if the criticisms were of him, but feeling they were unwarranted. Andrew started an extra-marital affair, recounting this in therapy in an excited, boastful way. Brian was critical of this 'acting out'. In fact, Brian was struggling with a number of issues himself, particularly with his father's current illness which made it difficult for him to deal with his long-term resentments towards him. There was a good deal of competitiveness in his supervisory relationship too and he tended to think of his supervisor as smug and over-clever. In the therapy, Brian would alternate between being critical of Andrew's behaviour and being rather intellectual about this 'phase of his development'. He was never able to deal with the anger Andrew felt towards him, or the competitiveness that was growing between them. Andrew's marriage collapsed and he felt overwhelmed by guilt and depression once again.

Areas in which therapists are vulnerable to subjective counter-transference reactions span the full range of potential difficulties. From a psycho-dynamic point of view, these responses most obviously include those such as:

- Aggression and hostility – in which some power struggle might develop with attempts to dominate, manipulate or control the client or else to submit to her and to feel controlled, persecuted and powerless.
- Sexuality and eroticism – in which a degree of mutual seductiveness develops, ranging from efforts to please each other through flirtatious-ness and more or less subtle sexualization and voyeurism all the way through to some overt sexual behaviour.
- Narcissism and dependency – in which a sense of low self-esteem and emptiness is avoided through one person being idealized (usually of course the therapist, though this can happen with certain clients) with the relationship becoming an essential prop to both parties.

These types of distortion of the therapeutic relationship are probably quite common and versions of them underlie many impasses, both those which are recognized as such and ones which are not (Robertiello and Schoenewolf, 1987). They are most likely to happen where there is some pathological fit between the vulnerabilities of the client and those of the therapist (Elkind, 1992).

A useful distinction can be made between what might be called 'situational' and 'characterological' counter-transferences. In the *situational* response, some distorting reaction of the therapist's arises substantially in response to something specific about the client's material and to that phase in the therapeutic process; an area of vulnerability in the therapist, nor-mally adequately protected or dealt with, is touched upon and the counter-transference reaction is 'ignited'. For example, a therapist may find herself passive or placatory to a subtly intimidating male client who has triggered something from her relationship with her authoritarian father. This is obviously close to an objective counter-transference and carries the poten-tial to be converted into one. It signals something difficult for the client and can be tracked back to that, but only after it is mastered through internal work by the therapist. The capability to become aware of and to process situational counter-transferences is one which is built and enhanced through the process of training and personal therapy. It requires an ability to contain strong feelings rather than be overwhelmed or propelled into action by them; the security to be aware of pain and anxiety rather than to defend against it; and the capacity for creating some distance from your responses in order to reflect upon them. Such abilities are always under pressure in therapeutic situations and they frequently require the added distance and awareness which supervision can provide.

Recognizing the therapist's vulnerability

Characterological counter-transferences are more problematic. These are 'ways of being' in therapeutic situations which typify distortions and restrictions in the therapist's overall approach, appearing repeatedly in stereotyped forms with many clients. For example, a therapist may have difficulties dealing with confrontation and anger generally, and adopt a conciliatory style throughout her work. These various characterological counter-reactions may be strong and pervasive or be a mild vulnerability intensified under particular pressure (pressure which may be intrinsic to the therapy itself or may be quite external, stemming from stresses and events in the therapist's life – see Chapter 13). In fact, they draw attention to the crucial issue of the ordinary human vulnerability of every therapist.

Such vulnerabilities will frequently be related to the very reasons we have chosen to do this kind of work. There are a variety of dubious benefits to be derived from the role of therapist and these fit a range of neurotic needs, emotional limitations and defensive patterns (Sussman, 1992). Some of the commonest of these dysfunctional motivations and the therapeutic dangers which they give rise to are outlined in Table 9.3. They are so pervasive that, in effect, every practitioner may be able to identify some elements of more than one of these patterns as forming some part of their own motives for undertaking the role. Such a listing is therefore a starting point for reviewing our own vulnerabilities to particular counter-reactions. The commonness of such motivations suggests that personal therapy is an essential part of preparation for anyone taking on the role, whatever their model of practice.

Unfortunately, the individual choice of a theoretical perspective and our affinity for it – something often strengthened by our relationship with a personal therapist – can in itself have the quality of a pervasive counter-transference, limiting each therapist's ability to respond flexibly and adaptively to the needs of individual clients. Factionalism, idealization of 'gurus' and denigration of professional enemies become part of our professional selves in ways which are particularly hard to see beyond. What is most needed from professional cultures – and which is often lacking – is encouragement and support for therapists' acceptance of themselves. This is what enables the open discussion of counter-transferences in their fullness and complexity. An honest examination of our responses in the role of therapist reveals many ways in which we are not pleasant or admirable. However, all too frequently this is not talked or written about in professional circles with real openness and specificity. For example, it remains awkward to be frank about the relatively common experience of sexual interest or arousal in relation to clients (Mann, 1997). Dislike and hostility

TABLE 9.3 *Motivations for becoming a therapist leading to common counter-transferences*

Motivating need	Underlying anxiety	Therapeutic enactments
Power/domination	Vulnerability Helplessness Humiliation	Being superior and invulnerable Emphasizing/maintaining client's neediness and dependency
Masochism	Fear Helplessness Abuse Aggression	Suffer along with client Provoke client to abuse therapist Over-helpfulness (as reaction formation)
Omnipotent healing	Worthlessness Emptiness Helplessness	Play saviour; try to love people better Take excessive responsibility Project blame for failure Work beyond competence
Exhibitionism/ display	Worthlessness Being ignored/invalidated	Requiring admiration Show-off wisdom Rejecting challenge Being competitive Being overactive and unreceptive
Voyeurism/ curiosity	Being shut-out Rejection Helplessness	Intrusiveness/prying Create sexualized/excited relationship

Professionalized
  intimacy
	Loss of control
	Merger
	Abandonment
	Ambivalence about
	  involvement/closeness
		Becoming over-involved/identifying
		  with clients
		Dependency on clients/holding onto
		  relationships
		Rejection of clients
		Being distant and emotionally over-
		  controlling

Being loved/needed	Worthlessness Rejection	Over-encouraging/reassuring/ supporting Rescuing Avoid confrontation Keep client dependent
Dependency	Loneliness Emptiness/non-existence	Turn clients into friends Break boundaries of therapy Excessive reciprocity/self-disclosure
Escape oneself	Emptiness Emotional deadness	Over-involvement Loss of separateness Dependency on clients

too are often so loaded with guilt that they are repressed or dealt with indirectly through humour (Searles, 1979). Counter-transference is often only acceptable – and so able to be acknowledged – when it has been mastered and used to therapeutic effect. Outside of this arena, there is a damaging culture of shame which inhibits therapeutic awareness and needlessly perpetuates impasses which could be remedied.

Every individual has her own unique complex of responses but one pattern is so common that it warrants particular exploration. A 'helping professions syndrome' has been observed which involves relating to and looking after our own neediness and vulnerability through the medium of our clients' hurt, using a process of projection (Sussman, 1995). One aspect of this is the failure to get our own needs met which so often leads to exhaustion and burnout. However, a covert side of this pattern is the envy felt for the client who is receiving our help and attention. Our need to heal and to repair the wounds of the client is very personal but our efforts often seem ineffective and are even rejected. The hostility we feel towards clients, both because of this rejection and because we are hostile and rejecting towards our own neediness, is frequently defensively denied. This driven need to heal has itself an aggressive quality and the experience of hostility that arises from it almost inevitably is unacceptable and causes considerable guilt. Hostility and guilt in fact seem almost endemic to the helping situation (Winnicott, 1958). They constitute a pervasive and intimately linked counter-transference which appears in many situations and in many guises. Hostility may be acted out more or less subtly. The therapist may try to push the client towards a particular point of view (even to browbeat her); she may take sides in the client's conflicts and disputes with the world outside, whether against the client or with her against her supposed enemies; or the therapist may find herself disparaging her client within sessions or outside them, making pejorative references or using pathologizing labels. Less obviously, there may simply be a battle for control which becomes personalized. More covertly still, there may be a kind of competitiveness and rivalry with the client which is increased when she starts to improve; the therapist evolves a subtle investment in keeping the client unwell.

Perhaps even more common and less easy to spot, is the therapist's fear of her own hostility, her denial of it and the subtle but pervasive sense of guilt which it creates (Searles, 1979). This can result in over-solicitousness and an excessive tendency to provide reassurance. The therapist is less likely to confront and deal with the client's own hostility, possibly setting up a situation in which she is taken advantage of through non-payment of fees or non-attendance at sessions. The therapist submits to the client and turns the relationship into one in which she is herself persecuted. This could be thought of as a form of therapeutic 'masochism'. Sometimes, it can result from the therapist having what amounts to an unconscious aim to fail, submitting to a part of her personality which sabotages success. Potency, effectiveness and being well come to be seen as dangerous, perhaps hostile and laden with guilt. This is a kind of negative therapeutic reaction on the part of the therapist herself (compare Chapter 8).

At worst, we have been discussing what might be termed the psychonoxious or pathogenic therapist whose characterological difficulty results in a widespread lack of awareness, a tendency towards intense, undifferentiated relationships, confusing and contradictory communication patterns and the exploitation of clients in the therapeutic situation as a vehicle for relief from personal difficulties. While such practitioners exist, they are relatively few. Rather, all therapists need to be alert to their own vulnerability and to the forms of counter-transference to which it gives rise. No-one is immune. It is important to recognize that we do not have a monopoly on 'sanity' and we need to acquire the security to be able to drop our own defensiveness. Focus on the vulnerabilities of 'high-risk' clients (as in Chapter 8) can distract from acknowledging the therapist's woundedness and her part in creating an impasse. Personally and as a profession, we need to recognize and validate the 'client in the therapist' without discrediting our capacity to help. For each of us, what can be useful is to identify the kinds of counter-transference reactions we are most prone to. Typically, difficulties arise for each individual therapist in relation to certain kinds of clients, issues and situations. An important piece of professional development is to review past cases where we encountered some difficulty and to identify our contribution and what we were responding to. Forewarned, we may actively avoid areas of work which might present intractable problems. At the very least, it facilitates identifying when we are – again – in some familiar pattern of response.

Impasse in the therapeutic transaction

The therapist's personal responses to her client are not only a distorted imposition stemming from her own history and assumptions, not just 'subjective': the counter-transference is also 'objective', a reality-based response to how the client presents herself and the interpersonal cues which she gives out. Such reactions are invaluable evidence of how other people too will respond to this person. Indeed, such responses can be clues to very subtle aspects of the client which are otherwise out of the therapist's awareness and so serve as a vital source of information about hidden features of the client's emotional world. Objective counter-transference is not an interference with the therapeutic process but a potential vehicle for understanding – but only when it can be made conscious and emotionally manageable.

Racker (1968) identifies two forms that this response might take: the concordant and the complementary. In a *concordant* counter-transference, the therapist feels as the client does or would do: she 'identifies' with the client. There is a strong predisposition to do this in the therapeutic situation and the capacity to resonate in this way with the client's experience is the source of empathy. However, without the emotional distance also to recognize this process for what it is, the therapist may over-identify with the client and an impasse can result from then colluding with a partial point of view. For example, client and therapist seem to find that they share values, implicitly supporting and admiring each other: they are 'the good guys' and others appear to them deluded, cruel or insensitive.

In a *complementary* objective counter-transference, the therapist's experience is that of being treated by the client as 'the other': the way the therapist feels and acts identifies with the client's internal model of how other people feel and act towards her. This happens when there is a failure of the attempt to empathize. The therapist is instead 'role-responsive' (Sandler, 1976). For example, the client presents as weak and pathetic and is deferential to the therapist; the therapist in turn feels strong and helpful, makes many 'wise' comments but ignores any signs of the client's competence. If the therapist can recognize this role-responsiveness for what it is, that is, 'convert' it into objective counter-transference, new understanding and different possibilities for relating are opened-up.

Rani was a competent secretary, intelligent, very well dressed. She had problems making friends. After the first few sessions, the therapist felt increasingly passive and unable to think of many useful things to say – nothing seemed particularly helpful; what she thought of didn't seem good enough. Shaking herself out of this state of mind, she began to detect what seemed a subtle superciliousness, a sense that Rani didn't need anything from anyone. The therapist reflected on the way that her client kept herself distant from those around her and began to think more clearly about her underlying sense of being inferior and unworthy of receiving from others.

This process of role-responsiveness is universal in human relationships: people are always *eliciting* responses from others which fit their rigid and distorted expectations of other people (Safran and Muran, 2000). Sometimes we select people who fit our expected roles to play a part in our lives but we also pressurize others through subtle aspects of our own behaviour to act in expected ways. We may dissociate parts of our experience, such as anger, but nonetheless communicate this non-verbally and evoke a frightened or rejecting response. The ways we deny feelings – for example, being cool and rational – may make other people less responsive to our emotional needs. Often, therefore, these processes result in 'vicious circles' in which the responses which we expect are the ones that we evoke from other people, confirming our narrow and fearful view of the world and locking us into limiting and self-defeating patterns of behaviour. A client who experiences her feelings as unmanageable and expects them to be rejected acts so as to distance other people who are then unresponsive to her needs. These 'cyclical maladaptive patterns' (Ryle, 1990; Wachtel, 1987) are often what bring clients into therapy.

In the therapeutic situation, the therapist's attempts to empathize and to be emotionally available to the client, intensifies the general human predisposition to be role-responsive. When the therapist's empathy wavers and her emotional distance is not retained, there is a strong chance that a complementary counter-transference will be evoked and acted on. The interpersonal pattern which may have brought the client into therapy in the first place is recreated in the consulting room. Whether simply on the level of feelings and subtle interpersonal communication, or in the form of the therapist's actions and distortions in the therapeutic framework, an impasse arises as a replication of the client's difficulties in her life outside therapy.

Moving from an individual level of understanding of the resistances of the client and the counter-resistances of the therapist to a transactional one like this, we can arrive at a fuller understanding of impasse and its trans-formation. Transference and counter-transference, resistance and counter-resistance are two components of a unity, each giving life to the other. They co-create the vivid reality of an interpersonal relationship: 'individual' therapy is best seen as a 'bi-personal field' (Langs, 1976). Elements from each person contribute to this new unity, responding to and seeking out corresponding aspects of the other person. Significant counter-reactions in the therapist are neither purely subjective nor simply objective: they respond to something in the client but do so out of the therapist's own personality repertoire, selecting something from her own range of attitudes and responses which matches or counterposes the activity of her client. Meanwhile, the client is always responding in turn to the personal element of what the therapist does – however rational or neutral or client-centred her technique may encourage her to be. Mutual participation in this transaction is inevitable and it is vital for the therapist to become aware of and acknowledge her own contribution.

The degree and intensity of such participation varies. Impasses typically become intractable when the vulnerabilities of therapist and client intersect (Elkind, 1992). The mutuality in the relationship then takes on a regressive, fused quality: a situation has been created in which, rather than experi-encing each other primarily as separate individuals, both the therapist and client substantially participate in the relationship as though the other was a part of her own internal drama. This is at one and the same time a permissive and a demanding point of view. It allows technical flexibility and encourages an acceptance of one's own mistakes; it suggests a stance of 'participant observation' for the therapist. However, in the context of an impasse, that observational quality is lost as the therapist fails to retain an appropriate sense of her own separateness. Participation becomes intense, confused and lacking in self-awareness, with both parties invested in its continuation. Ferro (1993) refers to the interpersonal structures developed in these situations as 'bastions' to indicate their defensive, rigid quality.

These mutual enactments are of two broadly contrasting types which Atwood et al. (1989) term 'conjunctions' and 'disjunctions'. *Conjunctive* enactments (based in concordant counter-transferences) are blind spots which result in a defensive collusion by the therapist with the client's current way of viewing the world. It is a kind of anti-therapeutic alliance or 'misalliance' (Langs, 1975).

Harry was an alienated young man in his 20s who had difficulties forming relationships with women and holding any job. In sessions, he talked a great deal about the exploitativeness and abusiveness of capitalist society and his activities in the environmental movement. His therapist shared many of his values and was also personally somewhat inclined to attribute personal difficulties to forces outside herself. The therapist also shared

Harry's fears about conflict within close relationships and failed to challenge his avoidance of more personally painful issues or to relate the abusiveness he was talking about to an experience of the therapeutic relationship. Both began to feel a kind of alienation and dissatisfaction with the therapeutic work but were unable to risk disrupting their unwitting collusion which served to maintain each person's defensive pattern. They managed to avoid frightening issues about the experience of anger and exploitation in close relationships. Harry eventually dropped out of therapy.

The *disjunctive* enactment (based on complementary counter-transferences) is an anti-therapeutic negative spiral in the alliance in which the therapist's reactions cause her to participate in a vicious circle where the relationship spirals down through a series of worsening ruptures which are never repaired.

Kathleen, a divorced woman in her 30s, tended to adopt a rather flirtatious style of relating both in and outside of therapy. She had experienced numerous disappointing or frankly abusive relationships with men in her life. Her male psychotherapist, in the name of maintaining boundaries, took quite a tough and distant stance towards her while interpreting her 'seductiveness' as covertly hostile. In fact, the therapist felt his sense of autonomy and control threatened by what seemed like intrusive, sexualized demands. These touched on his own relationship with his controlling mother. He became increasingly withholding, critical and covertly angry while Kathleen started to alternate between increasing coquettishness and moments of rage. Her underlying need for both safety and emotional responsiveness was never met.

Resolution through the therapeutic transaction

The high probability of the therapist participating in an enactment with the client of the very difficulties for which she is seeking help represents an opportunity as much as it does a problem. It provides the therapist with a vehicle not only for learning about those problems but for putting them right. The issues are recreated in the concrete immediate experience of the interpersonal field. They are live 'examples', rather than things talked 'about' at a generalized level. Access is gained to the details of the client's world in a way that might not be possible without the experience of participation. Unarticulated issues find a route to expression in the relationship. As the therapist becomes reflectively aware of her participation and of its emotional character, its defensive nature and the anxieties and pain which are involved, she is better placed to understand and clarify the client's struggles with her. She is also in a position to *do something different*. The construction of this intersubjective field provides an arena within which the therapist has an opportunity: she acquires the capacity to transform the relationship and the client's experience of it. Impasse has been described by

Stolorow et al. (1987) as the 'royal road' to understanding and to trans-formation (updating Freud's famous dictum about dreams).

For personal change to take place, there needs to be not only an under-standing of how things are going wrong – the 'old-bad' experience – but also an experience of something different and positive on which to build. Resolving the continuing problems within the therapeutic alliance is a major vehicle for this process of change, providing client and therapist with an occasion for risking something new (Safran and Muran, 2000). Repeated cycles of rupture and repair in the relationship can create faith that it is possible for things to work out, even when they don't go perfectly. The experience of manageable disappointment can enable a growing acceptance by the client of her own feelings and needs. The client gets her needs responded to in some measure but learns acceptance of the fact that this may not be the ideal she dreamt of. At the same time, the anticipated catastrophe – the unmanageable pain which is expected and against which the client defends herself – may be tested out and found to be less dreadful than was feared. Weiss and Sampson (1986) refer to this as a 'transference test' in which the therapist does not simply repeat the pattern which the client has come to expect and the client in turn finds that she survives a change in her defensive patterns. Different ways of responding to our vulnerabilities, expanded awareness and greater flexibility are developed. It gradually becomes less frightening and more acceptable to experience ourselves (both therapists and clients) as separate from others and responsible for our own actions.

The route to transformation lies through the 'eye of the storm' of impasse. This places significant emotional demands upon the therapist. Letting go of her defensive, restricted participation creates the space to engage in an authentic encounter rather than to talk 'about' the problems. As human beings, we are always going to be ambivalent in wishing both to explore bravely and to collude safely. Internal work is required from us to resolve the conflicts and metabolize the painful experiences which are ones that, though generated in parallel with the client, have become our own. In a sense, the solution to an impasse is complementary for both therapist and client: it is not a solution to an external problem nor a new understanding, but a changed relationship to oneself. The therapist restores her equilibrated sense of self, differentiating from her immersion in the enactment and obtaining access to both the experiencing and the observing parts of herself. This might sound too cognitive however: it means restoring a sense of risk and the possibility of failure, stepping outside the safety of what has become an accustomed position. It is an 'act of freedom' that, in accepting the emo-tional reality of the encounter, sets in motion a creative interpersonal process so that something new can happen (Symington, 1983). A change of this kind can transform the whole interpersonal field, allowing new identities to emerge.

Frequently, in dropping the defensiveness towards disowned aspects of ourselves and by recognizing what there is of the client within our own experience, for example, in the acceptance of our own hostility and spite-fulness, the impasse can be seen to have been a situation of relative safety, one in which there has been a struggle to control the other person, with both parties validated in feeling someone else is responsible for her difficulties. On the therapist's part, this has resulted in interpretations which subtly blame the client for the impasse but which are doomed to perpetuate it. She must emerge from this sado-masochistic position and restore a sense of freedom, acceptance and responsibility and a willingness to strive for discovery and emotional contact. Whether any of this internal work is disclosed by the therapist is partly a matter of therapeutic style. Perhaps more importantly, it requires a judgement about what self-disclosure of her own contribution would mean to this client in the context of the rela-tionship at this moment (Maroda, 1991). What is important is that the internal work is done – its effects will be felt.

Gloria was a woman in her middle 40s who was experiencing tearfulness, low mood and lack of energy at the point in her life when her children were leaving home. She was seeing John, an experienced male therapist who also managed the Centre she was attending. She was consistently pleasant and accommodating and tried to work hard. Although John tried to discuss her 'niceness', it felt to him as though, after a dozen sessions, things were going nowhere. On two different sessions, the therapist came 10 and 15 minutes late; even though he wasn't able to make up the time, Gloria was quite accepting of this. John was a busy man and he rationalized his late-ness in this way, but normally he was very seldom late. He cancelled another session in order to accommodate an urgent meeting and sub-sequently found himself questioning what he was doing. He realized how accommodating Gloria was and that he had come to take her for granted, to the point of actually exploiting her niceness. Looking inside himself, he found that he was actually quite irritated with her: she was just 'too bloody nice' – and that hopeful smile! He also realized that he had not taken the case to supervision because he was feeling rather guilty about such reactions. Indeed, he realized that Gloria reminded him of what he found most difficult about his own mother – and he thought he had dealt with all that! He did take the case to supervision and talked a little about his associations to Gloria, about how his mother indulged him but was emo-tionally remote and he was helped to wonder about a kind of comple-mentary counter-transference – the contemptuous, exploitative relationship which he had formed and the guilt he felt about it. Moving out of this position, he found himself much better able to help Gloria look at her own resentment about being unappreciated and her fears of being abandoned if she pushed for her own needs to be met.

In this case, as in the failed cases cited earlier, there was a particular 'fit' between the personal issues of the therapist and the client. Such issues of fit are a risk and an opportunity at the same time, and perhaps the therapy professions should develop a deeper knowledge of how this 'chemistry' works. Through linkages of this kind impasses may be created but work at depth can be achieved – but only if we do not take on more than we are equipped to bear.

Conclusion

Working with the resistance in an interactional way, being sensitive to the state of the alliance, responding to and rectifying ruptures is a challenging business. If we fail in this task and participate more fully and less consciously in the client's defensive repetitions, a true impasse develops. It may be necessary to live through it without letting hope for the client or faith in ourselves fail. In a sense, the existence of an impasse confirms the existence of the bond between the therapist and the client and its crucial importance to both. Perhaps the therapist may be waiting to become equipped to appreciate fully the client's pain and to deal boldly with her own fears. But in waiting and trusting, there must also be working. It is not enough to rely blindly on a kind of magic within the therapeutic relationship to bring about change by itself. Constant internal work is required as the therapist attempts to find a new and authentic relationship with herself and her client.

Often, for this to be achievable, the support system around the therapist needs to provide the kind of security which will allow the therapeutic relationship to unfold and without which the difficulties of undertaking the work may simply be too great. Indeed, the containment provided by the entire culture of the therapy professions may need to develop new, less guilt-inducing conceptions of impasse and less perfectionist expectations of therapists in order to provide an environment which sustains the process of transformation. The kind of self-acceptance that supports liberating therapeutic work needs a context of disciplined but accepting colleagues.

10 Impasse and Resolution: Changing the Pattern

When you find yourself stuck as a therapist, the problem is compounded by a dilemma. As a feeling of paralysis takes hold, there is on the one hand a temptation to resign oneself to passively opting out: it can bring a sense of relief. On the other hand, there will often be a mounting sense of frustration: stuckness can be a profoundly unpleasant experience and the only alternative seems to be to *do* something *now*. There is a temptation to resort to dramatic interventions, random experimentation, changing the style of therapy or ending it suddenly. Sometimes, of course, this will 'work'. However, more usually it will be useless or damaging. There are serious risks of acting out our frustration towards the client.

If you have turned to this chapter first – perhaps even in desperation – go back: do not start here! The thrust of the previous chapters has been to try to *think through* impasse. Recognizing that we are stuck should lead to reflection about our client and our own inner process. This in itself changes something about the situation: by standing back, we are already doing something subtly different – 'space' is introduced within an interaction that had been narrowed in its possibilities. Out of this can emerge an alteration in the pattern of the work and the reintroduction of movement and a possibility of growth while avoiding any aggressive 'acting out'.

Impasse implies stuckness for the therapist as much as for the client. If we are in the business of learning from our clients, an impasse may be a crucial point in our own development: what we know and what we are doing seems not to be enough and some new capability has to be found. Sometimes this is simply a greater freedom or confidence within the boundaries of our current professional self, perhaps putting into practice what we already know in theory. However, on other occasions it can be a significant step in growth associated with some qualitative change in our work. What may be demanded is an expansion of our personal capacities to bear or express feeling, to be more fully aware of the range and diversity within ourselves, to risk emotional contact with others. However, at times what may be needed is a major change – even a reconstruction – of our theoretical and technical foundations. Several eminent practitioners have reported stuckness and repeated frustration as reasons for creating new therapeutic approaches (Dryden, 1985). Nonetheless, it is wise to stay within your own base orientation in most cases, certainly in the initial steps and in terms of conceptualizing whatever it is that you decide to do. Good therapeutic work in a situation of impasse requires a demanding combination of flexibility and disciplined thought.

The various strategies and tactics briefly described below must be understood in this context. Each situation is unique and there is no suggestion that any of the procedures would be appropriate in every situation. There is no trick to perform and no routine to resort to. It is helpful to think of going through a spiral process: creating some space for reflection on the work (whether in or out of the session, alone or with a supervisor); taking some action which comes out of that reflection; and using it as an experiment with an implicit hypothesis which is then tested against the client's response and the effects on the therapeutic situation as a whole. Thus, resolving impasse is part of the tentative, exploratory style of any good therapy. In responding to impasse we are seeking better questions, not an answer. The following strategies are not set out in an order which implies where to start and what to try next. They need to be considered according to what best suits your specific situation.

Review the alliance

Reviewing the state of the therapeutic relationship is the obvious thing to do. Taking stock of whether the collaborative framework is in place and what elements of resistance are apparent in the process of the sessions may allow us to think afresh. Is the stuckness within the context of a smooth, over-comfortable bond or of one which is precarious and mistrustful? Are the client's full range of resources being utilized? Is the original contract in place and still appropriate or has it been compromised? Have the goals changed subtly and do they still seem realistic? Pause and ask yourself some of these questions – but crucial to such a review is the spirit of collaboration. This means involving the client in the process; it means speaking about the sense of stuckness. Simple as this at first seems, it requires both tact and courage and is often avoided. We may feel ashamed to hear what the client has to say about the work. In order to address this, it will often be most productive to start from some immediate, concrete instance where there is a fairly obvious sign of resistance or rupture in the alliance: for example, some task that was not completed; or an indication of emotional withdrawal in response to one of the therapist's comments. It should be possible to ask about the client's experience of that occasion and then to widen the scope of the review in whatever direction emerges as appropriate. This can be easier to do when the original framework for therapy included an agreement to review the process at regular intervals.

Clients may not find it easy to be honest, especially where trust is low or they wish to please their therapist. This has to be handled tactfully, gauging the client's willingness and ability to discuss the relationship. The therapist needs to participate frankly, giving her point of view. Doubts may need to be shared about the appropriateness of goals initially agreed. It is important to identify any difficulties which you see the client experiencing in managing the process and tasks of therapy. It is vital to tackle violations of the contract, particularly around boundaries, by referring to the original agreements – but also to understand the client's views on the difficulties, rather than taking an authoritarian, rule-bound approach. It may be necessary to renegotiate a more explicit contract and set of ground rules than was done in the beginning. With all these it may also be appropriate to share your view of the rationale for the contract and tasks and perhaps also for the original or revised therapeutic goals.

This approach is a 'reasonable' starting point – but it may be inadequate and there are some dangers. If mishandled, confronting the stuckness can leave the client with a sense of failure and shame; it can degenerate into accusation towards either party; and it can unhelpfully increase pressure when the underlying need is to decrease it. It can also reinforce a sense of superficiality in the therapy, when what is required is an opportunity to engage with what is difficult and unknown.

(Re-)Formulate

It is helpful to stand back and review what you know about the 'case' overall. Reliance on experience and intuition, an initial sense of recognizing what is going on, pressure of work, counter-resistance, puzzlement or the wish to let things unfold – all might stand in the way of explicitly conceptualizing the therapy early on. For those who are uneasy about procedures which seem to objectify the client and fear that using a formulation will create a barrier, there is nonetheless a need to seek *some* way of creating the distance needed to obtain a fresh and widened perspective. There has to be a pulling together of different strands of case material and an attempt to retell the story of the person's life in the therapy. It should be wider than just the client in the consulting room and the therapeutic relationship: it should encompass the person's life situation and the professional networks around the work. This retelling should be generative, drawing attention to gaps and neglected issues, offering new ways of seeing and reframing the experience of stuckness. If an impasse proves intractable at first, reformulation is a professional obligation.

It is possible to undertake this in an ad hoc way, but it may be helpful to proceed more systematically. Formulations depend on theories and there are many different ways to approach the task. Various structures have been described in the preceding chapters, drawing on theory in an eclectic manner. These have included the idea of a force-field, the various elements of the therapeutic alliance, the systemic relationships surrounding the client and her referral, the physical and psychiatric aspects of the client's problem, the state of the person's self-structure and the relational dynamics reflected in therapy and life interactions. More specific structured processes are tools to be experimented with according to what each therapist finds appealing:

the activity of reformulating has to be undertaken in ways compatible with your approach to therapeutic work. Getting a new view, however, is vital and it will be helpful to seek consultation from others to assist you with this. If those who share your approach turn out not to help generate a sufficiently new perspective, it can be wise to seek consultation from someone with another approach who can assist you to put things together from a different angle.

Having gone through a process of reformulating, what next? One possibility is to explicitly share the formulation with the client. Ryle (1990) suggests using a letter to the client in which the formulation is articulated in ordinary language. Cognitive therapists may also use diagrams in the context of sessions to help the patient see their difficulty in the light of the therapist's understanding (Beck, 1995). This is not only collaborative and respectful but also very powerful, challenging the client's current views of herself and evoking new perceptions. It creates coherence out of confusion, pulling things together into a different pattern and can take hold in the client's mind as a new focus for the work.

A formulation – and we always have one, implicitly – implies a 'plan' of intervention, at least in terms of broad strategic direction. In reformulating, our current strategy is held up for reappraisal. In increasing order of the degree of change required in the therapeutic strategy, the questions facing the therapist which may arise from this process are:

- Do the therapeutic relationship and process embody what needs to be worked on or are they trapped in some form of *circular resistance*? The therapy may have become 'part of the problem' as now understood, rather than part of the solution. Can this new intellectual awareness help to rebalance the work and free it from this trap – or does some more personal work need to be done by the therapist?
- Is the *focus* of the therapy accurate and are the *goals* reachable in the light of our current understanding – or does the direction of the therapy need to be redefined with the client to more appropriately reflect how we now see the problem?
- Is the *style* and the *format* of the therapy right for this client, for what she needs to work on and what she is capable of at this time? Is the relational framework of the therapy appropriate, with the right people involved in the session or in support around the session? If not, does the therapist feel able to change her therapeutic style or manage a new format for the therapy, or is referral to a different therapist or therapeutic context the best way forward for the client?
- Is *psychotherapy* actually appropriate for this problem at this time at all? Perhaps an ending needs to be negotiated.

The process of reformulation may bring home to the therapist that there are some hard choices to be faced if she is to act responsibly and in the client's best interests.

Using supervision (better)

Throughout this book, reference has been made to the need for support and input from a supervisor. But there is a surprising lack of guidance about how to use supervision to the maximum advantage. The profession of counselling has always placed a premium on the value of supervisory support throughout one's career and increasingly other therapeutic professions have come to take this view. There has been a burgeoning literature on the supervision of therapists in recent years but it is focused on carrying out the supervisory role. There is little published on how best to *be* a supervisee (with Inskipp and Proctor, 1993 a rare exception). While the supervisor's contribution is obviously vital, as therapists we should be active in the process of choosing, building and sustaining supervisory alliances which will provide us with the context of safety and challenge which enables exploration and the facilitation of movement. It is essential to feel an active and empowered participant in a collaborative relationship, rather than one who is passive and fearful in a way which is too common and which parallels unproductive therapeutic interactions.

One obvious aspect of this is the degree to which we feel able to grant a supervisor access to the work we do. Research suggests that there is a fairly high level of non-disclosure of relevant information and an element of impression management in therapeutic supervision (Ladany et al., 1996). The need to maintain the appearance of competence not only during training but even once qualified is a powerful force. For example, clients to whom we are experiencing some significant counter-resistance are very often those whom we don't take to supervision. The issue of shame for all therapists in relation to the (inevitable) mistakes and uncomfortable personal reactions within the therapeutic process is an issue for everyone. Of the wide range of formats for supervision (Watkins, 1997), some are much more 'exposing' than others. Developing forums in which relatively more access is given to the work widens the uses to which we allow supervision to be put. Verbatim transcripts, audio recordings, video recordings and live supervision expose work to an increasing degree. Developing confidence about using these techniques provides a powerful counter to some forms of relational impasse. Disclosing our inner experience while reviewing in detail the therapeutic process opens things up further. A willingness to take risks that is validated by results can encourage more experimentation. Getting the help we need to respond to an impasse may well involve going beyond our 'comfort zones' within a consultative context.

Three functions of supervision are relevant in the context of resolving impasse:

- To provide a general background of support and 'holding' which enables the therapist to utilize her own capabilities better. This is an issue in handling all therapeutic setbacks to which we will return in the final chapter.

- To help the therapist understand the client and the scope of her work better through reviewing her understanding (formulation by whatever name) to arrive at a deeper appreciation of the difficulty. For example, Omer (1994) describes a group consultation format designed to generate multiple new perspectives on an impasse and to synthesize these into a significantly different 'critical intervention' which re-orients the therapist and restarts the therapeutic process.
- To enable the therapist to work through her own participation in the therapeutic relationship and respond more constructively to the challenges the client poses for her. For example, Saretsky (1981) describes a group supervision format designed to help therapists explore experientially counter-transference entanglements in their work with particularly challenging clients.

As in therapy itself, there needs to be a balance between challenge and support in supervision. Balance is always easier if it rests on a broad base: it seems probable that a single supervisory relationship is not necessarily the best context within which to manage the more challenging elements of the therapeutic role. This is most obvious on those occasions where a different viewpoint is needed from the therapist's own model. Many impasses seem to go unchallenged because supervision has become part of an over-validating context which constitutes part of the problem. There should be a network of different consultative relationships available. As the above examples suggest, there may be particular advantages to group formats in working with issues of stuckness.

Change the communication pattern

Sometimes direct ways of addressing the therapeutic issues seem to go nowhere. In these circumstances, using an indirect style of communicating with the client may be helpful. A change of tack can take the pressure off and may allow new options to emerge. A number of tactics share this feature of changing the pattern of communication and shifting to an indirect approach.

Thinking aloud

Rather than speaking directly to the client, the therapist might think aloud and let her client 'overhear' her words. The therapist looks down or away while speaking and soliloquizes as empathically and thoughtfully as possible about an aspect of the client's situation or about the therapeutic interaction. It might be an opportunity to reframe problems as attempts at communication or to communicate an inner experience of the client. For example, the therapist might muse about her frustration and growing sense of futility at pursuing a client who seems always elusive – this is quite likely to lead to the client seeking the therapist's attention more directly! The approach is related to the systemic therapy technique of discussion with colleagues in front of the client (see 'in-therapy consultation' below). Gans (1994) describes this technique well in a psychodynamic context, as a means of utilizing and communicating counter-transference responses productively. However, it can be used within most therapeutic approaches. People do not have to be looked at and spoken to directly to feel recognized and cared about. It can replace a growing sense of antagonism and passivity with an opportunity to reactivate collaboration and may locate the interaction in a more 'playful' mode. It can also provide the therapist with a degree of distance in the session that enables her to work on intense affect or immobilizing conflict. For example, it can be very useful under pressure, such as when a client announces unilaterally that this will be her last session; the therapist's response can be more thoughtful, weighing up pros and cons and considering possible reasons without appearing panicked, irritated or (in reaction) over-caring.

John, a man in his late 20s, had come to therapy for help with his difficulties settling to any career. After ten sessions he was still struggling with his ambivalence about whether he really needed to change. As a youngest child, he had been shielded from responsibility by his mother and had a fraught relationship with his distant and critical father. The therapist chose to think aloud about her sense of being caught between being either critical or indulgent and linked that in a positive way to John's negativity and reluctance to be forced to change. She concluded by speculating about some of the issues that might be being avoided – John's self-doubt and a longing for help and direction. John gave little immediate response but was thoughtful. In ensuing sessions, he seemed to feel more in charge of the process and to gradually move into revealing his sense of neediness and doubt about his masculinity.

It is important with such a technique to set it up carefully with a brief introduction of what you are going to do, being careful not to appear weird or controversial. It should be avoided with clients who are deeply troubled by shame or aloneness; and it must not be used as a vehicle to be hostile from a safe distance or try to 'disprove' a client's accusations rather than explore them.

Strategic responses

Strategic responses aim to resolve stuckness and arrive at a therapeutic goal by using an indirect approach (Fish et al., 1982). They avoid open confrontation, explicit interpretation or the use of rational argument. Understanding and awareness may in fact be viewed as irrelevant to change. The type of intervention one might use may be only slightly indirect – for example, rather than asking a client, 'What would be useful?', in a given situation, one might say 'Do you think you know what might be useful?'.

More frequently, strategic approaches employ an intervention which is surprising and dramatic. The 'critical interventions' used by Omer (1994) – described above – are designed to be highly impactful so as to jolt the therapy out of its old patterns and turn the work in a new strategic direction.

Sometimes strategic interventions may seem to be the opposite of what is intended. They can involve proscribing change in a problem, or encouraging an increase in its frequency or intensity. For example, a marital couple who are stuck about whether to continue their relationship or separate and have gone round the same circle many times, might be advised to ensure that no decision was reached, since it is clear that it is much too early to be sure and that much more time and argument are needed to reach the best outcome for them. A man with a compulsive ritual who has not responded to attempts at treatment by response prevention could be told to significantly increase his checking and to do so in a ritualized manner. These 'paradoxical injunctions' have the capacity to disrupt the stability of stuck situations in a meaningful way. If they are used, it is essential that a positive rationale be developed concerning the desirability of the status quo and that this have some reality to it; it should be developed on the basis of an appreciation, in systemic terms, of what keeps the person stuck. Thus, the compulsive client above may be told how clear it had become that safety and control is important to him and that he needed to achieve a greater degree of control before he felt it would be safe to be free of his problem. Such explanations should embody, in a para-doxical way, the conflicts and ambivalences at the heart of the relational system, reframed in positive terms. They are, to some degree, unpalatable but they bypass the usual objections. This approach depends to some extent on Milton Erickson's 'utilization' technique and the solution-focused approaches deriving from it (Dolan, 1985): that is, seeing problems and resistances as potential resources; joining the client, rather than getting into battles with her; and going 'with the grain' of the resistance but in such a way as to free the situation and promote change. This tactic involves accepting apparently unacceptable states of affairs and amplifying them in order to unbalance the previously over-stable situation.

Strategic responses are useful when the therapeutic interaction is itself locked in some implicit battle. Thus, when the therapist has found herself manoeuvred into doing all the work, she might declare her confusion and uncertainty about what to do, with the expectation that the client might take up the slack. Where ambivalence is frozen into 'black and white' thinking – for example, the client feels stuck with a boring, unsatisfactory lifestyle but the therapist seems to her to be proposing improbable and risky changes – the polarization might be amplified by pressing both views to extremes; or the therapist's views might be attributed to an outside authority, perhaps her supervision group or 'the wisdom of the profession', creating space to be better allied and explore the client's objections. All of these attempt to unlock a hidden power struggle and introduce the possibility of a realignment of forces. There are dangers in such strategic techniques: they can be tricky, disrespectful and a vehicle for hostile frustration. However, if based in understanding and respect, they can be extremely productive.

Using metaphor

Metaphor in its many guises is a flexible and powerful way of addressing issues indirectly. It can be adapted to various different therapeutic styles: by emphasizing or elaborating the metaphorical meanings of words and images; or by telling stories with a thematic relationship to the issue; or by suggesting clients experiment with taking some action (for instance, a weekend break) designed to evoke broader meanings (perhaps, leisure or freedom or exploration). Metaphors resonate with non-conscious processes and the clients make their own connections in response to them. They can be highly involving, precisely because their ambiguity can encourage clients actively to search for sense while still offering them choice. It will often be possible to utilize the imagery provided by the client herself and to encourage her to elaborate it. Equally, images and evocative words often occur to therapists spontaneously and may be used without necessarily being clear as to what their meaning might be. Metaphor can deepen the resonance of any therapeutic process which has begun to feel dead or stale.

Changing the modality

The option of changing the therapeutic style and format may need to be considered. However, within an existing therapeutic strategy it may be possible to introduce a new medium of expression which can expand the client's breadth of awareness and so move the work to a new level. Therapeutic trainings vary enormously in what is regarded as acceptable in introducing different modalities and structures for expression: we will outline a few which may be helpfully used across a range of therapies but which may not yet be within the usual practice of many. Of course, it is essential that any new medium be appropriate to the individual client, that it is seen to be optional, and that it is introduced in a context of safety which includes the therapist being both clear and confident about what she is proposing.

Writing

Writing is used spontaneously by many clients as an adjunct to their own growth. Poetry, stories, private journal entries can all form part of people's personal development (White and Epston, 1990). However, it can be helpful to suggest some specific exercises in certain impasse situations. *Unsent letters* can be extremely useful in moving forward 'unfinished business' with some important figure from the client's past: writing a letter to that person – not to be sent – expressing the full range and intensity of feeling towards them without any concern for its impact; and perhaps writing an imagined reply from the person, followed by the reply the client would liked to have received. These tasks can be very moving and will often allow the client to realign her relationship with her own past, with only supportive help from the therapist needed. The *personal development journal*, a diary written with some degree of structuring, is useful when worries about privacy and loss of personal control appear to be inhibiting work within sessions, with the sense of the therapist acting as a background presence who 'holds' the private work. These features deepen work which might have reached a plateau. A *life review project* is often undertaken as part of a journal but can also be developed as a task in itself. The client is invited, in a structured way, to search through and order memories of all kinds across her entire lifespan, perhaps involving specific research, the drawing of genograms and even a real journey to significant places from her past. This can be helpful during developmental transitions when it is unclear what direction therapy should take.

Experiential guidance

Where therapy is stuck on a seemingly superficial level but efforts to understand the resistance have not moved things on in spite of the client seeming to be willing to take things further, it may be appropriate to use procedures, such as meditation and guided fantasies, which help to access other levels of awareness. Two less well-known approaches are experiential focusing and streaming. Gendlin's (1981) *'experiential' focusing* is designed to help get in touch with a pre-symbolic level of experience, a 'felt-sense' which underlies responses to situations and wider mood states, allowing them to take symbolic form. This requires a relatively sophisticated and responsive client, but can be useful for people who tend to over-intellectualize. *'Streaming'* (Mahoney, 1991) is a version of the classical psychoanalytic procedure of 'free association' in which a client attends to and reports as best she can, her ongoing thoughts, images, sensations and feelings within a defined part of the session. It is made explicit that the client is allowed to keep control over her privacy and to decide what she actually reports. This is an emotionally intense procedure, needing care and a clear decision from the client to try it out. It can be extremely helpful in facilitating the recall of dissociated material where this appears to be the cause of a block in the development of therapy.

Other evocative procedures

Many other interactions may be used in order to encourage a wider range of exploration than seems to be available in a 'talking heads' format. The therapist might encourage the client to attend more to her experience of embodiment, by trying out various *physical disciplines* such as yoga, dance, sports and massage, as a complementary approach outside therapy. *Role play* and *dramatization* can be used within sessions, not only as a preparation for handling some real life event, but to allow a freer elaboration in an 'as if', playful version of a relationship. *Rituals* – particularly those for resolution and completion of relationships – can be vital in enabling clients to move on from some previous obsessive involvement. *Art, music* and *guided reading* can act as vehicles for deepening a therapeutic dialogue, inviting the client to explore any of these realms and bring to therapy experiences which they find personally meaningful.

It should be emphasized once again that widening the sphere of the therapeutic dialogue through any of these modalities can be used unwisely in ways which attempt to avoid difficulties rather than work with them. If you choose to work in a flexible way that incorporates a range of activities, then discipline and thought about the specific situation and the purpose of using any technique is essential.

Engaging in-therapy consultation

The term consultation is sometimes used as an alternative expression for clinical supervision. It may also imply a one-off case discussion with someone with specific expertise or a different set of skills – we have already recommended the value of this at times. By 'in-therapy consultation', something different and more unusual is meant: it is the procedure of involving a third party directly in the therapeutic system in a consultative role. This is a 'drastic' procedure and there are many legitimate reservations and concerns to be expressed about it. It is more commonly employed in the United States than it is currently in Britain. However, we should not deceive ourselves that it does not happen in an *ad hoc* manner in any case: clients who feel dissatisfied and stuck do from time to time consult alternative therapists. While such actions can frequently be unhelpful, there is a case for exploring whether and in what ways this impulse to seek further external help can be put to constructive use in resolving an impasse. Broadly, there are two distinct formats for in-therapy consultations: separate individual consultations with client and therapist; and joint in-session consultations.

Separate consultation

Elkind (1992), working within a psychodynamic framework, discusses situations in which longer-term therapies are approaching a point of breakdown. Clients may still be very involved and attached to their therapist but in a state of fear, doubt or confusion. Consultation is generally initiated by the client but also sometimes by the therapist. The consultant meets separately with each party between one and three times, seeing the client first. The focus of the consultation is on the problematic intersection of the vulnerabilities and resistances of both parties to the therapeutic interaction, on the assumption that impasses of this kind stem from such interpersonal mismatches. The function of the consultant is to provide non-judgemental feedback about the interaction and identify the transference matrix in a way which models for the client a way of thinking about the impasse and endeavours to link it to other relational themes in the client's life. The therapist is enabled to see how an alliance might be restored if she can be supported in stopping her retreat to an unhelpfully self-protective or hostile stance. These relatively direct communications enable both parties to see their impact on each other.

In-session consultation

A number of therapists working from a systemic perspective describe the introduction of a consultant on a one-off basis directly into the therapeutic sessions (Connel et al., 1990; Hoffman et al., 1994; Rickman et al., 1990). Typically, this procedure is used in family and couple work, but Hoffman describes its use in individual therapy, with very similar techniques. The therapist initiates the consultation and takes care to prepare the client for it. Procedures for briefing the consultant range from using the therapist's regular supervisor with whom the case has been discussed in detail, through briefing the consultant only about therapeutic process and goals (not about the client's problems), to no prior briefing so that all the information is supplied openly before the client. The aim is to focus on here-and-now therapeutic interactions and to act as a catalyst, re-activating the therapeutic system rather than dealing directly with the client's problems. The consultant's expert power gives leverage very quickly and enables her to increase productive disequilibrium and open up communication boundaries. Interventions often have a strategic quality – such as splitting the negative transference onto the consultant so as to strengthen the client's alliance with the therapist, while providing a point of future reference to the consultant's provocative statements.

While both of these procedures (separate or in-session) might seem an unwelcome and perhaps even dangerous intrusion into the privacy of the therapy room, conducive to inappropriate splitting, diluting the intensity of the work and acting out hostility either to therapist or client, these concerns may be misplaced if the process is handled carefully. Privacy can become secrecy and isolation when therapy starts to go wrong. The consultant needs both expertise and authority, together with the trust and respect of the therapist. She can act as a third party providing a holding environment which both creates the space for thought and normalizes appropriate helpseeking. Consultation enlarges the relational context within which therapy is being conducted in a way that should be supportive.

Giving up

Perhaps you have tried your best. Nothing seems to work. This therapy just doesn't seem to be going anywhere, however hard-working or creative or patient you are, whatever tactics you try, whatever understandings you may offer, and in spite of good supervision. It may be time to give up. You can't win them all!

There is, however, more than one way to give up (Leigh, 1998). We have already discussed referral to another format or style of therapy on the basis of reformulating the needs of the client: a hypothesis has been made that a different therapy will make a positive difference. It may be, though, that you refer on to someone else without having any clear conceptualization, or even belief, that they could be more effective: you may simply have had enough or feel that the client needs a fresh start. Occasionally there might be a hope that having 'defeated' one therapist, the client could 'allow' someone else to make more impact.

Alternatively, it might seem appropriate to just stop. This raises issues of how much time and energy to put into working through the ending in what are presumably disappointing circumstances for both people. Some form of review of the work from each person's point of view is essential, with enough time for the impact of the ending to be taken on board and worked with if possible. This may involve discussion of future therapeutic possibilities; but having decided not to refer or make some similar recommendation, a balance must be struck between not avoiding the impact of the decision to stop by escaping into offering some false hope, and, on the other hand, not wiping out the client's reasonable sense that things may change with time or that she may be better able to use help in the future.

Finally, you might decide to give up hope of change but stick with the therapy anyway. Irvine (1984) describes this experience of despair in the therapeutic context. This decision has to be presented to the client in some way so that they are not coming under false pretences. The subtle pressure of the hope for change may constitute a final resistance for the client which can only be given up through facing a profound sense of despair (Safran, 1999). It can be the case that giving up hope, 'giving in' to despair on the part of the therapist, can prompt a breakthrough – but this is not the final 'trick' to be 'pulled out of the hat'. Such hopelessness is real and deeply painful and has to be endured. It may seem that the offer of human companionship in the face of a hopeless impasse in the client's life is what is worth offering and it may even be accepted with gratitude.

11   Understanding Relapse

Rosemary Kent

'Relapse' – the word has depressing connotations: it implies not just a temporary setback, but a scenario of efforts having been all in vain, a sense of hopelessness. Its dictionary definitions refer to 'backsliding' and 'failure following improvement' and thus the sense that energy expended to achieve positive change was fruitless: it implies disappointment and weakness. For clients and therapists alike it may even suggest something worse than trying and failing – they may feel that if their efforts or interventions were at first successful, then it is not the approach that failed, but they themselves: they didn't 'have what it takes' to stick with it. In the world of psychiatry and general medicine, 'relapse' is used without implications of personal blame, but refers to the re-emergence of symptoms which existed prior to treatment – implying that the interventions themselves were ineffectual. In this chapter and the next each of these ideas will be challenged. We will explore how therapy can deal constructively with relapse, in spite of its negative connotations.

We will refer to the types of psychological and behavioural problems where relapse is most likely to occur, and explore its meaning for different models of therapy. We will go on to consider how relapse connects to crisis and impasse and how – like them – it can be both an interruption and an opportunity in the therapeutic process.

How common is relapse?

Relapse can, of course, happen either during therapy or after it is completed. However, the topic is often avoided within some therapeutic approaches – including the possibility of relapse either being managed effectively during therapy, or it leading to the end of the therapeutic relationship, or it occurring soon after therapy ends. A notable exception to such avoidance is the research and treatment literature on relapse in the addictions field, since the 1970s (see, for example, Gossop, 1989; Wanigaratne et al., 1990). For certain other conditions, such as major depressive disorders, there is a tendency to assume that successful outcomes are 'usually' achieved, when in fact carefully conducted research studies often reveal the ubiquity of post-treatment relapse.

Research into the effectiveness of counselling and psychotherapy is playing an increasing part in guiding the practice of practitioners and organizations. However, it is noticeable that many studies compare severity of problems before and immediately after treatment, and have a very limited follow-up period for measuring change, thus obscuring the possibility of identifying post-therapy relapse episodes. Given that depression, eating disorders and addictive behaviours in particular are characterized by their chronic relapsing nature, it would seem that a minimal duration of the period of improvement should be specified before a participant in a research study is classified as recovered and the intervention deemed to be effective. Roth and Fonagy (1996) point out that in major depressive disorders, for example, long-term follow-up of at least two years would be necessary to provide a conclusive indication of improvement, which is not confounded with the natural history of the disorder. Effectiveness of therapy cannot be judged simply by how an identified episode was managed: reduction in frequency and intensity of occurrences and the perceived and experienced consequences of the relapse or relapses is more relevant. Outcome research into those conditions where a relapsing course can normally be anticipated also requires particularly complex methodology. Individuals move from one time point to another: for example, outcome classifications from the first six months in terms of behaviour amongst problem drinkers have been found to be unrelated to long-term outcome status, and the vast majority of cases shift status during the first year of follow-up, with less (but still substantial) variability thereafter (Miller et al., 1992).

Terminology is also a problematic aspect of outcome research, for instance in depression studies, with 'recurrence', 'relapse', 'remission' and 'recovery' having to be carefully differentiated (Frank et al., 1991). Nonetheless, there have been some significant studies investigating what types of interventions (pharmacological and psychotherapeutic) might reduce the recurrence – either severity or frequency or both – of depression in treated patients. It has been estimated that six out of ten people who become depressed recover spontaneously, but the likelihood that they will have another episode in the next two years is greater than 50 per cent. Studies of treatment of depression tend to show discouraging results, including findings that 25 per cent of patients relapsed within 12 weeks after treatment, and 75 per cent suffered a further depressive episode within ten years (Piccinelli and Wilkinson, 1994). Large-scale research trials in North America, such as the National Institute of Mental Health Study (NIMH) (Elkin, 1994), of patients receiving cognitive, interpersonal and pharmacological therapies, have found little indication of the differential effect of any therapeutic approaches used on the severity or frequency of relapse in the six to 18 months of follow-up. NIMH researchers themselves emphasized that more serious attention needed to be given to the limitations of short-term treatments for depression and to investigating alternatives, including maintenance treatments and 'booster sessions'.

One of the few studies of treatment outcome in depression to concern itself explicitly with relapse prevention was that of Frank et al. (1991). As part of the three-year follow-up after treatment, consisting of psychotherapy plus antidepressant medication, some patients continued to receive interpersonal therapy. An interesting finding was that although relapse rates generally were higher in these groups than in the medication-only group, the median survival time was very different: detailed analysis of the data, using audiotapes, investigated the degree to which the interpersonal therapy was implemented as intended. Patients whose therapists had adhered closely to therapy manuals had a median survival time to relapse of approximately two years; those whose therapists did not, had a median time of only five months.

It is important for practitioners to become familiar with outcome research literature and to know how common relapse is amongst certain types of problems. On an individual level, therapists, particularly those in private practice, have no way of knowing whether their clients relapse once therapy is over. Some therapeutic approaches specifically discourage clients from re-contacting their therapist once an agreed conclusion has been reached. In other situations, clients themselves are reluctant to re-contact either because they are feeling better and sufficiently independent, or because they are feeling worse and ashamed or angry. Perhaps clients who relapse after the end of therapy are right in believing that therapists 'won't want to know'. There is no straightforward answer as to how, when or with whom we can legitimately find out the relapse status of ex-clients. This can result in carelessness, a lack of accountability and ignorance of potentially useful feedback. In the period leading up to completion, clients need careful preparation for the time when they no longer have access to expert help and it is reasonable to suggest that wherever possible we should seek to find out if we have done this preparation adequately. It is important to explore our reasons for bringing therapy to an end and the timing of it (Leigh, 1998). We need to ensure we are not just 'getting out while the going's good'. The question to be addressed is: will postponing ending decrease or increase the client's ability to cope on her own?

The fact that it is not always easy, or that it is not common practice, to find out how our clients cope after therapy ends, does not mean that ideas about follow-up should go unchallenged. If it is mentioned at the right time during therapy, it is likely to prompt the client into thinking in concrete terms about what it will be like to reflect on progress after leaving therapy. It may help the client internalize the 'coping with setbacks' aspects of the therapy: both she and the therapist are recognizing that she will feel vulnerable but that the therapist is interested in how she copes with this on her own. In many agency settings, it is relatively easy to set up arrangements for a short, one-off return visit for feedback and review. Alternatively, the client could be sent a letter or questionnaire which provides the opportunity for her to comment on how she is getting on, what she has found difficult and whether she has experienced recurring problems. In independent practice or when payment for an additional session may be an issue, a questionnaire or a structured form may be more acceptable.

Theoretical approaches to relapse

During the process of therapy, we usually recognize that clients have relapsed, or may be about to relapse, because of what we observe or what they tell us in relation to their behaviour. Thoughts and feelings will play a part, but it is what clients *do* that normally leads us to define something as 'a relapse'. It is likely to be a *pattern* of behaviour, over a short space of time, that client or therapist (or both) recognize, which is both familiar and unwelcome. It may be a slow slippage back into that state or it may very quickly begin to dominate the person's life again. Sometimes a client will have progressed in therapy to a point where she believes she has developed more control in her life, so that the return of old patterns of behaviour seems alien and threatening. Alternatively, in spite of therapy, another person may still believe she has little choice about her behaviour and a return to familiar patterns may feel inevitable and possibly even reassuring. In both cases, the sense of exerting voluntary control over what one does and thinks is undermined.

Craig had spent many weeks in therapy talking about his violent father, and how this must have contributed to his growing up prone to aggressive behaviour. During the first months of therapy, he was very pleased that he seemed to have overcome his outbursts of temper in relation to his son and his wife. During a two-week holiday, however, he had returned to being verbally abusive at home, and on his return to therapy admitted that it had somehow felt reassuringly familiar to 'let fly' at them again. Nonetheless, he regretted it happening and was very keen to continue to work to reduce the likelihood of this behaviour continuing.

Baljinder came into therapy specifically to get help to reduce her overeating and to work on her shyness. She made excellent progress, learning about developing normal eating patterns and gradually reducing her social phobia. Therapy seemed to have worked very well for her but nevertheless, six months after leaving, she was involved in a minor car accident and following this event her eating binges returned and she avoided going out of her flat for days at a time. She felt despondent and helpless, and was reluctant to contact her therapist again.

Both examples involve a return to familiar behaviour which appears undesirable, but there are differences in how upsetting it is seen to be, and the likely explanation for why it occurred.

The emphasis on patterns of behaviour, as well as on the beliefs associated with the behaviour, is one of the reasons that cognitive therapy and cognitive-behavioural approaches are at the forefront of theory, research and clinical practice in attempts to understand relapse. In contrast, it is not a concept which is given particular emphasis in those psychotherapeutic models which focus on personal growth, systemic change, social transitions and the resolution of developmental crises.

Although most therapists accept that working through a setback is a necessary part of therapy, the specific word 'relapse' may not be part of their professional vocabulary. Many within a humanistic and experiential tradition of psychotherapy regard problems or psychological disturbance as resulting from people being prevented by adverse experiences from actualizing their potential. Distressing or unwanted behaviour and ways of thinking are viewed as manifestations of underlying blocks in their experiential processing. Within therapy, they are offered a supportive context for working towards self-awareness and personal meaning: the manner in which this process will occur is assumed to be idiosyncratic and will not necessarily progress in a linear fashion, nor are behavioural symptoms targeted as things simply to be got rid of. Feelings and experiences are explored and reflected upon, without an emphasis on categorizing them as 'dysfunctional' – at whatever point they occur during the therapeutic encounter.

Within a psychodynamic approach too, the emphasis is on exploration and a search for the meaning of 'symptoms' but there tends to be a more elaborated, predetermined approach to understanding their structure. Problematic behaviours are viewed as coded expressions of emotional conflict: they are 'compromise formations' by which the client endeavours simultaneously to defend against a painful or unacceptable thought or feeling, to keep it out of awareness, while also allowing it some degree of outlet. For example, obsessional checking to ensure 'safety' is likely to be a hidden reversal of aggressive impulses while also discharging them (by giving both oneself and other people a hard time). There is an expectation in psychodynamic therapies that such behaviours will be resolved as the associated anxieties are brought to awareness and made tolerable. All setbacks in the progress of therapy are viewed as grist to the mill, part of the material contributing to the development of insight and the assimilation of previously warded-off aspects of the self. The meaning of these fluctuations is sought by relating them to the client's responses to changes in her life or developments in the relationship with the therapist. Life events may stir up elements of old conflicts even after there has been some degree of resolution. For example, a client's obsessional checking may resume when aggressive and competitive strivings are evoked by someone being promoted over her at work.

Equally, changes in the transference relationship may touch on significant anxieties, perhaps ones which had earlier been allayed by the more 'holding' aspects of the therapy: again, anger with and worry about the therapist who cancelled a session through illness might result in resumption of checking. Such a return of symptoms would not necessarily be labelled as a 'relapse' by the therapist. Uncovering, understanding and containing these meaningful difficulties is regarded as central to the therapeutic process: they provide the possibility of a direct experience of the underlying conflicts and the opportunity for further resolution and 'working through' – that is, revisiting and re-experiencing with greater awareness in order to re-integrate painful and cut-off elements of the 'inner world'. In both psychodynamic and experiential therapies, relapse within therapy tends to be viewed as much as an opportunity as a problem. Both of these psychotherapeutic approaches might be said to share a *developmental model* of relapse.

Psychodynamic theory in particular makes it clear that exploratory therapy is likely to involve some degree of regression: this might involve, or look very similar to, a relapse. Regression is a return to developmentally earlier and less differentiated and integrated modes of experience and action (Sandler et al., 1976). Therapy is an invitation to 'break down' in a safe way, to let go of some habitual but limiting ways of holding oneself together in order to re-work early anxieties. This is the source of the idea that a client might have to get worse before she gets better. There is a danger of therapists misusing this notion, perhaps avoiding taking responsibility for the therapeutic process. However, it is essential for therapists to 'keep their nerve' in the face of an apparent relapse and to continue to work at understanding. Some dangerous aspects of regression are dealt with in Chapter 8. Malan (1979) suggests that clients in exploratory therapy are quite likely to 'relapse', however briefly, to a state similar to the worst they have experienced, at some point in the process. Circumstances must be such that this can be tolerated and used productively. Regressions and relapses can be viewed as an opportunity but also as a defence, that is, clients may be refusing to be more directly aware of anxiety and conflict. This element seems to predominate in 'negative therapeutic reactions' in which progress is almost immediately cancelled and the client relapses in the face of anxiety which improvement creates; this form of relapse can easily lead to an impasse and is addressed in detail in Chapter 8.

The main feature of humanistic and dynamic therapies with regard to relapse is the focus on establishing its meaning, in order to utilize it as a normal part of therapy with the behaviour itself being given no specific emphasis. Those approaches to therapeutic change in which the concept of relapse figures more prominently and specifically are – broadly speaking – the bio-medical model, and the coping skills model.

In the *bio-medical model*, the notion of relapse is located in relation to understanding an individual's physical or mental vulnerability, and the potential for symptoms or problem behaviour to re-emerge as a result of stress. Relapse can be minimized and sometimes prevented by buffering those suffering from conditions which make them vulnerable, from certain environmental, physical, interpersonal or psychological pressures ('stressors'). In acknowledging that relapse is better described as a process than a sudden event, this model emphasizes the importance of recognizing 'prodromal symptoms', or early indications of deterioration. In many mental health treatment settings therefore, a range of interventions are used, both to protect people from relapse (for example, in-patient respite care, long-acting medication) and to teach them and their carers to recognize the warning signs of a potential relapse.

The *coping skills model* also emphasizes the importance of acknowledging and tackling relapse. In particular, cognitive and cognitive-behavioural therapies seek to predict and so enable better control of psychological functioning. These therapies also focus less on what the recurrence of difficulties 'represents' and more on identifying what may precipitate them. Nonetheless, they are also clearly distinct from a bio-medical model. Cognitive therapy views a relapse 'event' as the end point of a relapse process: it is the consequence of triggering events combined with thoughts or beliefs a client holds about herself, her world and her vulnerability.

The more behavioural therapies emphasize an understanding of relapse as the reactivation of habitual response patterns to particular triggers. They argue that creating initial changes in thinking and behaviour is not where most of the therapeutic work necessarily needs to be focused – it is *maintaining change* and preventing relapse which is crucial. Homework tasks, relaxation exercises, social skills training and anxiety management may all be used as an adjunct to therapy, but these should be in the service of establishing new patterns of coping and self-control which can be maintained in the face of future triggering situations. The goal in this model is the unlearning of dysfunctional patterns and acquiring and consolidating new, more adaptive ways of responding: when this process is incomplete or has been inadequate, relapse occurs.

How – or whether – the term 'relapse' is used, will depend very much upon the therapist's overall theoretical position. Nonetheless, each of the theoretical models referred to has a useful contribution to make to our practice when it comes to dealing with this phenomenon. The approach of the humanistic and psychodynamic practitioner focuses on how clients view their experience – what meaning they give to it, what it represents for them. The bio-medical model reminds us that many people have a layer of vulnerability which predisposes them to succumb to particular life events or experiences which are felt to be stressful. They are 'relapse prone' and appropriate psychological, social and, in some cases, pharmacological support may be required over long periods of time. A cognitive-behavioural therapy framework is useful in its emphasis on anticipating relapse and its focus on enabling clients to practice overcoming the difficulties they are likely to encounter when therapy is over, by exploring them whilst it is still in progress.

Processes of change

In practice, relapse is most usefully regarded as a phenomenon occurring at some point during the *process* of change – a process which has distinctive markers. There is not a single shift from the existence of problems to their absence, but a series of smaller shifts in the person's thoughts, feelings and actions. Some schools of thought in psychotherapy would emphasize that one of these shifts involves moving from the wish for something to be different to the decision to change. As has been discussed in previous chapters, there is inevitably a co-existing *resistance* to change. For therapists working with problems such as eating disorders, obsessive-compulsive disorders, addictive behaviours, and some phobias, these shifts – including the decision to change and resistance to change – are comparatively easy to identify, if not to work with. This is true too of so-called 'life style' decisions, for example, embarking on a programme of regular exercise. Of particular importance in understanding relapse in a process model of change, is the concept of ambivalence: whilst clients may recognize dysfunctional and painful consequences of their current psychological situation, giving up that which is familiar and brings short-term benefits may be equally painful. There may also be doubts about their *ability* to change, and conflict develops about whether it is even worth making the decision to try. From this perspective, relapse is a manifestation of ambivalence reasserting itself at a later time in the process of change, and therefore similar interventions will be needed to help the person after a relapse as were provided when the initial shift in decision-making occurred.

Not all theoretical approaches would use the term 'resistance', but most would agree that ambivalence is important: the therapeutic process needs to include reducing or resolving the ambivalence which inevitably surrounds the initial decision to change, if relapse is to be prevented. Cognitive-behavioural therapists and most humanistic and problem-orientated therapists would maintain this can be addressed at a conscious level, by exploring thoughts, feelings and behaviours; psychodynamic therapists would argue that ambivalence and resistance may be substantially unconscious. For our purposes here we will consider a transtheoretical model which was developed for understanding the process of change in 'addictive behaviours' – that of Prochaska and DiClemente (1984) – ideas which were developed from Janis and Mann's (1977) work on conflict, choice and commitment. This highlighted that decisions made under stress, and decisions relating to highly conflictual behaviours, are particularly vulnerable to being reversed. Later versions of these models discuss how these reversals are related to initial ambivalence and may be temporary – people may well return to and later commit themselves to their original decision.

This model identifies five stages through which those attempting to change habitual patterns of behaviour move. *Precontemplation* is a stage when others around the person are aware that her behaviour is causing problems, but she appears unaware of this or is unwilling to make changes. This is followed by the *contemplation* stage, which is characterized by ambivalence: the person vacillates between the wish to change, and reluctance to do so. She is aware of her problems but has not yet made a commitment to take action. The *action* stage follows, when visible change

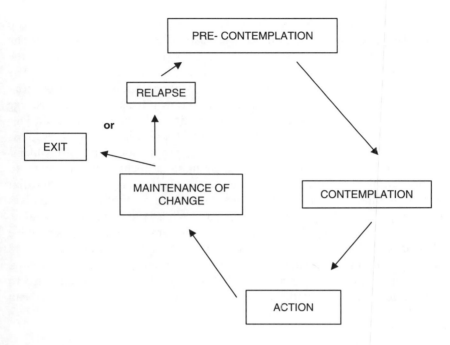

FIGURE 11.1 *'Model of change' (adapted from Prochaska and DiClemente, 1984)*

occurs and the person often makes alterations to her environment or lifestyle, possibly including telling others of her new decisions. She then enters the *maintenance* stage, characterized by consolidating her commitment and the changes achieved in the action stage, either with or without professional help or self-help groups. Psychological work on preventing relapse takes place at this stage. Although not included in their original model, Prochaska and DiClemente added *relapse* as the fifth stage. This seems to imply a dispiriting revolving door syndrome, but recent conceptualizations regard it rather as a 'spiral' model – a more accurate and more optimistic view of the process of change. Although there have been criticisms of this model (Davidson, 1998), it has been very useful in shifting the thinking of many practitioners away from simplistic assumptions about people being either ready and motivated to change, or not ready to change and having no motivation. By encouraging clients and therapists to think about a continuum of change, there is the opportunity to work out what sort of help may best suit people at each stage in their progress from the old, problematic behaviour to new, healthier behaviour.

There is much to be said for therapists having a model in their heads which reminds them that *maintaining* changes in thinking, feeling and acting is a struggle. And when the struggle is temporarily given up on and relapse occurs, the process can nonetheless continue. Both therapist and client will need to consider carefully what the relapse has meant in terms of how ready the client is to continue the journey. Is she disillusioned, ready to give up completely, convinced that she is just wasting her time – that is, has she returned to the pre-contemplation stage? Or is she back to weighing up the pros and cons, recognizing the part of her that is resisting change as well as the part of her that wants to change – contemplation? Or is she more determined than ever, having re-experienced how it feels to not be in charge of her own lifestyle, to pick up where she left off – the action stage? This recognition of a process, which probably exists whether or not therapy is taking place, is useful and relevant to work with a wide range of problems where setbacks commonly occur, from habitual behaviours through to anxiety and pathological grief. It is reassuring for clients to know that change is rarely a total transition from one state to another, but involves gradual progress through phases or stages. Whilst these are not inevitable, discrete categories, it is likely that, for example, ambivalence precedes active change, and that a relapse is preceded by a period of working on – and so consolidating maintenance of – the newly established style of coping. The feelings and thoughts associated with each of the phases may also to some extent be anticipated, thus guiding the type of work the therapist can best do.

Relapse and addictive behaviours

Of all conditions and problem behaviours a therapist is likely to deal with, it is amongst the so-called addictions that the notion of relapse is most often discussed. Nonetheless, as Gossop (1989) and many others point out, what counts as an addictive behaviour or evidence of addiction is not straightforward. For the purpose of looking at relapse in this context, we will regard addiction as including all or most of the following features:

- a strong desire or sense of compulsion to engage in the particular behaviour (especially when the opportunity to engage in such behaviour is not available);
- impaired capacity to control the behaviour (notably in terms of controlling its onset, staying off, or controlling the level at which the behaviour occurs);
- discomfort and distress when the behaviour is prevented or stops;
- persisting with the behaviour despite clear evidence that it is leading to problems.

These characteristics indicate that addictive behaviours are conflictual: there is discomfort when the behaviour is being indulged in and when it is being resisted. Making resolutions to change but finding this impossible to maintain is a common, psychological phenomenon, which has puzzled those who study addictive behaviours for many decades. Explanations have tended to have either moral or medical overtones – or both. In the recent past there has been increasing interest in the psychological processes which underlie the development of the addictive behaviours, heralding a move away from both a medical and moral domain. It is social learning theory which has contributed most (Heather and Robertson, 1997), in particular the model of the relapse process developed by Marlatt and Gordon (1985).

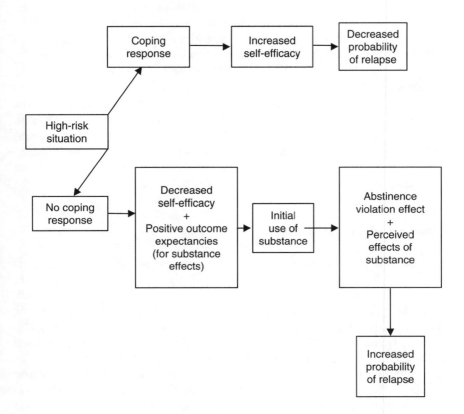

FIGURE 11.2 *Model of the relapse process (adapted from Marlatt and Gordon, 1985)*

This model relates to the use of substances such as alcohol, nicotine or other so-called addictive drugs, following a voluntary decision to stop. It highlights the importance of 'high-risk' situations and can be applied to other behaviours which have both a compulsive and a tension-reduction element to them such as food bingeing or repeated self-harm. The sequence of events (that is, the process of relapse) occurs as follows: when the individual does not deal with the risky situation by putting in place new or different coping strategies, she will experience herself as less capable, lacking in self-efficacy, and will also start to anticipate the short-term benefits that she had learned to expect from the 'old' behaviour. The combination of these may lead to the beginning of 'indulgence'. This is followed by the *rule violation effect* which is the tendency for people to tell themselves they 'may as well be hung for a sheep as for a lamb'. They perceive themselves as having switched from being in control of their situation, to being out of control. This, combined with becoming intoxicated or experiencing some other tension-reducing physical response, will considerably increase the likelihood of a full-blown relapse ensuing.

Marlatt and Gordon's model has its limitations, particularly in its over-emphasis on rationality and its de-emphasis on affect, but it provides a much needed alternative to disease models of addictive behaviour and it has stimulated research, theory and practice in relapse prevention generally. Their own research has included identifying the most common precipitants for alcohol, nicotine and heroin relapse: negative emotional states, inter-personal conflict and social pressure. They and others have described the specific interventions which can be used to help clients cope effectively with high-risk situations, trigger events and initial 'lapses'. In the next chapter, we will adapt this model and extend it to cover a range of potential relapse situations, rather than just substance misuse, and identify appropriate interventions for different phases of the relapse process.

Relapse and mental illness

A broad-based medical approach to psychiatric problems normally incor-porates a 'stress-vulnerability model', which suggests that some people are more vulnerable than others to environmental stressors because of both psychological and biological factors. This provides a context for thinking about relapse which is very different from those described so far in this chapter. It contrasts with models which regard both initial 'recovery' from a problem behaviour, and a later return to it, as involving some degree of intentionality, whether conscious or out of awareness. There are of course ongoing debates about the role played by genetic, physiological, social and developmental factors in the causality of mental ill-health – but there is a common belief that people can be helped at least to manage and limit, if not prevent, relapse. Contemporary good practice in psychiatry uses a wide variety of interventions aimed at stress reduction, as ongoing vulnerability to relapse is seen to be worrying for the individual sufferer and to those around her. At best, there is a genuinely holistic approach to mental illness, tackling family dynamics, the living situation, medication, individual counselling, education about the condition and general stress management interventions. Although this orientation may be unfamiliar to some coun-sellors and psychotherapists used to an individualistic approach, there is much to be learned about relapse from psychosocial orientations, particu-larly the role of family interventions.

Research in the last twenty years has highlighted the significance of how families interact with people diagnosed as schizophrenic, and there has been a focus on the potential for relapse prevention which exists in providing psycho-educational family interventions. It has been established that patients who had recovered from an episode of schizophrenia and who returned to families where levels of criticism, emotional over-involvement or hostility were high, had markedly higher rates of relapse. The concept of 'expressed emotion' was developed (Leff and Vaughn, 1985) and linked to a 'stress-vulnerability' model (Zubin and Spring, 1977) to explain how psychotic episodes are triggered. Family intervention techniques were developed, including establishing a collaborative working alliance between the therapist and the whole family, the sharing of information about the condition, identifying and practising coping skills to reduce interpersonal stress and conflict, learning about constructive ways of interacting with one another and reducing demanding, nagging and critical comments (Fadden, 1998). This type of targeted relapse prevention, focusing on the whole family, has been found to be highly effective: a four-fold decrease in relapse at nine months post-intervention, and relapse rates of less than 10 per cent, being reported in the intervention groups compared with rates of 40–50 per cent in the control groups; results remained impressive at a two-year follow-up (Tarrier et al., 1988).

The relationship of expressed emotion to a variety of other conditions suggests that there may be useful relapse prevention work to be done with the families of people suffering from eating disorders, bipolar disorders and depression. For example, a study by Hooley et al. (1986) found that high expressed emotion in spouses of depressed patients was significantly related to nine-month relapse rates, and the single best predictor of relapse in this study was patients' perception of criticism by the spouse.

Another aspect of relapse prevention which has been mainly developed in work with people who have experienced psychotic illnesses is identifying and responding to early indications or 'prodromal symptoms' of reduced well-being (Birchwood and Tarrier, 1992). Its emphasis is on careful discussion between patients, carers and the therapist to establish what an individual's 'relapse signature' might be and then assisting her to self-monitor and to seek out appropriate interventions to reduce the severity of a relapse. This might involve a variety of stress-reducing interventions, including a short period of respite care away from the normal environment. The person is empowered to take an active role in affecting the course of her difficulties, whilst her intrinsic vulnerability is acknowledged. This might be regarded as a form of early or preventative crisis intervention. As discussed in Chapter 2, the term 'stress' refers to pressure on the individual's coping processes, and both 'crisis' and 'relapse' occur only when these are overloaded.

Establishing that social factors can influence the course of an 'illness' is no more or less radical than observing that social factors play a part in the process of personal behaviour change. What is significant, however, in terms of dealing with relapse, is that non-medical interventions (for example, psychosocial intervention with families, cognitive therapy) are seen as effective in augmenting pharmacological treatments. We would suggest that there is scope for research and more flexible practice in a variety of fields in order to explore what counsellors and psychotherapists could usefully borrow from this approach to mental health problems.

Theory and practice – an overview

When trying to understand relapse, some profound questions arise. Some clients will argue that they cannot control certain actions, or that they experience thoughts, feelings or impulses which seem to override any sense of personal choice. How much does stress and vulnerability erode purposeful decision-making? If someone *intends* to exert self-control, and then fails to do so, does this suggest wilfulness, ignorance, illness, or over-learned habit? Even if we feel unable to give categorical answers to these questions, we need to be open to a diversity of perspectives and to recognize our own beliefs about apparently 'involuntary' ways of behaving. Many different views about preventing or minimizing relapse have something useful to contribute to our practice. There is the issue of vulnerability and the individual's perception of impaired control, which encourage us to look at the social situation, family circumstances, genetic elements and physiological potential of individual clients as being relevant to relapse. Medical and social models remind us that some clients will want and need something outside of themselves to help them avoid relapse, whether this is medication, spiritual fulfilment, social support, a change in material circumstances, or identifying with others who are in a similar situation. The humanistic and dynamic psychotherapies, with their emphasis on the exploration of experience, highlight the importance of working with the client to understand the significance or symbolism of their return to the unwanted behaviour, thoughts and feelings and the place that this has in the course of her personal development. The cognitive-behavioural approach should always be included insofar as it emphasizes both the situations and the automatic thoughts and beliefs that can trigger a particular pattern of action and perpetuate it. By doing our best to look at every facet of vulnerability to relapse and its reduction, we will avoid the danger of providing a therapeutic intervention which focuses only on how to *avoid* doing or feeling something, rather than on an approach which emphasizes change, the maintenance of change and the promotion of personal growth.

It is also important to avoid an over-preoccupation with preventing relapse at all costs, as this can blind us to the fact that in reality people tend to oscillate between sometimes quite extreme ways of acting and reacting. There are rhythms in our lives, and during therapy clients may need to adjust gradually to new rhythms, sometimes involving a reduction in the intensity of certain experiences, rather than these disappearing completely. Many clients will regard therapy as having been successful if they oscillate less wildly and unpredictably in their behaviour, experience these fluctuations as somewhat more under their control, and are able to see that the consequences of their behaviour are less distressing or harmful. In the next chapter, we will look at the way in which therapists can work with clients both on anticipating relapse, and reducing it to something more manageable and less frightening.

12   Managing Relapse

Rosemary Kent

Our premise is that relapse – no matter how ambiguous the term – is a setback that occurs relatively often, and it is good practice to acknowledge it rather than avoid it. Therapist avoidance is most likely to happen either as a result of believing that relapse is an inevitable part of certain illnesses or syndromes which therapy is powerless to eradicate, or feeling that it is a sudden, inexplicable phenomenon which can overwhelm the client at any time – leaving the therapist with the sense that she and her client are helpless in the face of it. Recognizing that unwelcome but familiar behaviours, thoughts and feelings will recur and are part of the process of achieving change and growth, is a more hopeful and also a more realistic belief, whatever your theoretical orientation.

Sometimes therapists may believe that discussing relapse with clients encourages negativity, or implies that therapy is not going to be successful. By not discussing it with them, there is a tacit assumption that relapse ought not to occur. This 'wishful thinking' may apply to all setbacks, but as was noted in Chapter 11, for certain types of problems and conditions relapse is more likely than for others. The prospect of relapse, therefore, can and should be worked with, whilst also recognizing that reducing the frequency and intensity of relapse episodes over time is our ultimate goal. More attention must be paid to limiting the harmful consequences of a relapse – psychologically (for example, shame, guilt, loss of self-confidence) and interpersonally, socially and physically. We learn by our mistakes – but only when there is the opportunity to view those mistakes from a new perspective, and in a supportive environment.

In this chapter we address practical ways of reducing the likelihood of relapse, and managing it by mitigating its negative consequences. This includes how we can help clients limit the length and severity of a relapse episode. Many of the approaches discussed are specifically cognitive-behavioural in origin as it is the literature on CBT which most often and specifically addresses this. A number of CBT ideas can be modified or included when working within other theoretical approaches – these include developing coping techniques or learning to recognize high-risk situations. It is likely that the empowering element of any therapeutic approach will increase the client's sense of control, reducing the frequency of unwanted feelings, thoughts and behaviours. There are also aspects of addressing relapse which require a completely different focus: for instance, early relapse resulting from unresolved ambivalence about the decision to change may require close attention to the nature of the therapeutic contract and relationship.

Early relapse

We need to consider the possibility that relapse may occur fairy early on in the therapy process. Reasons for this may include a failure of client and therapist to achieve a satisfactory working alliance: an apparent return to 'the problem' may indicate that therapy hasn't really got started. It may also imply that motivation to change is not sufficient, or not *yet* sufficient, and a robust decision to tackle problems and engage fully in the process has not yet been made. Early relapse can often present itself as a crisis, and may be followed by an impasse: to resolve this cluster of setbacks, the therapist needs to return to re-examine the contract, the original working alliance and the extent to which the client has really explored and resolved her ambivalence about change (see Chapter 7). This should be discussed in supervision, and should also be raised within the therapy session, so that client and therapist can together figure out the meaning of this early relapse episode: this enables it to be 'reframed' as a point of learning and can improve the capacity of the therapy to withstand future difficulties.

The timing of the client coming to feel and believe that she is ready to change may not coincide with the timing of others expecting that she *should* change. There is a danger that if other people around her have clamoured loudly enough, the therapist and client may both convince themselves that a commitment to change has actually been made when it has not. As may occur in relation to early impasse, there is the illusion that a therapeutic contract has successfully been formed, but the client is more invested in staying the same than in starting a process of change or growth. As therapists, we are particularly likely to fall into this trap when working with any behaviours which are seen to be socially undesirable or dangerous – there is so much pressure from others for the individual to change, that we may too readily believe that the client shares the desire for change in equal measure and we act as if this is the case. In fact, she may be a long way from having made a firm commitment to change (that is, she is a pre-contemplator) or she may be at a stage of intense ambivalence about it (a contemplator), and the therapist will need to work with her to strengthen the therapeutic alliance and re-establish a more realistic contract, before any work focused on changing has a realistic prospect of success.

Helping people to make overt decisions to change any aspect of their lives involves reviewing with them what is desirable and what is undesirable, or frightening, or alien about change. It also involves exploring how confident they are about their ability to make changes – that is, their self-efficacy. As both 'desirability' and self-efficacy increase, readiness to change increases – see Figure 12.1. Many therapists will automatically address this, both in assessment and by focusing during therapy on small achievable goals at first, and then encouraging clients to recognize that they have proved to themselves that they are able to change. Within every therapeutic approach we need to pay attention at an early stage (once a client has committed herself to the therapy process) to talking about what may undermine the client's confidence about changing. It may be a major theme for the whole therapeutic process. Indeed, it may be that the client has recognized something specific which undermines her ability to achieve self-change, which has brought her into therapy in the first place. It is also not uncommon that clients say that they believe they will manage change for a short time but will then be unable to sustain it. Building up the client's belief in herself will involve reviewing what has happened in the past to lead her to this point, discovering areas of her life in which she is competent, and ensuring that she recognizes positive achievement when it does occur, in addition to focusing on problematic feelings and behaviours.

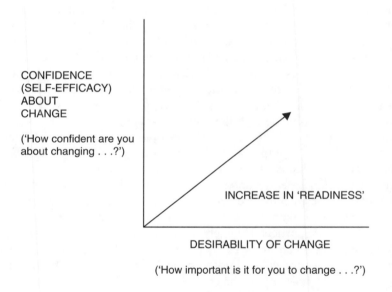

FIGURE 12.1 *Readiness to change*

Of course, ambivalence about change does not disappear completely because a client has progressed, with or without therapeutic help, to the stage that she can acknowledge, express or embrace a commitment to change – the *action* stage. Ambivalence will, however, gradually recede, and she is likely to feel less resistant and more confident as therapy progresses. We need to acknowledge that it may be very difficult for her to keep this up consistently in the face of all kinds of vulnerabilities that may beset her. *Maintenance of change* – in all its forms – is the vital next step.

Tackling vulnerability

Apart from the potential for relapse which occurs at an early stage, related to unresolved ambivalence, 'pseudo-decisions' and failure to establish an adequate therapeutic bond or contract, the possibility of relapse remains very real throughout therapy and, of course, after it. Much of the therapeutic business of 'relapse prevention' involves recognizing and tackling the vulnerability of the individual client. Shiffman (1989) describes three 'levels' at which vulnerability may exist, and sees them as differing in their temporal relation to relapse – enduring personal characteristics, background variables and precipitants. This conceptualization overlaps with Marlatt and Gordon's (1985) model of the relapse process, and with the 'stress-vulnerability' model. We have adapted some of these ideas in order to provide a practical framework for interventions suited to the different levels of vulnerability, which applies to a wide range of problems.

Level 1 – Enduring personal characteristics and life circumstances

Some individuals can be assumed to have certain relatively stable characteristics which predispose them to relapsing when other (temporary) stresses occur. These include personality variables (for instance, low self-esteem) and the experience of mental illness. Rather than regarding a relapse as a random, unexplained variable, a thoughtful and detailed consideration of such an individual's life story and social circumstances usually allows us to arrive at an understanding of the specific set of vulnerabilities which beset that person. Therapists are then in a position to consider how the frequency of relapse episodes can be reduced, however vulnerable someone is. This may take forms other than psychotherapeutic intervention, such as practical help (for example, the single mother prone to depression may be offered day care for her young child), or social support (a severely anorexic young woman joining a self-help network) or medication (a low-dose neuroleptic prescribed as a maintenance dose for someone prone to outbursts of aggression). Accurate assessment, diagnosis and understanding of vulnerable individuals makes it more likely that they will get the prophylactic help they need. Whatever is provided, it is likely that such help will need to be reasonably long term.

Where vulnerability is created by life circumstances, it is important for therapists to acknowledge and assess the extent to which counselling and psychotherapy can realistically influence these. Clients vulnerable to relapse may be poor or isolated, lacking access to social support or an environment which encourages psychological health – for example, young people in areas of high unemployment. They may be physically impaired or prone to ill-health. Many people are vulnerable to relapse because of their day-to-day living habits or a lifestyle which cannot easily be changed – for instance, they are in a job where there are constant 'triggers' to return to old habits. They may be trapped because of their marital situation, or

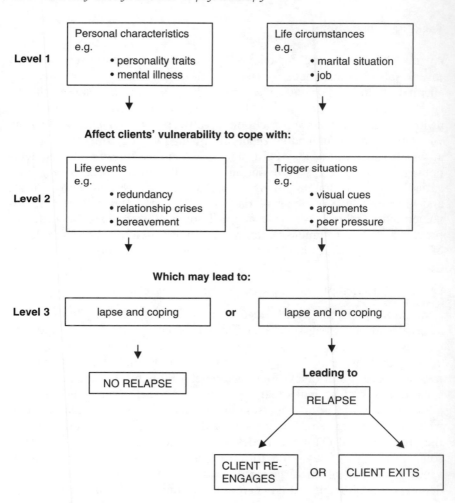

FIGURE 12.2   *Levels of vulnerability to relapse*

because they are a carer. They may be socially excluded or victims of prejudice through appearance, background or cultural beliefs.

Given the many different ways in which life circumstances contribute to vulnerability to relapse, it could be said that family, structural or social change, rather than an individualistic approach, is required. However, therapy can and should contribute to empowering people, starting by addressing their perceptions of powerlessness and aspects of choice and control in their own lives.

Level 2 – High-risk situations – life events and triggers

High-risk situations set the stage for relapse: they are background factors which relate not to the enduring character or circumstances of the individual client, but to the person's experiences during the 'maintenance stage'. In our framework we include what Shiffman refers to as 'background factors' as well as 'precipitating factors': these refer to less immediate and possibly cumulative antecedents to relapse, and to the immediately antecedent, triggering incidents, respectively. Thus, high-risk situations include a range of life events which most people would regard as stressful, such as redundancy, illness, relationship crises; and also specific events or situations which are perceived by the individual as potential triggers to relapse, and may be unique to that person, for example, seeing a favourite brand of beer advertised, or being involved in an argument. These may be very strongly associated with the relapse behaviour, particularly if it is an appetitive or habitual behaviour related to eating, drinking, drug use or sexual behaviour, or to aggression or self-harm.

The therapist may encourage the client to identify and monitor risk-creating background factors and also precipitating factors. The specific interventions which may be used to prevent relapse are:

- identify high risk situations;
- identify and monitor precipitating factors;
- identify, test and challenge negative thoughts;
- learn distraction and avoidance strategies;
- learn coping strategies, problem-solving and relaxation;
- enhance self-efficacy through realistic goal setting.

Thus, the relapse prevention focus of cognitive-behavioural therapy, which is used for a wide variety of client difficulties, is aimed quite specifically at tackling situations in which the client feels vulnerable, and helping her to generalize these strategies to other situations if necessary.

Many other therapeutic approaches do not attempt to be as concrete or situation-specific about vulnerability – they are likely to work more at Level 1 and then use specific stressful situations as examples to illustrate how clients could apply their new insights as they emerge in therapy. Clients who describe such scenarios and relate feelings of vulnerability may be encouraged by the person-centred therapist to explore these in a safe counselling environment; the transactional analysis therapist might suggest identifying what interpersonal games were being played out; the psychodynamic therapist may enable her client to recognize what echoes there are in the situation with earlier patterns in her life. Within most theoretical frameworks however, there should be a space for considering the *habitual* element of relapse vulnerability. Cognitive-behavioural therapy reminds us that often negative, automatic ways of thinking produce a pattern of learned helplessness which may be effectively tackled by focusing on life events and precipitating factors in specific, familiar, vulnerable-making circumstances. These may then shift from being 'high-risk' to 'potential for growth' situations.

Level 3 – lapses

Marlatt and Gordon (1985) have been credited with the idea that returning to familiar but unwanted patterns of behaviour is not an event, but a process. This is mainly applicable to those types of difficulties where the short-term tension-reducing effects contribute to long-term harm or distress. It begins with a lapse or the initial violation of a self-imposed rule, which can either be nipped in the bud or, alternatively, be allowed to continue. The biggest danger for the client who has not initially coped, and begins to relapse, is that she will 'catastrophize'. Her vulnerability increases as she recognizes the familiar thoughts, feelings and behaviours associated with failing. A key intervention is to stop the client thinking in extremes ('I'm either in control, or totally out of control'). Therapy may encourage the client to recognize that her own insistence on being perfect 100 per cent of the time has perpetuated fluctuations between extremes of behaviour and prevented her learning to deal with the inevitable imperfections of life, other people and herself. She will also need to work on self-acceptance, the acknowledgement of guilt and tolerating her sense of frustration. Whenever possible, the idea of relapse as a sudden 'event' should be discouraged so that a client's self-efficacy is enhanced: she *can* successfully avoid repeating familiar patterns.

We can see, then, that there are helpful interventions drawn from various therapeutic approaches that can reduce a client's vulnerability to relapse – at any or all of three different levels. The probability of setbacks needs to be anticipated and normalized at the same time as we aim to reduce their frequency. There are major therapeutic advantages to a client handling a lapse or a relapse without panicking and in a way that keeps her willing to reflect on it and develop her understanding of herself.

Post-relapse therapy

The essential features of post-relapse therapy are:

- managing crisis-related aspects of the relapse, if the situation requires it, and helping the client to be safe and the therapy viable;
- providing an accepting, non-judgemental context to enable emotional containment and allow exploration of distressing thoughts and feelings, and;
- helping clients make sense of their experiences within the framework established for the therapy, in order to promote learning and development.

Relapse is not a crisis situation. However, there may be instances when a relapse leads to a crisis within therapy, and there may sometimes be occasions when relapse poses risks to the client herself or to others. The continuation or integrity of the therapy itself may also be greatly threatened by elements of the relapse behaviour. These aspects of relapse management are dealt with in Chapter 5 – the general principles of risk assessment and crisis management apply.

Post-relapse therapy requires giving full attention to a client's initial sense of 'things having gone horribly wrong' and being able to empathize with this, whilst at the same time avoiding either colluding or catastrophizing. The core condition of acceptance provides reassurance for those who have been scarred by previous experiences of relapse. Friends and families are likely to have expressed anger, disappointment, frustration, false reassurance, or have inappropriately attempted to rescue. Significant others frequently express criticism when people in therapy relapse, as they will have seen the individual improving or coping and may be especially annoyed at the apparent irrationality of a sudden sliding backwards. A calm, impartial approach by the therapist will provide some counterbalance to the reactions of others, whether real or imagined. The emphasis in the past may have been on the consequences for others of this person's behaviour. The therapist will need to ensure that the client has permission to put herself centre stage in reviewing what has happened, rather than focusing on what effect it had on other people or situations. Indeed, she might have to press for this to happen, and it may be useful to explain to clients how various roles may get played out following a relapse. It is not uncommon for clients to take up the position of victim, whilst family members or others are behaving either as persecutors or rescuers. Therapists need to take a stance of benign neutrality to avoid being drawn into psychological game-playing. This is discussed in the section below on the therapist's response.

When working with people who resume habitual behaviour which they have struggled to give up and which they feel badly about, it is particularly important to help them cope with the shame and guilt they experience following a relapse episode. We discussed earlier the 'rule violation effect': a major component of this is often self-disgust at having failed to keep to a decision. The initial lapse may bring immediate but temporary relief and escape from feelings of vulnerability, confusion and distress. As this effect wears off, other powerful negative thoughts and feelings will emerge, which are perceived as intolerable: they need to be fended off. Continuing with the lapse/relapse behaviour is likely to feel overwhelmingly familiar as the forces of self-loathing and desire for indulgence combine with a lack of self-efficacy, to produce a vicious circle which is hard to break. When a client has failed to prevent the initial lapse developing into a repetition of previously avoided behaviour, she may feel intense guilt because she has not used therapy properly, or because she feels she has let down her therapist, as well as significant others. Her sense of shame and loss of self-respect may increase as she indulges in the drug use, the self-cutting, the binge-eating or whatever behaviour it is that she had previously managed to limit or avoid.

She feels she now needs those behaviours to cope with the feelings which they produce. A period of low mood which many people would label to themselves as being 'down in the dumps' can become an occasion for self-recrimination and condemnation in someone who fears a depressive relapse: she sees herself as 'not coping'; her unhappiness is testimony to her worthlessness. This lapse into depression produces a similar downward spiral – unless these feelings can be contained.

The shame and guilt can be sufficiently strong that the client feels unable to admit to having relapsed. Within a good therapeutic relationship, if a client hints about 'things going wrong', the therapist should ask her to be concrete about how this has manifested itself. In the example of Mike quoted below, the therapist said, 'It sounds as if the stress was becoming almost too much for you to bear. I guess having a few drinks was a very tempting option? Is that what you did?' A balance was struck between not enabling him to continue to avoid the subject, and not appearing to assume that he had failed in some way.

Cultural norms, the setting in which therapy takes place and sub-cultural attitudes will play a significant part in how people feel and behave after a relapse. These will also affect what defences are erected to deal with the situation. Denial is, of course, a reaction to confrontation and may in the past for a client have been an automatic initial response to fend off fear, guilt, shame and loss of self-esteem. The norms of certain institutions, such as eating disorder clinics, or the probation service, are likely to engender various defensive postures which may make it difficult for honest and productive post-relapse therapy to take place. Other defensive strategies include minimizing, avoiding through 'not remembering' details, extreme dissociation ('it wasn't really me') or extreme passivity. The possibility of not being frank about setbacks should be acknowledged and discussed early in the development of the therapy – if necessary it should be addressed in the initial contract. Behind the defences, therapists may find that the degree of guilt, shame and sense of failure which beset their clients is almost overwhelming. Clients may view the therapy room as a 'confessional' – but rather than the therapist being in a position to offer forgiveness and absolution, she needs to help the client to survive the intense feelings that are elicited, to explore them and to continue with the therapy process.

Mike was living in a flat owned by a landlord sympathetic to the fact that Mike had previously been a very heavy drinker, but was now receiving counselling and had been alcohol-free for four months. The landlord had made it clear to Mike that if he relapsed, he reserved the right to give him notice to leave. During weekly counselling sessions Mike struggled with the stresses of establishing a sober lifestyle for himself, including taking care of himself physically. At a psychological level, he made slow but steady progress and recognized the importance of identifying emotional discomfort as it emerged, and talking it through either in counselling sessions or with a supportive friend. He decided that he needed to deal with a major fear related to his not putting on weight – he arranged to have an AIDS test. The therapist helped prepare him for this. The following week in the counselling session he spoke about having been totally miserable, uptight and terrified for the past few days. He talked to a number of people about how he was feeling, but it didn't seem to help. When the therapist asked him if he had decided to have a few drinks, he admitted he had, but went on to cross-examine the therapist about confidentiality and the importance of his landlord not finding out. The therapist gently brought the discussion back to Mike's feelings – his shame, guilt, and sense of inadequacy, loneliness and fear. He was helped to understand the wish to deny that the relapse had happened – to himself and to others – and he was able to experience, for the first time, another person wanting to understand rather than criticize his drinking.

The third key feature relating to post-relapse therapy is that of locating the relapse episode within the process of change, and exploring its meaning within the framework of the therapeutic modality within which the work is taking place. Challenges and conflict will occur during the therapy process and good theories will offer a way of constructing a meaning for them. What clients experience as 'relapse' can be worked on and understood as having at least some elements which make sense. In exploring these, it is likely that the therapy will need to emphasize the re-establishment of self-esteem, self-efficacy and improved coping responses. It will also be helpful to discuss the 'spiral' model of change with the client, indicating how insight and experiences gained as a result of a relapse episode will enable her to return either to re-evaluating her choices about changing, or working on maintaining previously achieved gains.

After seven sessions of apparently successful cognitive therapy with Jay during which she looked at many aspects of her anxiety and developed a number of effective strategies for dealing with it, she came to session eight looking extremely frightened. She described how, the day before, she had unexpectedly had to organize the catering for a lunchtime meeting, when her colleague – who would normally have done it – was not at work. She had become increasingly anxious as the morning wore on and had at one point left the building and started to drive home. She managed to turn back but by then another colleague had been asked to take over. Jay was tearful at first in describing this but was able to calm down within a short while and worked on analysing the whole episode. Though at first she regarded it as a 'catastrophe', the therapist enabled her to identify precipitating factors, the return of some (but not all) of her old 'automatic thoughts', the recognition of where she had 'caught' herself and reminded her that this experience – though unpleasant – was not the same as the previous experiences of anxiety for which she had originally sought help. By the end of the session she was focusing on what she had learnt about herself on this occasion and congratulating herself on having had the courage to return to work after initially driving off in her car.

The therapist's response

In the preceding section, we have emphasized the importance of the core conditions of empathy and acceptance in responding to relapse and the need to help clients use the experience as an opportunity to learn. Unfortunately, it is quite possible that the therapist's initial feelings on hearing that someone has relapsed could be anything from disappointment through to despair, puzzlement through to disbelief, mild irritation to downright anger. Pride in our work with clients and optimism about their future can be overturned in an instant. All these feelings are entirely understandable but they can certainly undermine therapists' willingness and ability to work effectively with lapse and relapse.

Relapse can have a dramatic effect on therapy, leading either to a sudden moving forward, or to crisis, or to an impasse. The latter is likely if the therapist fails to maintain her neutrality, or ignores her own feelings and allows them to leak into the therapy sessions – for example, setting an inappropriately difficult homework task for a client, following discussion of a relapse, may be a way of punishing her. The resulting resistance may lead to impasse and further feelings of frustration in the therapist. Sometimes the therapist expresses her annoyance or disappointment directly – either verbally or non-verbally and the client feels she has no choice but to leave therapy, carrying the sense that she is entirely to blame.

Other feelings which may overwhelm the therapist and get in the way are associated with taking up the position of 'rescuer' or 'victim'. These are the roles complementary to that of 'persecutor', identified above, and have been vividly described by Karpman (1968) who refers to the playing out of these interactions as the 'Drama Triangle'. Two, three or more people temporarily move into one of the three roles in response to a situation and to the role taken up by another significant person. If played out in a therapeutic situation, impasse or unplanned endings are inevitable. Thus, the therapist who feels great sympathy for the client who has relapsed may try to 'rescue' her from a 'persecutory' world, colluding with or even pushing her into the role of 'victim'. Sometimes the therapist may see the client as the persecutor and herself as the victim, (for example, believing that the client 'deliberately' started cutting herself again just before the therapist's holiday, making her feel guilty). In this case, the therapist's supervisor may end up being expected to take the role of rescuer.

Acknowledging and reflecting on our emotional responses to relapse contributes to normalizing the situation and moving forward. This may be done within supervision or outside of it – acknowledging disappointment or frustration in private with a colleague may be sufficient – prior to thinking about and then exploring how the client feels about it. Colleagues and supervisors need to beware of collusion (or rescuing or persecuting) and to be alert to the feelings in the therapy situation being replicated within supervision. There is no shame in feeling upset by a client's relapse:

the therapist can in fact model for the client ways of dealing with it which are both honest and constructive.

Consolidating change and ending therapy

It is helpful to have a model which regards improvement as cumulative, when relapse is a likely part of the change process. This encourages a pragmatic, optimistic approach to therapy. We can also work towards relapse episodes occurring less frequently, and with less serious consequences. This can be achieved not just by the techniques described above, but also by addressing some of the practical frameworks of the therapy.

The way therapy is organized within a time frame plays a crucial part in reducing the frequency of relapses. As clients grow stronger, increase their self-understanding, resolve conflicts and make positive decisions, there is a danger that therapists can become seduced by apparent 'success' and consistently avoid exploring possible setbacks. Either consciously or unconsciously they may then decide to finish 'whilst the going's good'. Clients in their turn feel optimistic and may be keen to assert their independence. They may convince themselves and their therapists that the 'bad old feelings' have now disappeared and even if they returned they would be able to handle them. Therapy is often terminated prematurely – but of course many therapists are unaware that it was premature as the relapse occurs later.

The setting in which therapy occurs and the model used influences how the ending of therapy is managed and how acceptable it is for clients to return to their therapists for further work (Leigh, 1998). Many therapists are highly unlikely to say, prior to finishing, 'but of course if the problem flares up again, just come back and see me . . .' – organizational, practical and theoretical considerations militate against such an approach. However, there are many ways of ensuring appropriate ending processes occur and building in safety nets, without encouraging excessive dependence.

Endings should be discussed at the start of the therapy, and the therapist needs to be clear to what extent the length of therapy will be influenced by the client's wishes and behaviour. Many clients may believe that if they relapse, they no longer 'deserve' help, so therapists should emphasize that attending sessions and being willing to discuss setbacks are crucial elements. If the number of sessions is open-ended, therapists need to be particularly aware of how they assess someone's readiness to finish: they should not be so frightened by the prospect of relapse that they constantly put off ending; they should not collude with the idea that handling a single difficult situation successfully is evidence that therapy should end immediately.

A helpful approach may be to provide a gradual reduction in frequency of sessions – signalled well in advance – with increasingly longer between-session gaps. This should be planned with the client, and dates written down by both parties so there is no confusion. Another approach is to build in booster sessions which are arranged before therapy is concluded, and which serve as mini-interventions (of between one and three sessions) to help clients stay on track, or re-establish gains previously made. With this approach, it may be best to obtain the client's permission to send a reminder letter, and also to agree that if she does not want or need the booster session at the time, she should let the therapist know.

In some therapeutic settings, there are no constraints on clients choosing to return for further periods of therapy if they want them, or simply opting to have occasional follow-up sessions. From an organizational point of view, this needs careful thinking through by therapists and their managers. Clients need to be given information about whether an additional session or sessions are regarded as crisis intervention (that is, an appointment will be offered very promptly), whether it is a consultation or review session, or whether it is a further period of therapy (and whether this will be long or short term) that is being provided.

Whether or not 'post-therapy therapy' is available to clients, planning to conclude a period of therapeutic intervention should always include considering how change can be consolidated. This may involve various practical approaches such as written work, consisting of a client writing down contingency plans to deal with difficult future scenarios. There may be life transition points where additional stress can be anticipated. Other aspects of a therapy package which are particularly relevant to the maintenance of change stage may include relaxation training and other stress management techniques, recommending the reading of appropriate self-help books, or referral on to different or additional therapeutic work focusing on issues which the current therapist is not competent to deal with – for instance, the therapist helping a client overcome her agoraphobia successfully may discuss her seeking help for sexual abuse issues which they both recognize could play a part in her becoming vulnerable again in the future.

Cautions and conclusions

In these two chapters we have tackled the issue of clients appearing to revert to old patterns of thinking, feeling and behaving which seem to occur in spite of the therapeutic process. As with attempting to understand crisis and impasse, we need to recognize that individual relapses may be integral to the whole experience of being in therapy: consisting of a decision to enter a new context, to confide in and work with a therapist, to examine closely the distressing and conflictual problems which have been experienced. Thus, relapses during and after therapy should not be seen as identical to the problem behaviours which occur without therapy (or a self-help programme) having been undertaken. During therapy, therapists are aiming, in a sense, to reduce their clients' naivety about how and why things are experienced as conflictual or problematic. Clients may cling to beliefs about the inevitability of their eating or drinking binges, or the comforting nature of their checking behaviour, but good therapists will challenge these in such a way that when temporary return to this behaviour occurs it will be *experienced as different*. It will have been 'spoilt' by therapy – the anticipated 'benefits' do not occur, or its original significance has been altered. It follows that the duration, intensity and subsequent frequency of the original behaviour is likely to be reduced.

It could therefore be argued that once clients have genuinely begun to see themselves and their problems in a new way, a precise re-enactment of previous behaviour is increasingly unlikely. Superficially, their actions or experience may appear the same, and in the absence of therapists helping clients to examine these more closely, they may conclude that they have failed. However, the process of therapy ensures new meanings are attached to familiar and habitual patterns.

Emphasis on quantitative methodologies, randomized controlled trials and assessing outcomes according to very limited time frames has also meant that research equates 'relapse' with unsuccessful outcome (Miller, 1996). It therefore falls to the therapist to challenge the self-fulfilling prophecy so deeply embedded in the word relapse: it may even be time to abandon it altogether or consider using a more everyday word, like 'setback'. Perhaps a way forward is to keep our attention at all times on the nature of the change process in which we are participating, with these experiences, like impasses and crises, serving to remind us of the complexity of change and the importance of the therapist's essentially affirmative role within it.

13   Responding to Developmental Challenges

Therapists are not exempt from the uncertainties of life. Like their clients, they are subject to the turbulence of their own developmental processes. They are immersed both in the flow of their own change and in the demands of their involvement with clients' troubled development. There is a double-sidedness to a therapist's relationship to her own change processes: her own life moves on and this affects her work in complex ways; at the same time, the experience of participating in the struggles of others feeds back into a changing sense of self. This reciprocity can be profoundly beneficial – but it can also contribute to therapeutic difficulties. Throughout the preceding chapters the therapist's impact on the course of the therapeutic work has been emphasized – the ways in which she is implicated in the formation and the resolution of crises, impasses and relapses. We know from the research literature how crucial 'therapist variables' are in influencing outcomes, much more so than differences in theory or technique (Beutler et al., 1994). Awareness of your own personal and professional development as a therapist plays a vital part in responding effectively to the developmental challenges of clients.

The therapist's life course

It is in the nature of the therapeutic process – its essentially non-reciprocal basis – that the therapist is expected to be a relatively stable figure. She provides a 'secure base' for the client (Bowlby, 1988). However, therapists are human and change in complex ways in response to challenges which they may not have anticipated. Their life course is likely to be influenced by the interaction of a number of factors:

- the impact of life events;
- the unfolding of their own continuing maturation and development, both personal and professional;
- the stimulation and demands of therapeutic work with clients.

Each of these may bring to light previously unsuspected problems or prove to be a challenge of such magnitude that it cannot be confronted without the therapist experiencing some setback of her own. These struggles impact in turn on the security and responsiveness which she can provide as a developmental context for her clients. As with all such challenges, however, they present both threats and opportunities for growth to client and therapist alike.

Events in the life of the therapist provide the clearest instance of the effect of her development on the therapy. This impact can on occasion be dramatic, creating substantial personal and technical challenges in the work. Divorce, bereavement and serious illness are all likely to have emotional resonances and practical implications within the therapy (Bellak, 1981). Even minor (less 'crisis-like') events may have repercussions which find their way into the consulting room. Depending upon the meaning of what has happened, such life events can be a substantial emotional drain on the therapist. There may be an increased sense of aloneness and an intensification of personal need. The energy available to invest in the client is reduced, the therapist's sense of personal vulnerability is heightened and it becomes more difficult to tolerate the client's demands or attacks. The therapist may start to retreat defensively, becoming less emotionally available in order to avoid the potential threat. She may start to feel needy towards the client, perhaps simply hoping for appreciation of the effort that she is making, or else expecting the client to make up for her suffering by seeking, subtly or overtly, to be loved and cared for. Thus, therapists can indulge their suffering at the client's expense – but they can also have a tendency to deny their experience of pain, disability and vulnerability in equally unhelpful ways. Those who have a limited 'safety net' of personal resources and social support are more likely to be seriously affected by the impact of life events. Those without good supervision are at greater professional risk. Everyone, however, needs to be aware of their own limitations at such times, identifying and protecting specific vulnerabilities and considering what kind of work and what kind of clients they can responsibly take on.

When there has been a significant event for the therapist, clients may have to be told something of what has happened in order to account for a break or other alteration in arrangements. Alternatively, they may find out about it in other ways: they may hear through their social network or they may become aware through changes in the therapist's circumstances or demeanour. Clients are often very aware of the smallest signs from their therapists and may know, consciously or not, more than we might imagine that they do. So the therapist should be alert to what the client may be making of these signs and how she is reacting to what the therapist is going through. The client may have difficulty tolerating the ordinary humanity and 'fallibility' of the therapist. There may be a sense of disappointment and disillusionment, or alternatively one of triumphant pleasure. The client may feel altruistic concern but she may also be afraid of damaging the therapist or anxious that she would be deserted were she to overburden someone who seems vulnerable. Thus, important therapeutic material is generated by the client's response to such events which may echo significant personal issues for her. This can lead to gains in understanding and a wider acceptance of both self and others. However, it can also lead to significant difficulties for the therapist, particularly where she is feeling threatened or depleted and so is less well equipped to respond: it can lead to the client's feelings – particularly negative ones – being blocked or avoided. The client may be worried about abandonment while the therapist needs greater emotional distance. The client may be angry and abusive when the therapist needs to feel valued. The client may wish to ignore an obvious difficulty which is too threatening or not what she needs to work on, while the therapist may long for some acknowledgement. The client may be preoccupied with the therapist's troubles when the latter is wanting to play them down. In these circumstances, the risk of a therapeutic impasse is significant.

Of course, where the therapist is well supported and functioning within her limitations at the time, this should all be 'grist to the mill'. This means making a judgement about what is in the client's interests: what she needs to know about the therapist's life and what she needs to explore in her reaction to it. The one sometimes has to be weighed against the other, since knowing the facts can get in the way of exploring fantasies and assumptions. Different therapeutic approaches adopt very different stances in relation to personal disclosure by the therapist and it is obviously important to work consistently from your own position. Either relatively frank self-disclosure or relative anonymity can be misused. Disclosure of personal difficulties by the therapist can obviously distract attention from the client's issues and subtly pressurize her to take care of the therapist. Withholding information can be rationalized as protecting the client or preserving neutrality when it is actually a defensive attempt to project an omnipotent façade. It is necessary to maintain the focus on the client's needs and struggles without hiding, deceiving, failing to respond or creating some artificial game around her concern or curiosity. It is unlikely to be helpful to bring in details of all the current upheavals in the therapist's life but if the client seems to have discovered something, or there is some obvious change in the therapy, the issues need to be addressed directly, otherwise the client's sense of what is real and what can be talked about will be further confused. A simple acknowledgement of what is happening, while leaving enough space to explore the client's reactions and their implications for the relationship, is generally what is needed. If the client must be aware of some change but has not mentioned it, it is essential to explore this. Keeping the focus on the client means continuing to listen and learn even when this might be difficult for the therapist to bear.

With some major life events, specific practical arrangements need to be put in place. It may be necessary to limit the therapist's caseload and careful thought should be given about how to do this. If the only responsible thing to do is to interrupt or even terminate a therapy, there should be both an attempt to prepare the client for this and to ensure that appropriate alternative arrangements are made and that the client is helped to utilize them. Of course, in the case of sudden illness, accident or incapacity, the therapist may not be in any position to inform clients or make arrangements for them herself. Giving proper consideration to this eventuality is a responsibility neglected or avoided by many: being well, we expect to remain that way and we are loath to think otherwise. If the therapist knows that she has a fatal illness or is unlikely to get well enough to resume work, then the practical aspects can and should be handled straightforwardly – making alternative arrangements, putting in place emergency cover and leaving adequate records. In effect, these are the things which should be in place at all times, as provisions against the unexpected.

Wendy was in her late 40s and had been practising as a counsellor for 12 years when her mother died. She was not so distressed that she felt unable to contact her clients herself; she cancelled their sessions for a month, since she knew that it would be a difficult time for her and that she would have a lot of sorting out of her mother's affairs to take on. With two rather fragile clients, she gave them the name of a colleague with whom she had a long-standing arrangement to act as each other's stand-ins. All her clients were told that there had been a 'family bereavement'. Over the month she found that her distress, though manageable, increased. On returning to work, she decided that it would be unwise to continue to work with two clients who had significant bereavement issues and one older lady whom she had always experienced as troublesomely similar to her mother: she gave them each two or three closing sessions and helped them make alternative arrangements. She had known from the therapy she had undertaken during training that her attraction to being a counsellor was in many ways bound-up with the care-taking relationship she had developed from an early age with her depressed and demanding mother. She felt that she had worked through this sufficiently and had made a good career, working hard and never doubting the wisdom of her choice of a second vocation after leaving teaching. Now, however, as the months passed following her loss, she felt some deep alteration in her relationship to her professional work: some longer-term 'sea change' seemed to be taking place within her. She no longer felt the intense interest and involvement with her clients that she once had; it was as if she didn't *need* to do it any more. She went for a brief period of therapy with someone whom she respected outside her local area and quite quickly came to the decision to scale down her practice. Her mother's estate allowed her some greater financial leeway and she felt a growing need to use that to explore a long-cherished dream to travel and to write. By two years after her bereavement, Wendy had reduced her practice to four or five short-term clients per week and two or three hours of providing supervision. She was at work on a book.

Events in the life of the therapist are always experienced in the context of the slower cycles of personal evolution across the lifespan (Guy, 1987). Individuals may enter their career as a counsellor or psychotherapist at different stages in their life cycle and there is a complex interrelationship between these two aspects of the therapist's development. Different phases of both personal and professional development have their own strengths and weaknesses in terms of the therapist's capacity to respond to clients' developmental challenges. At different times, both in response to the events of life and independent of them, every therapist will experience fluctuating levels of involvement and changing forms of satisfaction within the work. The wise therapist endeavours to be sensitive to these rhythms in her changing needs – and in respecting them, offers the best to her clients. Over time, changes in interests and outlook can create an incompatibility with some or even most aspects of the therapeutic role. This creates a major professional developmental challenge and it may take considerable courage and imagination to find a way out of this professional impasse.

Therapeutic work is a profoundly personal enterprise and professional growth will often involve the most intimate aspects of our being. People in all walks of life change and grow in interaction with the events and demands of their work. It is a unique feature of a psychotherapeutic career that this dialogue is with the intimate developmental challenges of other people. Formative events will often be particularly challenging experiences with clients which call for change in how we see our work and perhaps ourselves (Dryden, 1985). This dialectic between the working and personal lives of therapists is a crucial feature of how blocks in the client's growth process are responded to.

The therapeutic self

When we make the choice to become a psychotherapist or counsellor, it is in itself a critical developmental decision with roots deep in our own history and aspirations which are complex and not entirely reality based: our motives are always mixed but the balance within them counts (Sussman, 1992; Wosket, 1999). Our personal needs may be more or less compatible with the therapeutic role. Guy (1987) identifies what he terms 'functional' and 'dysfunctional' motivations for becoming a therapist. Problematic motivations were discussed in the context of counter-transference in Chapter 9: they are a crucial contribution to the interactive dimension in the creation of therapeutic impasses, sometimes in their most damaging and abusive forms. They also contribute to real difficulties in sustaining a viable therapeutic self. These problematic motivations may be divided very crudely into two categories. Firstly, there may be an excessive wish for self-healing – gaining insight from others, taking risks vicariously, receiving care at second-hand, overcoming loneliness and finding intimacy in a safe, artificial form. In its positive form, this 'wounded healer' position can mean the therapist has faced her own vulnerability and struggled with her own existential predicaments and so can be more understanding of the client's pain. However, if a poor resolution has been achieved, the therapist remains needy and provides little hope of well-being. In the second problematic type of motivation, the therapist needs to display herself as the embodiment of well-being, exercising almost magical power over the client and receiving her love and admiration. Again this 'guru' stance has a positive element: inhibitions about being effective and influential have been overcome. However, the need to be the perfect practitioner, free from all problems, imposes all the neediness on the client and disables the therapist from learning from her own mistakes. These dysfunctional motivations are often intermingled in subtle ways: wishes to rescue, protect and nurture the client become primarily projections of the vulnerable and needy aspects of the therapist herself.

Becoming a therapist often seems to be related to early life experiences – of feeling isolated and set apart, of pleasing and caring for a parent, of being a mediator or peace-maker (Guy, 1987). Although these may lead to the vulnerabilities and dysfunctional needs outlined above, they are often translated into positive motivations for therapeutic work: curiosity, empathy and an interest in the personal dimension of life, together with capacities for self-denial and a tolerance of ambiguity. These intertwining needs interact with the rewards and demands of the work in the growth of what might be termed a 'therapeutic self'. This professional or therapeutic self is a kind of 'second' self which the therapist responds from in the context of her work (Schafer, 1983). It is not false or inauthentic to respond out of a part of ourselves in a therapeutic context. On the contrary, it is built out of the effort to bring the best of ourselves to our work – to put the needy, destructive or immature elements of ourselves 'on hold' to some extent and to bring to the therapy those aspects which are most affirmative and resilient. It is these most developed parts of ourselves out of which we are best equipped to respond to the challenges of therapeutic work. It has often been proposed that a therapist cannot take her client further than she has travelled developmentally herself (Fine, 1982). These capabilities in the therapist require developing and sustaining in order to meet the demands of the role. This element of distance between the therapeutic self and wider personal life allows storms to be weathered in the short term, but the vitality of the self as a whole requires continuing dialogue and an effort towards integration.

The practice of counselling and psychotherapy can and should be a constant source of developmental challenge: participation in the growth of others is itself rewarding and inspiring as well as calling on us to exercise our capacities for understanding, creativity and effectiveness. All of these demands are likely to promote personal as well as professional growth in the therapist. However, this continual pressure for personal development in the therapist has its own double-edged quality: there may be times in our life when we may need to 'coast' rather than constantly strive. Constant self-sacrifice or compulsive self-reliance are developmental impasses which are potentially inherent in the therapeutic role.

Stress in the therapeutic role

Many aspects of working as a therapist are significantly stressful (Sussman, 1995). An element of isolation is intrinsic to the role. The nature of the working conditions tends to promote interpersonal isolation, with long hours spent without interruption or contact with colleagues. This is increased by the tendency to overwork, caused both by the financial insta- bility of independent practice and by sometimes guiltily dutiful motivations to help others. The depriving quality of the therapeutic relationship for the therapist contributes to a psychological isolation, needing as she does to set aside personal problems, withhold personal information, control emotional expression and constantly monitor her own reactions. Finally, and most closely linked to the issue of developmental challenges, are the emotional demands of being the witness to others' distress and struggles. Extending herself empathically while endeavouring to retain separateness in the face of interpersonal pressure can leave the therapist feeling repeatedly churned-up or depleted. Painful personal issues are reactivated. Reactions to the client may evoke feelings of shame or inadequacy. It is precisely in the areas of crisis, impasse and relapse that these issues are most prominent. The client behaviours rated most stressful by therapists are: suicide threats and attempts; hostility and the constant communication of intense suffering; slow progress, resistance to change and premature termination (Farber, 1983). As emphasized throughout the book, these difficulties can leave the therapist feeling ineffective, incompetent and helpless. They can easily result in demoralization. All of these elements of the work constitute a real risk to therapists' long-term functioning.

These risks inherent in the work can produce a range of problematic responses. At one level, they may result in some form of chronic, defensive posture on the part of the therapist – the magical healer, the self-sacrificing rescuer, the detached interpreter and so on. These fixed self-protective attitudes may spill over into private life, creating difficulties in intimate relationships: the therapist may become subtly superior, secretive and withholding, or bland and empty of genuine feeling. A narrow, highly defended version of the therapeutic self 'takes over' the whole personality. These damaging effects on ordinary relationships due to personal defen- siveness may contribute to a vicious cycle of withdrawal, growing isolation from real involvements and the exacerbation of emotional depletion and defensive distancing. The reactions of people in the helping professions to the pressures of their work have been summarized under the heading of *burnout*, a topic which has generated an extensive literature over the past quarter century (Firth-Cozens and Payne, 1999). Classically, this has identified a 'syndrome' characterized by:

- emotional exhaustion and loss of energy;
- loss of concern and depersonalization of clients;
- development of negative attitudes to self and work.

Most therapists have experienced some of these symptoms at some stage in their career and there is probably a continuum of degrees of professional impairment which may take various forms. Research suggests that 35–40 per cent of therapists report levels of personal difficulty which have reduced the quality of their work significantly at some point in their career, while about 5 per cent report having provided inadequate treatment as a result (Sherman, 1996). Vulnerability is heightened by a range of personal, work and contextual factors outlined in Table 13.1 to which therapists need to be alert. In spite of most therapists being aware of their responsibility to safeguard their fitness to practice and to obtain guidance when impaired, it appears that many still find it difficult to seek help at times when they are experiencing personal distress. The needs that brought them into the work may predispose them to deny disability, while the culture and organization of the professions may make finding appropriate help problematic.

TABLE 13.1   *Risk factors for depletion, burnout and impairment*

Personal characteristics
  loners, socially and professionally isolated
  idealistic, dedicated, self-sacrificing
  compulsive givers, care-taking, rescuing
  over-controlling, omnipotent
  perfectionist, competitive
  undergoing prolonged crises/transitions
Client characteristics
  suicidal – threats or attempts
  hostile, angry, critical
  passive-aggressive, covert resistance
  slow to change
  communicate chronically intense suffering
Work organization characteristics
  role ambiguity
  role conflict
  role overload
  inconsequentiality, professional doubt
  lack of recognition or pay-off
  lack of results or efficacy

States in which the therapeutic self is depleted or impaired are probably a major factor in creating therapeutic crises, impasses and relapses. Impasses may arise due to the therapist's inability to extend herself at critical moments in the work: she needs sufficient 'reserves' to call upon. Being overextended or burnt out is liable to result in a variety of negative, therapy-damaging reactions: inflexibility and rigidity of responses; pessimism and a readiness to give up, too readily terminate or push the client out of therapy; lack of patience and stamina; emotional withdrawal and unavailability; irritability, hostility and a tendency to blame the client; conciliatory avoidance of the client's frustration; and impulsiveness, sudden changes of technique or taking excessive risks. All of these are commonplace stress reactions; all have been identified earlier as tending to give rise to an impasse or provoke a crisis or relapse.

Professional cultures need to engender and support an understanding of these difficulties and a commitment to looking after ourselves in the interests of our clients. This means actively working to maintain a web of relationships and involvements around professional work which sustain the vitality of the therapeutic self: contact and interaction with colleagues; maintaining a balanced caseload; diversification in types of work and roles; attention to physical and recreational needs; and wider interpersonal involvements beyond professional circles which provide alternative sources of support and validation. Creating this context for our own work and development involves using our expertise on our own behalf. To care genuinely for other people, it is essential to have sufficient self-regard to care for ourselves and to be capable of allowing ourselves to be cared for. We need a world view that validates honesty and compassion about our shared experience of vulnerability.

'Containing the containers'

Individual counselling or psychotherapy is never really just something which takes place between two individuals. Whoever you see as a client in therapy – an individual, a couple, a family or a group – there is always a wider context for the therapeutic relationship. The 'therapeutic self' also exists within a professional, organizational and social context which spans the various specific therapeutic relationships in which it plays its part. This social context can be crucial in influencing the development and resolution of therapeutic difficulties. It provides 'containment' for therapists in ways analogous to that which the therapeutic relationship provides for clients: it enables anxiety and psychological pain to be tolerated and processed; it facilitates thinking and gaining fresh perspectives; it promotes integration. In situations of developmental challenge, there is a regressive pull away from performing the necessary therapeutic task which in these circumstances can become intensely anxiety provoking; instead, there is pressure towards finding some form of safety and security. This is true for the therapist herself (as has been emphasized throughout the book) and also for the organizational structures which surround and support her (Obholzer and Roberts, 1994). The entire therapeutic team and the social system around the work may respond to the client's distress, confusion and the pressure this puts on those around her: powerful forces are unleashed throughout the helping network.

In the commonplace observation of 'splitting' within staff teams, different members of the therapeutic network take up opposite and competing positions. This painful and destructive process is best understood as a result of the difficulties in tolerating the client's intensely ambivalent feelings. In a sense, it can be seen as the client 'externalizing' these feelings as a way of coping with them herself – but this must not be used as a way of blaming the client. It is a failure of the therapeutic staff to synthesize their own ambivalence about responding to her. Treating the disagreements as valid points of view and exploring the complex feelings of the staff behind them, enables the social system to move towards a resolution within itself. This is a necessary precursor to any resolution in the therapeutic relationship and provides the principal therapist with the sense of safety needed to explore and synthesize ambivalent feelings in the work with the client. Without this, the therapist is liable to fear that she will herself become a 'target' – that she will be disparaged or abandoned by her colleagues.

Organizational systems which are chronically under stress are less capable of withstanding these regressive pressures arising from difficult moments in the work. 'Real' problems contribute to this lack of security: inadequate staffing and role overload; the constant change which some organizations experience; the isolation of a team or agency; fears of financial instability and competition with colleagues. The culture and interpersonal atmosphere of the organizational or professional system can also undermine its capacity to provide a containing function for the therapist. Fragmentation and poor communication, chronic rivalry and conflict, lack of trust or lack of energy and direction all undermine the therapist's sense of safety and commitment.

In order to 'contain the containers', the social system needs to support the 'therapeutic self' in being secure, and free to perform its integrating and empowering functions for the client. Supervision and consultation are the usual mechanisms within counselling and psychotherapy for directly providing this containment. As with all institutions, there is the danger that supervision functions in a ritualized fashion which fails to offer containment of sufficient quality. Institutional arrangements depend for their vitality on the quality of the organizational and professional culture which supports them. A 'community' of therapists is needed which provides an environment in which individuals are free to be in touch with and expose their vulnerabilities, a culture which is mutually valuing and validating and which strengthens therapists to face the intense anxieties unleashed by developmental challenges. Cultures in which people feel under threat, criticized or scorned are all too common. In order to create an environment which provides this sense of safety, the development of clear organizational boundaries which are maintained in a flexible, non-authoritarian fashion is essential together with a shared philosophy and approach to the therapeutic work. Good management and leadership contains the organization as a whole. We are all dependent on our contexts for nurturing our sense of purpose, our values and our overall vision. These are at the core of every individual's therapeutic self and it is a rare person indeed who can sustain them in isolation.

Therapeutic morale

The morale of the therapeutic self – the degree to which an individual feels energized, committed, adequately resourced and secure in performing her therapeutic role – is an idea which brings together a range of factors which contribute to the therapist's investment in working effectively, even under trying circumstances. These ideas were developed in the context of working with client groups who were perceived to be difficult and unattractive, such as drinkers and violent men (Cartwright, 1980; Manley and Leiper, 1999). The concept applies equally well to therapeutic situations which are experienced as problematic – such as crises, impasses and relapses. The model is outlined in Figure 13.1.

There are three broad classes of factors influencing therapeutic morale. *Therapeutic commitment* is the personal investment of the therapist in undertaking the work and persisting with it even when the going gets tough. Several different elements go to make up an individual's therapeutic commitment:

- *Motivation* – her drive to undertake the work and succeed in it, with its roots in her own life history.
- *Work satisfaction* – the degree to which she derives and expects to derive personal fulfilment from undertaking the work itself.
- *Therapeutic self-esteem* – the degree to which she feels confidence in her competence in this type of work.
- *Personal resilience* – her capacity as a person to see difficulties as a challenge rather than as a threat.
- *Personal support* – the availability of diverse sources of support and renewal outside of work.

Role security represents the degree to which the therapist's sense of competence, efficacy and authority in the therapeutic role is sustained. It is made up of:

- *Role adequacy* – the degree to which training and experience have equipped her with the skills and capabilities to meet therapeutic challenges.
- *Role support* – the availability of resources such as supervision, consultation and a positive collegial culture which contain, encourage and inform her work at difficult moments.
- *Role legitimacy* – the extent to which her organizational context validates the type of therapeutic work in which she is engaged and acknowledges its difficulties.

Finally, *role structure* consists of those factors which ensure adequate organizational foundations and enable the work to be performed to a satisfactory standard:

- *Role clarity* – the degree to which expectations about what kind of work is to be done are unambiguous and consistent.

- *Role balance* – the presence of adequate diversity and richness within an individual's overall work tasks to ensure energy and interest is sustained.
- *Task resourcing* – the extent to which it is possible for the therapist realistically to undertake the required work, both therapeutic and administrative, without overload.

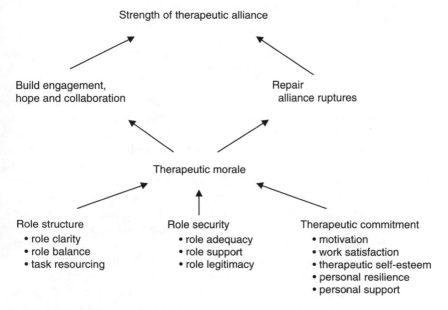

FIGURE 13.1   *Therapeutic morale*

This list of factors is not exhaustive but summarizes the issues discussed above. How they combine and interact in creating the level of therapeutic morale is extremely complex rather than simply summative. Interactions of certain factors may be particularly powerful – for example, low role legitimacy combined with poor therapeutic self-esteem; whereas in other individual cases, many negative factors may be substantially overcome – for instance, the combination of strong personal resilience and reasonably functional motivation may equip an individual to survive even quite poor organizational environments. However, it is unrealistic, on the whole, to place too much reliance on an individual therapist's capacity for self-containment. It is essential to ensure that she is also role secure and appropriately resourced if she is to sustain her level of response to developmental challenges.

The model suggests that therapeutic morale could be of crucial importance in meeting challenges to the developmental process because of its influence on securing the therapeutic alliance (see particularly Chapter 7). The therapist needs to believe in the efficacy of the therapy she is offering and in her own competence in order to convey assurance and realistic hope to a client who is demoralized, and to engage the client in a collaborative effort when she is feeling desperate or hopelessly stuck. The therapist also needs commitment, security and emotional reserves to support her in the face of setbacks and to give her courage to deal with the client's lost sense of trust or belief (Safran and Muran, 2000). Promoting the therapeutic alliance or restoring it when it weakens is the foundation for the therapist's capacity to deal productively with crises, impasses and relapses in the client's struggle to grow.

Responding to developmental challenges

A therapist is vulnerable to being seduced, entangled, bullied, downcast, intimidated or paralysed. In spite of these pressures, she has to persist with efforts to find meaning and a way through the difficulty. This is where therapeutic morale and personal resilience contribute, by enabling her to see the blockage in the process of growth as a challenge, one in which she can utilize and enhance her therapeutic skills and deepen her understanding of the client and her commitment to growth. To do this she needs to achieve a kind of balance within herself. Resilience and commitment must not turn into an attempt to bully or dazzle the client into 'getting better'. It must not shut-off her own emotional availability or exclude her openness to the client's struggles. This striving for balance occurs in many dimensions of the therapeutic relationship: the therapist must be effective and in control of herself without trying to be omnipotent; she must be committed without being self-sacrificing; she must limit her identification with the position of victim without denying her own sense of vulnerability; she must respect the client's defences but not fall into helplessness and passivity. Above all, perhaps, she needs to maintain her personal boundaries without retreating into some form of isolation.

Maintaining clarity about our separateness and a sense of responsibility for our own feelings without becoming detached and emotionally distant is never as easy as it sounds. The subtle loss of a well-bounded sense of separateness underlies many impasses and creates many therapeutic crises or relapses. Feelings of guilt and shame about our hostile or contemptuous reactions to the client or our sense of vulnerability or our inability to help are inevitable and pervade therapeutic work, particularly at difficult junctures. Slipping into some degree of personal or professional isolation is a constant danger which is inherent in the tensions of a therapist's role. Responding to therapeutic challenges is to a significant degree an internal struggle in which the therapist strives to achieve and sustain a position of detached concern.

Achieving this balanced stance can only be the product of a persistent commitment to sustaining the therapeutic self. It is this commitment which respects the privilege and maximizes the rewards of the opportunity to participate in the personal growth of other people. It enables us to be enlivened rather than depleted by the challenges of our work. Our motivations to be a therapist, rooted in our own needs and history, are shifted towards those elements which favour curiosity and creativity and so enable us to learn from mistakes and failures rather than to retreat into isolation and omnipotent thinking. Life-long learning and the humility which goes with it become part of a personal project: we need not to be seduced into encouraging clients in the illusion that certainty is achievable or that we are responsible for providing it. We thus become less liable to compromise our professional or personal safety through naivety, over-involvement, martyrdom, or the need to be needed.

Curiosity, creativity and the capacity to play – qualities which are so intimately tied up with the discovery of options, the construction of new meanings and the resolution of seemingly intractable dilemmas – depend upon the construction of a basic foundation of safety and security. In the therapeutic situation, as in life generally, this security stands constantly in a dialectical relationship with what is unfamiliar and threatening. 'The processes of human psychological development may be best served (or least violated) when the quest for change is appreciated in a context broad enough to include and respect change-resisting continuities' (Mahoney, 1991: 375). It is a fundamental paradox of therapy that personal change is best accomplished in the context of acceptance of the situation as it is (Safran, 1999). The capacity to accept both our client as she is and our own responses to her, frees us to be curious and to discover new possibilities. In therapy, as in life, we never learn anything new when things go as we had hoped. Only when our expectations and assumptions are challenged by some obstacle to our smooth progress are we provoked into appreciating the situation anew and endeavouring to know it in depth. It is in those painful moments of therapy when development appears to be blocked that we truly have the opportunity to think, to learn and to grow.

References

Adams, G. and Hopson, B. (1976) *Transitions.* London: Martin Robinson.

APA (American Psychiatric Association) (1994) *Diagnostic and Statistical Manual of Mental Disorders.* (4th edn). Washington, DC: A.P.A.

Appleby, L. (1992) 'Suicide in psychiatric patients: risks and prevention', *British Journal of Psychiatry,* 161: 749–758.

Aguilera, D.C. and Messick, J.M. (1982) *Crisis Intervention.* (4th edn). St Louis: Mosby.

Armor, D., Polich, J. and Stambul, H. (1978) *Alcoholism and Treatment.* New York: Wiley.

Atwood, G., Stolorow, R. and Trop, J. (1989) 'Impasses in psychoanalytic psychotherapy: a royal road', *Contemporary Psychoanalysis,* 25 (4): 554–573.

Baldwin, B.A. (1979) 'Crisis intervention: an overview of theory and practice', *Counselling Psychologist,* 8 (2): 43–52.

Balint, M. (1968) *The Basic Fault: Therapeutic Aspects of Regression.* London: Tavistock.

Baranger, M., Barranger W. and Mom, J. (1983) 'Process and non-process in analytic work', *International Journal of Psychoanalysis,* 64: 1–15.

Barnes, M. and Berke, J. (1971) *Mary Barnes: Two Accounts of a Journey Through Madness.* New York: Harcourt Brace Jovanovich.

Bateson, G. (1972) *Steps to an Ecology of Mind.* New York: Ballantine Books.

Bauer, G. and Kobos, J. (1987) *Brief Therapy: Short-Term Psychodynamic Intervention.* New Jersey: Jason Aronson.

Beck, A. and Freeman, A. (1990) *Cognitive Therapy of Personality Disorders.* New York: Guilford.

Beck, A., Rush, A.J., Shaw, B. and Emery, G. (1979) *Cognitive Therapy of Depression.* Chichester: Wiley.

Beck, J.S. (1995) *Cognitive Therapy: Basics and Beyond.* New York: Guilford.

Beck, U. (1992) *The Risk Society.* London: Sage.

Bellak, L. (1981) *Crises and Special Problems in Psychoanalysis and Psychotherapy.* New Jersey: Jason Aronson.

Berne, E. (1964) *Games People Play.* New York: Grove Press.

Beutler, L. and Clarkin, J. (1990) *Systematic Treatment Selection: Toward Targeted Therapeutic Interventions.* New York: Brunner/Mazel.

Beutler, L. and Harwood, T. (2000) *Prescriptive Psychotherapy: A Practical Guide to Systematic Treatment Selection.* Oxford: Oxford University Press.

Beutler, L., Machado, P. and Neufeldt, S. (1994) 'Therapist variables', in A. Bergin and S. Garfield (eds), *Handbook of Psychotherapy and Behaviour Change.* (4th edn). New York: Wiley.

Birchwood, M. and Tarrier, N. (eds) (1992) *Innovations in the Psychological Management of Schizophrenia.* Chichester: Wiley.

Bisbey, S. and Bisbey, L.B. (1998) *Brief Therapy for Post-Traumatic Stress Disorder: Traumatic Incident Reduction and Related Techniques.* Chichester: Wiley.

Blumenthal, S. and Lavender, T. (2000) *Violence and Mental Disorder: A Critical Aid to the Assessment and Management of Risk.* Hay-on-Wye: Zito Trust.

Bond, A. and Lader, M. (1996) *Understanding Drug Treatment in Mental Health.* Chichester: Wiley.

Bond, T. (1993) *Standards and Ethics for Counselling in Action.* London: Sage.

Bongar, B. (ed.) (1992) *Suicide: Guidelines for Assessment, Management and Treatment.* New York: Oxford University Press.

Bordin, E. (1979) 'The generalizability of the psychoanalytic concept of the working alliance', *Psychotherapy: Theory, Research & Practice*, 16: 252–260.

Bordin, E. (1983) 'A working alliance based model of supervision', *Counselling Psychologist*, 11 (1): 35–42.

Bowlby, J. (1988) *A Secure Base.* London: Routledge.

Boyer, L.B. (1983) *The Regressed Patient.* New Jersey: Jason Aronson.

Breakwell, G. (1995) *Management of Violence and Aggression in Health Care.* Leicester: British Psychological Society.

Brooke, R. (1994) 'Assessment for psychotherapy: clinical indicators of self-cohesion and self-pathology', *British Journal of Psychotherapy*, 10 (3): 317–330.

Campbell, D. and Hale, R. (1991) 'Suicidal acts', in J. Holmes (ed.), *A Textbook of Psychotherapy in Psychiatric Practice.* London: Churchill Livingstone.

Caplan, G. (1964) *Principles of Preventive Psychiatry.* New York: Basic Books.

Carr, A. (1990) 'Failure in family therapy: a catalogue of engagement mistakes', *Journal of Family Therapy*, 12: 371–386.

Cartwright, A. (1980) 'The attitude of helping agents towards the alcoholic client: the influence of experience, support and self-esteem', *British Journal of Addiction*, 75: 413–431.

Cartwright, A. and Gorman, D. (1993) 'Processes involved in changing the therapeutic attitude of clinicians towards working with drinking clients', *Psychotherapy Research*, 3 (2): 95–104.

Clark, M. (1989) 'Anxiety states: panic and generalized anxiety', in K. Hawton, P. Salkovskis, J. Kirk and M. Clark (eds), *Cognitive Behaviour Therapy for Psychiatric Problems.* Oxford: Oxford University Press.

Clarkson, P. (1995) *The Therapeutic Relationship.* London: Whurr.

Connel, G., Whitaker, C., Garfield, R. and Connel, L. (1990) 'The process of in-therapy consultation: a symbolic-experiential perspective', *Journal of Strategic & Systemic Therapies*, 9 (1): 32–38.

Daines, B., Gask, L. and Usherwood, T. (1997) *Medical and Psychiatric Issues for Counsellors.* London: Sage.

Dallos, R. and Draper, R. (2000) *An Introduction to Family Therapy: Systemic Theory and Practice.* Buckingham: Open University Press.

Davidson, R. (1998) 'The transtheoretical model: a critical overview', in W.R. Miller and N. Heather (eds), *Treating Addictive Behaviours.* (2nd edn). New York: Plenum Press.

Dolan, Y. (1985) *A Path with a Heart: Ericksonian Utilization with Resistant and Chronic Clients.* New York: Brunner/Mazel.

Douglas, M. (1992) *Risk and Blame: Essays in Cultural Theory.* London: Routledge.

Dryden, W. (1985) *Therapists' Dilemmas.* London: Harper & Row.

Duncan, B., Hubble, M. and Miller, S. (1997) *Psychotherapy with 'Impossible' Clients: The Efficient Treatment of Therapy Veterans.* New York: Norton.

Edwards, G. and Dare, C. (eds) (1996) *Psychotherapy, Psychological Treatments and the Addictions.* Cambridge: Cambridge University Press.

Eigen, M. (1993) *The Electrified Tightrope.* New Jersey: Jason Aronson.

Elkin, I. (1994) 'The NIMH treatment of depressions collaborative research programme: "Where we began and where we are"', in A.E. Bergin and S.L. Garfield (eds), *Handbook of Psychotherapy and Behaviour Change.* (4th edn). New York: Wiley.

Elkind, S.N. (1992) *Resolving Impasses in Therapeutic Relationships.* New York: Guilford.

Erikson, E. (1963) *Childhood and Society*. (2nd edn). New York: Norton.

Erikson, E. (1968) *Identity Youth and Crisis*. New York: Norton.

Fadden, G. (1998) 'Family intervention in psychosis', *Journal of Mental Health*, 7 (2): 115–122.

Fairbairn, G.J. (1995) *Contemplating Suicide: The Language and Ethics of Self-harm*. London: Routledge.

Farber, B. (ed.) (1983) *Stress and Burnout in the Human Service Professions*. New York: Pergamon.

Feltham, C. (ed.) (1999) *Understanding the Counselling Relationship*. London: Sage.

Ferro, A. (1993) 'The impasse within a theory of the analytic field: possible vertices of observation', *International of Journal of Psycho-Analysis*, 74: 917–929.

Fine, R. (1982) *The Healing of the Mind*. (2nd edn). New York: Free Press.

Fingarette, H. (1963) *The Self in Transformation: Psychoanalysis, Philosophy and the Life of the Spirit*. New York: Basic Books.

Firth-Cozens, J. and Payne, R. (eds) (1999) *Stress in Health Professionals: Psychological and Organizational Causes and Interventions*. Chichester: Wiley.

Fish, R., Weakland, J. and Segal, L. (1982) *The Tactics of Change: Doing Therapy Briefly*. San Francisco: Jossey-Bass.

Ford, D. and Learner, R. (1992) *Developmental Systems Theory: An Integrative Approach*. London: Sage.

Frank, E., Kupfer, D., Wagner, E., McEachrn, A. and Cornes, C. (1991) 'Efficacy of interpersonal therapy as a maintenance treatment of recurrent depression', *Archives of General Psychiatry*, 48: 1053–1059.

Freeman, A., Pretyer, J. Fleming, B. and Simon, K. (1990) *Clinical Applications of Cognitive Therapy*. New York: Academic Press.

Freud. S. (1926/1961) *Inhibitions, Symptoms and Anxiety*. (trans. J. Strachey). Standard Edition. London: Hogarth Press.

Gans, J. (1994) 'Indirect communication as a therapeutic technique: a novel use of countertransference', *American Journal of Psychotherapy*, 48 (1): 120–140.

Garfield, S. (1994) 'Research on client variables in psychotherapy', in A. Bergin and S. Garfield (eds), *Handbook of Psychotherapy and Behaviour Change*. (4th edn). New York: Wiley.

Gendlin, E. (1981) *Focussing*. New York: Bantam Books.

Ghent, E. (1993) 'Wish, need and neediness', *Psychoanalytic Dialogues*, 3 (4): 495–507.

Gilliland, B. and James, R. (1997) *Crisis Intervention Strategies*. (3rd edn). London: Wadsworth.

Glaser, M. (1992) 'Problems in the psychoanalysis of certain narcissistic disorders', *International Journal of Psychoanalysis*, 73: 493–503.

Golan, N. (1982) *Passing Through Transitions: A Guide for Practitioners*. London: Collier MacMillan.

Goldberg, D., Benjamin, S. and Creed, F. (1994) *Psychiatry in Medical Practice*. (2nd edn). London: Routledge.

Gordon, R. (1978) *Dying and Creating: A Search for Meaning*. London: Society of Analytical Psychology.

Gossop, M. (ed.) (1989) *Relapse and Addictive Behaviour*. London: Tavistock/Routledge.

Gould, R. (1980) 'Transformational tasks in adulthood', in S. Greenspan and G. Pollock (eds), *The Course of Life: Psychodynamic Contributions Towards Understanding Personality Development*. Vol. III. Washington, DC: N.I.M.H.

Green, R.J. (1988) 'Impasse and change: a systemic/strategic view of the therapeutic system', *Journal of Marital and Family Therapy*, 14 (4): 383–395.

Guy, J.D. (1987) *The Personal Life of the Psychotherapist*. New York: Wiley.

Heather, N. and Robertson, I. (1997) *Problem Drinking: A New Approach*. Harmondsworth: Penguin.

Herbert, M. (1993) *Working with Children and the Children Act*. Leicester: British Psychological Society.

Hodgkinson, P. and Stewart, M. (1998) *Coping with Catastrophe: A Handbook of Disaster Management*. (2nd edn). London: Routledge.

Hoff, L.A. (1978) *People in Crisis: Understanding and Helping*. Menlo Park: Addison-Wesley.

Hoffman, S., Gedanhem, S., Lahat, E. and Zim, S. (1994) 'Intervention by a consultant to overcome therapeutic impasse', *International Journal of Short Term Psychotherapy*, 9 (1): 61–65.

Holmes, J. (1993) *John Bowlby and Attachment Theory*. London: Routledge.

Hooley, J.M., Orley, J. and Teasdale, J. (1986) 'Levels of expressed emotion and relapse in depressed patients', *British Journal of Psychiatry*, 148: 642–647.

Horowitz, M. (1974) 'Stress response syndromes: character style and dynamic psychotherapy', *Archives of General Psychiatry*, 31: 768–781.

Horowitz, M. (1997) *Formulation as a Basis for Planning Psychotherapy Treatment*. Washington, DC: American Psychiatric Press.

Horvath, A. and Greenberg, L. (eds) (1994) *The Working Alliance: Theory, Research and Practice*. New York: Wiley.

Horvath, A. and Symonds, B. (1991) 'Relation between working alliance and outcome in psychotherapy: a meta-analysis', *Journal of Counselling Psychology*, 38: 139–149.

Hutchins, D. (1984) 'Improving the counselling relationship', *Personnel and Guidance Journal*, 62: 572–575.

Inskipp, F. and Proctor, B. (1993) *The Art, Craft and Tasks of Counselling Supervision. Part I: Making the Most of Supervision*. Twickenham: Cascade.

Irvine, F. (1984) 'Untransformed toads or talking frogs', *Psychological Perspectives*, 15 (1): 9–26.

Jackson, C. and Birchwood, M. (1996) 'Early intervention in psychosis: opportunities for secondary prevention', *British Journal of Clinical Psychology*, 35: 487–502.

Jacobson, G.F. (1980) *Crisis Intervention in the 1980s: New Directions for Mental Health Services*. San Francisco: Jossey-Bass.

Janis, I.L. and Mann, L. (1977) *Decision-making: a Psychological Analysis of Conflict, Choice and Commitment*. New York: Free Press.

Jenkins, P. (1997) *Counselling, Psychotherapy and the Law*. London: Sage.

Kareem, J. and Littlewood, R. (eds) (1992) *Intercultural Therapy: Themes, Interpretations and Practice*. Oxford: Blackwell.

Karpman, S. (1968) 'Fairy tales and script drama analysis', *Transactional Analysis Bulletin*, 7 (26): 39–43.

Kernberg, O., Selzer, M., Koenigsberg, H., Carr, A. and Applebaum, A. (1989) *Psychodynamic Psychotherapy of Borderline Patients*. New York: Basic Books.

Kluft, R. (1992) 'Paradigm exhaustion and paradigm shift – thinking through the therapeutic impasse', *Psychiatric Annals*, 22 (10): 502–508.

Ladany, N., Hill, C., Corbett, M. and Nutt, E. (1996) 'Nature, extent and importance of what psychotherapy trainees do not disclose to their supervisors', *Journal of Counselling Psychology*, 43 (1): 10–224.

Langs, R. (1975) 'Therapeutic misalliances', *International Journal of Psychoanalytic Psychotherapy*, 4: 77–105.

Langs, R. (1976) *The Bipersonal Field*. New Jersey: Jason Aronson.

Lambert, M. and Bergin, A. (1994) 'The effectiveness of psychotherapy', in A. Bergin and S. Garfield (eds), *Handbook of Psychotherapy and Behaviour Change*. (4th edn). New York: Wiley.

Lazarus, R. and Folkman, S. (1984) *Stress, Appraisal and Coping*. New York: Springer.

Leff, J. and Vaughn, C. (1985) *Expressed Emotion in Families*. New York: Guilford.

Leigh, A. (1998) *Referral and Termination Issues for Counsellors*. London: Sage.

Lerner, S. and Lerner, H. (1983) 'A systemic approach to resistance: theoretical and technical considerations', *American Journal of Psychotherapy*, 37 (3): 387–399.

Levinson, D.J. (1986) 'A conception of adult development', *American Psychologist*, 42: 3–13.

Lewin, K. (1951) *Field Theory in Social Science*. New York: Harper & Row.

Linehan, M. (1993) *Cognitive-Behavioural Treatment of Borderline Personality Disorder*. New York: Guilford.

Litman, R.E. (1994) 'When patients commit suicide', in E. Schneidman, N. Farberaw and R. Litman (eds), *The Psychology of Suicide*. Revised edition. New Jersey: Jason Aronson.

Little, M. (1981) *Transference Neurosis and Transference Psychosis*. New Jersey: Jason Aronson.

Littlewood, J. (1992) *Aspects of Grief: Bereavement in Adult Life*. London: Routledge.

Luborsky, L. (1984) *Principles of Psychoanalytic Psychotherapy: A Manual for Supportive-expressive Treatment*. New York: Basic Books.

McCormick, E.W. (1988) *Breakdown: Coping, Healing and Rebuilding after Nervous Breakdown*. London: Optima.

McLeod, J. (1997) *Narrative and Psychotherapy*. London: Sage.

Mahoney, M.J. (1991) *Human Change Processes: The Scientific Foundations of Psychotherapy*. New York: Basic Books.

Main, T. (1957) 'The ailment', *British Journal of Medical Psychology*, 30: 128–145.

Malan, D. (1979) *Individual Psychotherapy and the Science of Psychodynamics*. London: Butterworths.

Manley, J. and Leiper, R. (1999) 'Therapeutic commitment and role security in work with men with violence-related problems: an investigation and test of a model', *British Journal of Medical Psychology*, 72: 371–384.

Mann, D. (1997) *Psychotherapy: An Erotic Relationship*. London: Routledge.

Manthei, R. and Mathews, D. (1982) 'Helping the reluctant client engage in counselling', *British Journal of Guidance and Counselling*, 10 (1): 44–50.

Marcia, J.E. (1966) 'Development and validation of ego identity status', *Journal of Personality and Social Psychology*, 3: 551–558.

Marlatt, G. and Gordon, J.R. (1985) *Relapse Prevention*. New York: Guilford.

Maroda, K. (1991) *The Power of Counter-transference: Innovations in Analytic Technique*. New Jersey: Jason Aronson.

Mays, D. and Franks, C. (1985) *Negative Outcome in Psychotherapy and What to Do About It*. New York: Springer.

Miller, W.R. (1983) 'Motivational interviewing with problem drinkers', *Behavioural Psychotherapy*, 1: 147–172.

Miller, W.R. (1996) '*What is relapse? Fifty Ways to Leave the Wagon*', *Addiction*, 91 (Supplement): 515–527.

Miller, W.R., Leckman, A.L., Delaney, H.D. and Tinkcom, M. (1992) 'Long-term follow-up of behavioural self-control training', *Journal of Studies on Alcohol*, 53: 249–261.

Miller, W.R. and Rollnick, S. (1991) *Motivational Interviewing: Preparing People to Change Addictive Behaviour*. New York: Guilford.

Milman, D. and Goldman, G. (eds) (1987) *Techniques of Working with Resistance*. New Jersey: Jason Aronson.

Mitchell, S. (1988) *Relational Concepts in Psychoanalysis: An Integration*. Cambridge, MA: Harvard University Press.

Modestin, J. (1987) 'Counter-transference reactions contributing to completed suicide', *British Journal of Medical Psychology*, 60: 379–385.

Mollon, P. (1996) *Multiple Selves, Multiple Voices: Working with Trauma, Violation and Dissociation*. Chichester: Wiley.

Morgan, S. (1998) *Assessing and Managing Risk*. Brighton: Pavilion.

Morse, S.I. (1973) 'The after-pleasure of suicide', *British Journal of Medical Psychology*, 46: 227–238.

Nathanson, D. (1992) 'The nature of therapeutic impasse', *Psychiatric Annals*, 22 (10): 509–513.

Obholzer, A. and Roberts, V.Z. (eds) (1994) *The Unconscious at Work: Individual and Organizational Stress in the Human Services*. London: Routledge.

O'Connor, R. and Sheehy, N. (2000) *Understanding Suicidal Behaviour*. Leicester: British Psychological Society.

Omer, H. (1994) *Critical Interventions in Psychotherapy: From Impasse to Turning Point*. New York: Norton.

Orbach, A. (1999) *Life, Psychotherapy and Death: the End of our Exploring*. London: Jessica Kingsley.

Orne, M. and Wender, P. (1968) 'Anticipatory socialization for psychotherapy: method and rationale', *American Journal of Psychiatry*, 124: 1202–1212.

Paniagua, F. (1998) *Assessing and Treating Culturally Diverse Clients: A Practical Guide*. London: Sage.

Parkes, C.M. and Weiss, R. (1983) *Recovering from Bereavement*. New York: Basic Books.

Parry, G. (1990) *Coping with Stress*. London: B.P.S./Routledge.

Parry, G. (1998) 'Guidelines on treatment choice decisions for psychological therapies', *Audit Trends*, 6: 110.

Perlin, S. (ed.) (1975) *A Handbook for the Understanding of Suicide*. New York: Jason Aronson.

Piaget, J. and Inhelder, B. (1969) *The Psychology of the Child*. New York: Basic Books.

Piccinelli, M. and Wilkinson, G. (1994) 'Outcome of depression in psychiatric settings', *British Journal of Psychiatry*, 164: 297–304.

Prochaska, J.O. and DiClemente, C.C. (1984) *The Transtheoretical Approach: Crossing Traditional Boundaries of Therapy*. Homewood, IL: Dow Jones/Irwin.

Puryear, D. (1979) *Helping People in Crisis: A Practical Family-orientated Approach to Effective Crisis Intervention*. San Francisco: Jossey-Bass.

Racker, H. (1968) *Transference and Counter-transference*. New York: International Universities Press.

Raphael, B. (1986) *When Disaster Strikes: A Handbook for Caring Professions*. London: Hutchinson.

Ratna, L. (1978) *The Practice of Psychiatric Crisis Intervention*. St Albans: Napsbury Hospital.

Rickman, J., Aitken, D. and Pranther, D. (1990) 'In-therapy Consultation: A Supervisory and Therapeutic Experience from Practice', *Clinical Supervisor*, 8 (2): 81–89.

Robertiello, R. and Schoenewolf, G. (1987) *101 Common Therapeutic Blunders*. New Jersey: Jason Aronson.

Robins, E. (1981) *The Final Months: A Study of the Lives of 134 Persons Who Committed Suicide*. New York: Oxford University Press.

Roth, A. and Fonagy, P. (1996) *What Works for Whom? A Critical Review of Psychotherapy Research*. London: Guilford.

Ryle, A. (1990) *Cognitive Analytic Therapy: Active Participation in Change*. Chichester: Wiley.

Safran, J.D. (1999) 'Faith, despair, will and the paradox of acceptance', *Contemporary Psychoanalysis*, 35: 5–24.

Safran, J.D. and Muran, J.C. (1996) 'The resolution of ruptures in the therapeutic alliance', *Journal of Consulting and Clinical Psychology*, 64: 447–458.

Safran, J.D. and Muran, J.C. (2000) *Negotiating the Therapeutic Alliance: A Relational Treatment Guide*. New York: Guilford.

Safran, J.D. and Segal, Z.V. (1990) *Interpersonal Process in Cognitive Therapy*. New York: Basic Books.

Sandler, J. (1976) 'Counter-transference and role responsiveness', *International Journal of Psychoanalysis*, 3: 43–47.

Sandler, J., Dare, C. and Holder, A. (1976) *The Patient and the Analyst: the Basics of the Psychoanalytic Process*. London: Maresfield.

Saretsky, T. (ed.) (1981) *Resolving Treatment Impasses: The Difficult Patient*. New York: Human Sciences Press.

Schafer, R. (1983) *The Analytic Attitude*. London: Hogarth Press.

Schiff, J.L. (1975) *Cathexis Reader: Transactional Analysis Treatment of Psychosis*. New York: Harper & Row.

Schneidman, E., Farberow, N. and Litman, R. (eds) (1994) *The Psychology of Suicide: A Clinicians' Guide to Evaluation and Treatment*. Revised edn. New Jersey: Jason Aronson.

Schoenewolf, G. (1993) *Counter-resistance: The Therapist's Interference with the Therapeutic Process*. New Jersey: Jason Aronson.

Scott, M. and Stradling, S. (1992) *Counselling for Post-Traumatic Stress Disorder*. London: Sage.

Searles, H.F. (1979) *Counter-transference and Related Subjects*. New York: International Universities Press.

Sherman, M. (1996) 'Distress and professional impairment due to mental health problems among psychotherapists', *Clinical Psychology Review*, 16 (4): 299–315.

Shiffman, P. (1989) 'Conceptual issues in the study of relapse', in M. Gossop (ed.), *Relapse and Addictive Behaviour*. London: Tavistock/Routledge.

Sills, C. (ed.) (1997) *Contracts in Counselling*. London: Sage.

Stark, M. (1994) *Primer on Working with Resistance*. New Jersey: Jason Aronson.

Stein, D. and Lambert, M. (1995) 'Graduate training in psychotherapy: are therapy outcomes enhanced?' *Journal of Consulting and Clinical Psychology*, 63: 182–196.

Steiner, J. (1993) *Psychic Retreats: Pathological Organizations in Psychotic, Neurotic and Borderline Patients*. London: Routledge.

Stern, D. (1985) *The Interpersonal World of the Infant: A View from Psychoanalysis and Developmental Psychology*. New York: Basic Books.

Stolorow, R., Brandchaft, B. and Atwood, G. (1987) *Psychoanalytic Treatment: An Intersubjective Approach*. New Jersey: Analytic Press.

Strean, H. (1985) *Resolving Resistances in Psychotherapy*. New York: Wiley.

Strean, H. (1993) *Resolving Counter-resistances in Psychotherapy*. New York: Brunner/Mazel.

Striano, J. (1988) *How can Psychotherapists Hurt You?* Santa Barbara: Professional Press.

Sugarman, L. (1986) *Life-Span Development: Concepts, Theories and Interventions*. London: Methuen.

Sugarman, S. and Macheter, C. (1985) 'The family crisis intervention literature: what is meant by "family"?' *Journal of Marital and Family Therapy*, 11 (2): 167–177.

Sussman, M. (1992) *A Curious Calling: Unconscious Motivations for Practicing Psychotherapy*. New Jersey: Jason Aronson.

Sussman, M. (ed.) (1995) *A Perilous Calling: The Hazards of Psychotherapy Practice*. New York: Wiley.

Symington, N. (1983) 'The analyst's act of freedom as agent of therapeutic change', *International Review of Psychoanalysis*, 10: 283–291.

Tarrier, N., Barrowclough, C., Vaughn, C., Bamrah, J.S., Porceddu, K., Watts, S. and Freeman, H.L. (1988) 'The community management of schizophrenia: a controlled trial of behavioural interventions with families to reduce relapse', *British Journal of Psychiatry*, 153: 532–542.

Taylor, R. (2000) *Distinguishing Psychological from Organic Disorders: Screening for Psychological Masquerade*. London: Free Association Books.

Van Gennep, A. (1960) *The Rites of Passage*. (trans. M. Vizedom and G. Caffee). Chicago: University of Chicago Press.

Wachtel, P. (1987) *Action and Insight*. New York: Guilford.

Wanigaratne, S., Wallace, W., Pullin, J., Keaney, F. and Farmer, R. (1990) *Relapse Prevention for Addictive Behaviours*. Oxford: Blackwell Scientific.

Watkins, C.E. (ed.) (1997) *Handbook of Psychotherapy Supervision*. New York: Wiley.

Watts, D. and Morgan, G. (1994) 'Malignant alienation', *British Journal of Psychiatry*, 164 (1): 11–15.

Weiner, M. (1982) *The Psychotherapeutic Impasse*. New York: Free Press.

Weishaar, M.E. (1996) 'Cognitive risk factors in suicide', in P. Salkovskis (ed.), *Frontiers of Cognitive Therapy*. London: Guilford.

Weiss, J. and Sampson, H. (1986) *The Psychoanalytic Process: Theory, Clinical Observations and Empirical Research*. New York: Guilford.

Wessely, S. Rose, S., and Bisson, J. (1998) *A Systematic Review of Brief Psychological Interventions ('debriefing') for the Treatment of Immediate Trauma Related Symptoms and the Prevention of Post-traumatic Stress Disorder*. In the Cochrane Library, Issue 2. Oxford: Update Software.

White, M. and Epston, D. (1990) *Narrative Means to Therapeutic Ends*. New York: Norton.

Williams, R. and Morgan, H.G. (1994) *Suicide Prevention: The Challenge Confronted*. London: HMSO.

Winnicott, D. (1958) 'Hate in the counter-transference', in *Through Paediatrics to Psychoanalysis*. London: Tavistock.

Winnicott, D. (1971) *Playing and Reality*. London: Tavistock.

Worden, J. (1991) *Grief Counselling and Grief Therapy: A Handbook for the Mental Health Practitioner*. (2nd edn). London: Routledge.

Wosket, V. (1999) *The Therapeutic Use of Self*. London: Routledge.

Yeomans, F., Selzer, M. and Clarkin, J. (1992) *Treating the Borderline Patient: A Contract-based Approach*. New York: Basic Books.

Yule, W. (ed.) (1999) *Post-Traumatic Stress Disorders: Concepts and Theory*. Chichester: Wiley.

Zubin, J. and Spring, B. (1977) 'Vulnerability: a new view of schizophrenia', *Journal of Abnormal Psychology*, 86: 103–126.

Index